The UK Mathematics Trust

Yearbook

2016 – 2017

This book contains an account of UKMT activities from 1st September 2016 to 31st August 2017. It contains all question papers, solutions and results as well as a variety of other information.

Published by the United Kingdom Mathematics Trust.
School of Mathematics, The University of Leeds, Leeds LS2 9JT
Telephone: 0113 343 2339
E-mail: enquiry@ukmt.org.uk
Website: http://www.ukmt.org.uk

Cover design: – The backdrop is a Penrose tiling whose complexity
reflects the activities of the UKMT.

The photographs are

Front Cover:

UK 2017 IMO team in Brazil

Back Cover:

Ruthin School, STMC 2016/17 National Final winners

Students from Prenton High School for Girls taking part in the JMC

ISBN 978-1-906001-34-6

Printed and bound in Great Britain by
H. Charlesworth & Co. Ltd, Wakefield

Contents

Foreword

It is a pleasure yet again to write the foreword for the splendid UKMT yearbook. I very much look forward to spending many hours working through the problems, and reminding myself how clever the young people are, who do them in a much shorter time than they take me.

The year 2016/2017 has yet again been a time of growth and success for the UKMT. The challenges continue to attract large numbers with a record number of entries this year. It is exciting that this is happening, despite the continuous pressures that schools are under to deliver the curriculum. It is very pleasing to see the positive role that the UKMT is playing in encouraging more young people to enjoy mathematics and to engage with the challenges that it poses.

This UK team at the International Mathematical Olympiad (IMO) in Brazil had great success. It returned from the IMO with three gold medals, two bronze medals, and an Honourable Mention. In particular it finished top of all of the European nations. Congratulations both to the team and to the team leaders for making this possible. There was a lot of very positive press coverage of the team and its success. It was a pleasure and an honour to celebrate this success in an excellent event at the Science Museum in September, complemented by a superb talk by Vicky Neale on prime numbers. The UK will host the IMO in 2019 and plans are well under way for this prestigious international event, which I hope will be something that the whole UK mathematics community can engage with.

A new development for the UKMT has been the planning for the Junior Algorithms Challenge (JAC), which has questions for students aimed to test their understanding of how algorithms work. Thanks to the hard work by a dedicated team, this challenge was piloted with a number of schools over the summer. We are now digesting the results of this pilot, and planning for the future.

The UKMT would not function were it not for the combined efforts of many volunteers and it is my pleasure (again) to thank both them and the fantastic team at Leeds that make all of its work possible.

The start of this calendar year sees the UKMT team engaged in a strategy planning away day as we consider both what it has achieved and the best way to face the challenges of the future (pun intended). I look forward in the next yearbook to report on exciting developments over the coming year.

Prof Chris Budd, Chair

January 2018

Introduction

Foundation of the Trust

National mathematics competitions have existed in the UK for several decades. Up until 1987 the total annual participation was something like 8,000. Then there was an enormous growth, from 24,000 in 1988 to around a quarter of a million in 1995 – without doubt due to the drive, energy and leadership of Dr Tony Gardiner. By the end of this period there were some nine or ten competitions for United Kingdom schools and their students organised by three different bodies: the British Mathematical Olympiad Committee, the National Committee for Mathematical Contests and the UK Mathematics Foundation. During 1995 discussions took place between interested parties which led to agreement to seek a way of setting up a single body to continue and develop these competitions and related activities. This led to the formation of the United Kingdom Mathematics Trust, which was incorporated as a company limited by guarantee in October 1996 and registered with the Charity Commission.

Throughout its existence, the UKMT has continued to nurture and expand the number of competitions. As a result, over six hundred thousand students throughout the UK now participate in the challenges alone, and their teachers (as well as others) not only provide much valued help and encouragement, but also take advantage of the support offered to them by the Trust.

The Royal Institution of Great Britain is the Trust's Patron, and it and the Mathematical Association are Participating Bodies. The Association of Teachers of Mathematics, the Edinburgh Mathematical Society, the Institute of Mathematics and Its Applications, the London Mathematical Society and the Royal Society are all Supporting Bodies.

Aims and Activities of the Trust

According to its constitution, the Trust has a very wide brief, namely "to advance the education of children and young people in mathematics". To attain this, it is empowered to engage in activities ranging from teaching to publishing and lobbying. But its focal point is the organisation of mathematical competitions, from popular mass "challenges" to the selection and training of the British team for the annual International Mathematical Olympiad (IMO).

There are three main challenges, the UK Junior, Intermediate and Senior Mathematical Challenges. The number of challenge entries in 2016-2017 totalled 687,130; once again, a pleasing increase in entry numbers year on year. The challenges were organised by the Challenges Subtrust (CS).

The Challenges are open to all pupils of the appropriate age. Certificates are awarded for the best performances and the most successful participants are encouraged to enter follow-up competitions.

At the junior and intermediate levels, we increased the number of pupils entering follow-up competitions from a total of around 18,400 to a total of around 20,300. The follow-up rounds consist of the Junior Olympiad and Kangaroo, and a suite of papers forming the Intermediate Olympiad and Kangaroo under the auspices of the Challenges Subtrust.

The British Mathematical Olympiad Committee Subtrust (BMOS) organises two rounds of the British Mathematical Olympiad. Usually about 800 students who have distinguished themselves in the Senior Mathematical Challenge are invited to enter Round 1, leading to about 100 in Round 2. From the latter, around twenty are invited to a training weekend at Trinity College, Cambridge. Additionally, an elite squad, identified largely by performances in the UKMT competitions, is trained at camps and by correspondence courses throughout the year. The UK team is then selected for the annual International Mathematical Olympiad (IMO) which usually takes place in July. Recent IMOs were held as follows: Athens (2004), Mexico (2005), Slovenia (2006), Vietnam (2007), Madrid (2008), Bremen (2009), Kazakhstan (2010), Amsterdam (2011), Argentina (2012), Colombia (2013), South Africa (2014), Thailand (2015), Hong Kong (2016), Brazil (2017). The BMOS also runs a mentoring scheme for high achievers at senior, intermediate and junior levels. There is a Kangaroo follow-on round at the senior level as well, and over 5,000 pupils are invited to participate each year.

Structure and Membership of the Trust

The governing body of the Trust is its Council. The events have been organised by four Subtrusts who report directly to the Council. The work of the Trust in setting question papers, marking scripts, monitoring competitions, mentoring students and helping in many other ways depends critically on a host of volunteers. A complete list of members of the Trust, its Subtrusts and other volunteers appears at the end of this publication.

Challenges Office Staff

Rachel Greenhalgh continues in her role as Director of the Trust and as does the Deputy Director, Steven O'Hagan. They were ably supported by the Maths Challenges Office staff of Nicky Bray, Janet Clark, Gerard Cummings, Jessica Davis, Sara Liptrot, Heather Macklin, Shona Raffle-Edwards and Jo Williams. Beverley Detoeuf continues as Packing Office Manager and leads the packing and processing team of Aurelija Maciuniene, Rachael Raby-Cox, Stewart Ramsay, Alison Steggall and Tabitha Taylor, ably assisted by Mary Roberts, Packing Office Supervisor.

An outline of the events

This is a brief description of the challenges, their follow-up competitions and other activities. Much fuller information can be found later in the book.

Junior competitions

The UK Junior Mathematical Challenge, typically held on the last Thursday in April, is a one hour, 25 question, multiple-choice paper for pupils up to and including:

Y8 in England and Wales; S2 in Scotland, and Y9 in Northern Ireland.

Pupils enter their personal details and answers on a special answer sheet for machine reading. The questions are set so that the first 15 should be accessible to all participants whereas the remaining 10 are more testing.

Five marks are awarded for each correct answer to the first 15 questions and six marks are awarded for each correct answer to the rest. Each incorrect answer to questions 16–20 loses 1 mark and each incorrect answer to questions 21–25 loses 2 marks. Penalty marking is used to discourage guessing.

Certificates are awarded on a proportional basis:- Gold about 6%, Silver about 14% and Bronze about 20% of all entrants. Each centre also receives one 'Best in School Certificate'. A 'Best in Year Certificate' is awarded to the highest scoring candidate in each year group, in each school. There is a downloadable Certificate of Participation which may be given to all candidates. The follow-on rounds are the Junior Mathematical Olympiad and Kangaroo (JMOK) which are held around 6 weeks after the JMC. Between 1,000-1,200 high scorers in the JMC are invited to take part in the Olympiad; the next 5,700 or so are invited to take part in the Kangaroo.

The Olympiad is a two-hour paper with two sections. Section A contains ten questions and pupils are required to give the answer only. Section B contains six questions for which full written answers are required. It is made clear to candidates that they are not expected to complete all of Section B and that little credit will be given to fragmentary answers. Gold, silver and bronze medals are awarded to very good candidates. In 2017, a total of 227 medals was awarded. The top 25% candidates got Certificates of Distinction. Most of the rest receive a Merit and of the rest, those who had qualified for the Olympiad automatically via the JMC received a Certificate of Qualification. In addition, the top 50 students were given book prizes.

The Junior Mathematical Kangaroo is a one-hour multiple-choice paper, with 25 questions (like the JMC, but more challenging!). Certificates of

Merit are awarded to the top 25% and certificates of Qualification to everyone else who takes part.

Intermediate competitions

The UK Intermediate Mathematical Challenge is organised in a very similar way to the Junior Challenge. One difference is that the age range goes up to Y11 in England and Wales, to S4 in Scotland and Y12 in Northern Ireland. The other difference is the timing; the IMC is held on the first Thursday in February. All other arrangements are as in the JMC.

There are five follow-up competitions under the overall title 'Intermediate Mathematical Olympiad and Kangaroo' (IMOK). Between 400 and 550 in each of Years 9, 10 and 11 (English style) sit an Olympiad paper (Cayley, Hamilton and Maclaurin respectively). In 2017, each of these was a two-hour paper and contained six questions all requiring full written solutions. A total of around 12,000 pupils from the three year groups took part in a Kangaroo paper. In the Intermediate Kangaroo papers, which last an hour, there are 25 multiple-choice questions. The last ten questions are more testing than the first fifteen and correct answers gain six marks as opposed to five. Penalty marking is not applied. The same Kangaroo paper (designated 'Pink') was taken by pupils in Years 10 and 11 and a different one, 'Grey', by pupils in Year 9. In 2017, the Olympiads and Kangaroos were sat on Thursday 16th March. In the Olympiads, the top 25% of candidates got Certificates of Distinction. Most of the rest receive a Merit and of the rest, those who had qualified for the Olympiad automatically via the IMC received a Certificate of Qualification. In the Kangaroos, the top 25% got a Merit and the rest a Certificate of Qualification. All Olympiad and Kangaroo candidates received a 'Kangaroo gift'; a specially designed UKMT key fob. In addition, the top 50 students in each year group in the Olympiad papers were given a book. Performance in the Olympiad papers and the IMC was a major factor in determining pupils to be invited to one of the UKMT summer schools early in July.

Senior competitions

In 2016, the UK Senior Mathematical Challenge was held on Tuesday 8th November. Like the other Challenges, it is a 25 question, multiple-choice paper marked in the same way as the Junior and Intermediate Challenges. However, it lasts 1½ hours. Certificates (including Best in School) are awarded as with the other Challenges except that we award Gold to 10%, Silver to 20% and Bronze to 30%. The follow-up competitions are the British Mathematical Olympiads 1 and 2 (organised by the British Mathematical Olympiad Subtrust) and the Senior Kangaroo.

The first Olympiad stage, BMO1, was held on Friday 2nd December 2016. About 800 are usually invited to take part. The paper lasted 3½ hours and contained six questions to which full written solutions are required.

About 100 high scorers are then invited to sit BMO2, which was held on Thursday 26th January 2017. It also lasted 3½ hours but contained four, very demanding, questions.

The results of BMO2 are used to select a group of students to attend a Training Session at Trinity College, Cambridge in March or April. As well as being taught more mathematics and trying numerous challenging problems, this group sits a 4½ hour 'mock' Olympiad paper. On the basis of this and all other relevant information, a group of about eight is selected to take part in correspondence courses and assignments which eventually produce the UK Olympiad Team of six to go forward to the International Mathematical Olympiad in July.

In 2016, the Senior Kangaroo paper, for pupils who were close to being eligible for BMO1, was held on the same day, with the number of participants rising to 6,000.

The growth of the Challenges

In the 2005 UKMT Yearbook, we showed the growth of the Challenges since UKMT was established and this has now been updated. The graphs below show two easily identifiable quantities, the number of schools and the number of entries. In each case, the lines, from top to bottom, represent the Junior, Intermediate and Senior Challenges. As those involved in the UKMT firmly believe that the Challenges are a very worthwhile endeavour, we hope that the upward trends are continued.

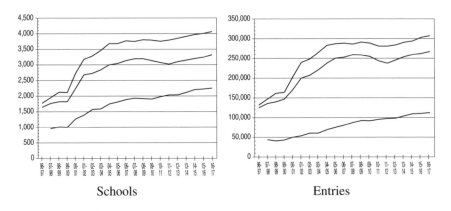

| Schools | Entries |

Team Maths Challenge and Senior Team Maths Challenge

This event is the successor of the Enterprising Mathematics UK which was run in conjunction with the IMO in 2002. A team consists of four pupils who are in Year 9 (English style) or below with at most two members being in Year 9. In 2017, 1642 teams took part in Regional Finals and 88 schools competed in the National Final held in the grand surroundings of the Lindley Hall, part of the prestigious Royal Horticultural Halls in Westminster, London, on Monday 19th June.

In addition, over 1200 schools took part in the Senior Team Maths Challenge which is aimed at students studying maths beyond GCSE. The final, which involved 88 teams, was held at the Lindley Hall, part of the Royal Horticultural Halls, London, on Tuesday 7th February 2017. Each team is made up of four student from years 11, 12 and 13 (S5 and S6 in Scotland, years 12, 13 and 14 in Northern Ireland) with a maximum of two older students per team.

Report from the Director

Many thanks to all of you who participated in the activities of the Trust during 2016/17. I hope you enjoy tackling the problems featured within the Yearbook, and reading about the varied activities.

It was another busy year for the Trust, and once again, we were particularly pleased to have so many young people take part in the Mathematical Challenges, with record entries for each of these competitions. Problem-solving is an important skill and essential for modern life, so we hope exposure to the Challenges helps to develop this.

This year's UK team at the International Mathematical Olympiad (IMO) had great success, returning from the IMO in Brazil with three gold medals, two bronze medals, and an Honourable Mention, and finishing top of all European nations. The UK will host this prestigious international event in 2019.

One of the highlights of my year was hosting a development and thank you event for our volunteers. The Trust has over 300 active volunteers, who together with the small core group of staff, do an amazing job and enable us to organise and run a wide range of activities and ensure these events run smoothly. If you would like to join this remarkable group of volunteers, please see our website for details about volunteering for the Trust. We'd love to welcome you on board!

My thanks also go to all who have supported us through sponsorship or donations during the year; in particular, thank you to the Institute and Faculty of Actuaries, who sponsor the Mathematical Challenges, and to Oxford Asset Management, who support the IMO team and our Mentoring Scheme. We are very grateful to receive donations large and small via www.donate.ukmt.org.uk.

Finally, it's great to have many schools, teachers, pupils and the public follow us on social media. To keep up to date with our activities, do follow us on Twitter @UKMathsTrust and Facebook https://www.facebook.com/UKMathsTrust/

Rachel Greenhalgh
director@ukmt.org.uk

Institute
and Faculty
of Actuaries

Profile

The Institute and Faculty of Actuaries (IFoA) is the UK's only chartered professional body dedicated to educating, developing and regulating actuaries based both in the UK and internationally.

What is an actuary?

Actuaries are experts in risk management. They use their mathematical skills to help measure the probability and risk of future events. They can work in lots of different industries like healthcare, pensions, insurance, banking and investments. The decisions that actuaries make in their roles can have a major financial impact on a company or a client, so it's important and very valuable work.

It is a global profession with internationally-recognised qualifications. It is also very highly regarded, in the way that medicine and law are. It is one of the most diverse, exciting and rewarding jobs in the world. In fact, due to the difficult exams and the expertise required, being an actuary carries quite a reputation.

How do I become an actuary?

To qualify as an actuary you need to complete the IFoA's exams. Most actuarial trainees take the exams whilst working for an actuarial employer once they have finished school or university. Exemptions from some of the exams may be awarded to students who have studied to an appropriate standard in a relevant degree, or have studied at Postgraduate level. The Fellowship qualification typically takes three to six years. Those on a graduate actuarial trainee programme can expect to earn around £35,000 a year. This will increase to well over £100,000 as you gain more experience and seniority.

Have you considered the CAA qualification?

The Certified Actuarial Analyst (CAA) qualification is a new qualification that we have launched. Do you love maths and problem solving? It's available to anyone with an aptitude for maths and problem solving and wants to use their great skills in the financial sector. Student and qualified CAAs will provide support in teams where the technical application of maths and risk modelling is essential to business success. It's not targeted at, nor does it specialise in, any particular business sector. What it does provide you with is a strong relevant, mathematical base and the tools and techniques which will open job opportunities for you as you progress in your career. It will take you two to three years to complete the six exams and one year of professional skills.

Do you not want to go to university?

Well, we have relationships with employers who offer apprenticeship opportunities, both at CAA and Fellowship level. You will leave school and enter straight into the work place, learning how to work in an office, learning actuarial techniques, taking exams and best of all… earning a salary! To find out more, see our Directory of Actuarial Employers or our website.

International outlook

The IFoA qualification is already highly valued throughout the world, with 42% of its members based outside the UK. Mutual recognition agreements with other international actuarial bodies facilitate the ability for actuaries to move and work in other parts of the world and create a truly global profession.

For more information on the qualifications and career path visit our website - http://www.actuaries.org.uk/becoming-actuary or join us on Facebook – www.be-an-actuary.co.uk

O*x*FORD
ASSET MANAGEMENT

HIGH LEVEL COMPLE*x*ITY

We are looking for people who can get to the root of high level challenges using innovative mathematical solutions. Could this be you?

O*x*FORD ASSET MANAGEMENT is an investment management company with a quantitative focus, based in central Oxford. We invest and trade world-wide, applying computational models to financial markets, analysing a range of data and information.

Our team of over 80 includes researchers, who identify opportunities and build our quantitative models and strategies, software engineers, who design the software that drives our investment strategies, and IT infrastructure specialists, who design and support our infrastructure.

We have a number of opportunities for talented mathematicians, logicians and computer scientists to join our team in the following roles:

- Researchers
- Data Analysts
- Systems Engineers
- Software Engineers
- Logic (Prolog) Programmers

We offer graduate and post-graduate roles, as well as internships for gifted students. For more information, please get in touch at recruitment@oxam.com.

www.oxam.com

The Junior Mathematical Challenge and its follow-up events

The Junior Mathematical Challenge was held on Thursday 27th April 2017 and over 265,000 pupils took part. Approximately 1000 pupils were invited to take part in the Junior Mathematical Olympiad, and a further 5700 to take part in the Junior Mathematical Kangaroo, both of which were held on Tuesday 13th June. In the following pages, we shall show the question paper and solutions leaflet for all of these.

We start with the JMC paper, the front of which is shown below in a slightly reduced format.

UK JUNIOR MATHEMATICAL CHALLENGE

THURSDAY 27th APRIL 2017

Organised by the **United Kingdom Mathematics Trust**
from the School of Mathematics, University of Leeds

Institute
and Faculty
of Actuaries

RULES AND GUIDELINES (to be read before starting)

1. Do not open the paper until the Invigilator tells you to do so.

2. Time allowed: **1 hour**.
   No answers, or personal details, may be entered after the allowed hour is over.

3. The use of rough paper is allowed; **calculators** and measuring instruments are **forbidden**.

4. Candidates in England and Wales must be in School Year 8 or below.
   Candidates in Scotland must be in S2 or below.
   Candidates in Northern Ireland must be in School Year 9 or below.

5. **Use B or HB non-propelling pencil only**. Mark *at most one* of the options A, B, C, D, E on the Answer Sheet for each question. Do not mark more than one option.

6. *Do not expect to finish the whole paper in 1 hour.* Concentrate first on Questions 1-15. When you have checked your answers to these, have a go at some of the later questions.

7. Five marks are awarded for each correct answer to Questions 1-15.
   Six marks are awarded for each correct answer to Questions 16-25.
   Each incorrect answer to Questions 16-20 loses 1 mark.
   Each incorrect answer to Questions 21-25 loses 2 marks.

8. Your Answer Sheet will be read only by a *dumb machine*. **Do not write or doodle on the sheet except to mark your chosen options**. The machine 'sees' all black pencil markings even if they are in the wrong places. If you mark the sheet in the wrong place, or leave bits of rubber stuck to the page, the machine will 'see' a mark and interpret this mark in its own way.

9. The questions on this paper challenge you to **think**, not to guess. You get more marks, and more satisfaction, by doing one question carefully than by guessing lots of answers. The UK JMC is about solving interesting problems, not about lucky guessing.

The UKMT is a registered charity
http://www.ukmt.org.uk

1. Which of the following calculations gives the largest answer?

   A $2 - 1$ B $2 \div 1$ C 2×1 D 1×2 E $2 + 1$

2. Nadiya is baking a cake. The recipe says that her cake should be baked in the oven for 1 hour and 35 minutes. She puts the cake in the oven at 11:40 am. At what time should she take the cake out of the oven?

   A 12:15 pm   B 12:40 pm   C 1:05 pm   D 1:15 pm   E 2:15 pm

3. What is the value of x ?

   A 43   B 47   C 53   D 57   E 67

   303°

   $x°$

4. A download is 95% complete. What fraction is yet to be downloaded?

   A $\dfrac{1}{2}$ B $\dfrac{1}{5}$ C $\dfrac{1}{9}$ D $\dfrac{1}{10}$ E $\dfrac{1}{20}$

5. What is the value of $201 \times 7 - 7 \times 102$?

   A 142 800   B 793   C 693   D 607   E 0

6. In a magic square, the numbers in each row, each column and the two main diagonals have the same total. This magic square uses the integers 2 to 10. Which of the following are the missing cells?

	10	5
8		4
7	2	

   A 6 / 9 / 3   B 6 / 3 / 9   C 3 / 9 / 6   D 3 / 6 / 9   E 9 / 6 / 3

7. If you work out the values of the following expressions and then place them in increasing numerical order, which comes in the middle?

   A $\dfrac{2}{3} + \dfrac{4}{5}$ B $\dfrac{2}{3} \times \dfrac{4}{5}$ C $\dfrac{3}{2} + \dfrac{5}{4}$ D $\dfrac{2}{3} \div \dfrac{4}{5}$ E $\dfrac{3}{2} \times \dfrac{5}{4}$

8. The diagram shows a rectangle $PQRS$ and T is a point on PS such that QT is perpendicular to RT. The length of QT is 4 cm. The length of RT is 2 cm.

   What is the area of the rectangle $PQRS$?

   4cm   2 cm

   A 6 cm^2 B 8 cm^2 C 10 cm^2 D 12 cm^2 E 16 cm^2

9. In William Shakespeare's play *As You Like It*, Rosalind speaks to Orlando about "He that will divide a minute into a thousand parts".

   Which of the following is equal to the number of seconds in one thousandth of one minute?

   A 0.24   B 0.6   C 0.024   D 0.06   E 0.006

10. Which of the following integers is not a multiple of 45?

    A 765   B 675   C 585   D 495   E 305

11. Seven squares are drawn on the sides of a heptagon so that they are outside the heptagon, as shown in the diagram.
    What is the sum of the seven marked angles?

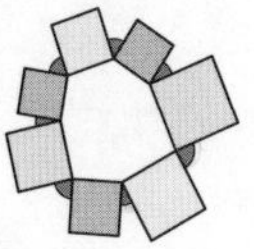

    A 315°   B 360°   C 420°   D 450°   E 630°

12. Last year, at the school where Gill teaches Mathematics, 315 out of the 600 pupils were girls. This year, the number of pupils in the school has increased to 640. The proportion of girls is the same as it was last year.
    How many girls are there at the school this year?

    A 339   B 338   C 337   D 336   E 335

13. Consider the following three statements.
    (i) Doubling a positive number always makes it larger.
    (ii) Squaring a positive number always makes it larger.
    (iii) Taking the positive square root of a positive number always makes it smaller.
    Which statements are true?

    A All three   B None   C Only (i)   D (i) and (ii)   E (ii) and (iii)

14. Mathias is given a grid of twelve small squares. He is asked to shade grey exactly four of the small squares so that his grid has two lines of reflection symmetry.
    How many different grids could he produce?

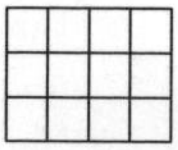

    A 2   B 3   C 4   D 5   E 6

15. What is the remainder when the square of 49 is divided by the square root of 49?

    A 0   B 2   C 3   D 4   E 7

16. In New Threeland there are three types of coins: the 2p; the 5p; and one other. The smallest number of coins needed to make 13p is three. The smallest number of coins needed to make 19p is three. What is the value of the third type of coin?

    A 4p   B 6p   C 7p   D 9p   E 12p

17. I add up all even numbers between 1 and 101. Then from my total I subtract all odd numbers between 0 and 100.
    What is the result?

    A 0   B 50   C 100   D 255   E 2525

18. What is the sum of the digits in the completed crossnumber?

ACROSS	DOWN
1. A cube	2. A square
3. A power of 11	

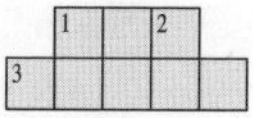

    A 25   B 29   C 32   D 34   E 35

19. The diagram shows a regular hexagon *PQRSTU*, a square *PUWX* and an equilateral triangle *UVW*.

    What is the angle *TVU* ?

    A 45°   B 42°   C 39°   D 36°   E 33°

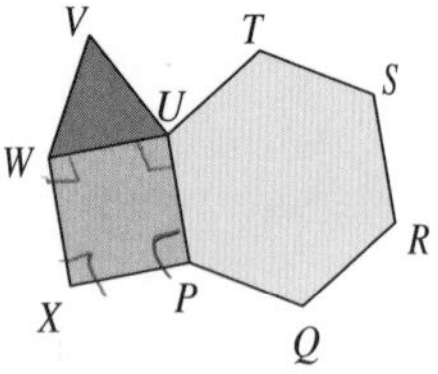

20. The range of a list of integers is 20, and the median is 17.
    What is the smallest possible number of integers in the list?

    A 1   B 2   C 3   D 4   E 5

21. The small trapezium on the right has three equal sides and angles of 60° and 120°. Nine copies of this trapezium can be placed together to make a larger version of it, as shown.

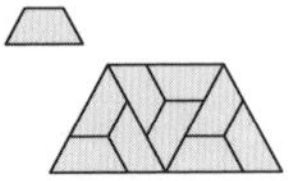

    The larger trapezium has perimeter 18 cm.

    What is the perimeter of the smaller trapezium?

    A 2 cm   B 4 cm   C 6 cm   D 8 cm   E 9 cm

22. In the window of Bradley's Bicycle Bazaar there are some unicycles, some bicycles and some tricycles. Laura sees that there are seven saddles in total, thirteen wheels in total and more bicycles than tricycles.

    How many unicycles are in the window?

    A 1   B 2   C 3   D 4   E 5

23. The positive integers from 1 to 150 inclusive are placed in a 10 by 15 grid so that each cell contains exactly one integer. Then the multiples of 3 are given a red mark, the multiples of 5 are given a blue mark, and the multiples of 7 are given a green mark.

    How many cells have more than 1 mark?

    A 10   B 12   C 15   D 18   E 19

24. A large solid cube is cut into two pieces by a single plane cut. How many of the following four shapes could be the shape of the cross-section formed by the cut?

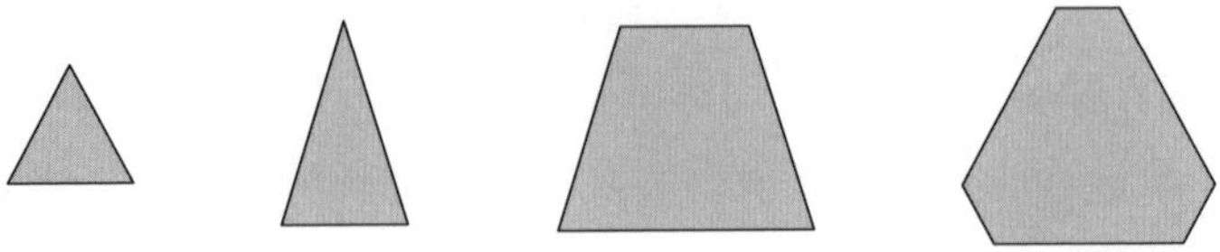

    A 0   B 1   C 2   D 3   E 4

25. The distance between Exeter and London is 175 miles. Sam left Exeter at 10:00 on Tuesday for London. Morgan left London for Exeter at 13:00 the same day. They travelled on the same road. Up to the time when they met, Sam's average speed was 25 miles per hour, and Morgan's average speed was 35 miles an hour.

    At what time did Sam and Morgan meet?

    A 17:00   B 15:55   C 15:30   D 15:00   E 14:40

The JMC solutions

The usual solutions leaflet was issued.

UK JUNIOR MATHEMATICAL CHALLENGE

THURSDAY 27th APRIL 2017

Organised by the **United Kingdom Mathematics Trust**
from the School of Mathematics, University of Leeds

http://www.ukmt.org.uk

Institute
and Faculty
of Actuaries

SOLUTIONS LEAFLET

This solutions leaflet for the JMC is sent in the hope that it might provide all concerned with some alternative solutions to the ones they have obtained. It is not intended to be definitive. The organisers would be very pleased to receive alternatives created by candidates.

For reasons of space, these solutions are necessarily brief. There are more in-depth, extended solutions available on the UKMT website, which include some exercises for further investigation:

http://www.ukmt.org.uk/

The UKMT is a registered charity

1. **E** The values of the options are A 1; B 2; C 2; D 2; E 3.

2. **D** Nadiya puts her cake into the oven at 11:40 am. So 20 minutes later, it will be 12:00. Then, there will still be 1 hour and 15 minutes before the cake is due to be taken out of the oven. So she should take her cake out at 1:15 pm.

3. **D** The angles which meet at a point sum to $360°$, so $y = 360 - 303 = 57$. As the marked lines are parallel, the angles marked $x°$ and $y°$ are equal (alternate angles). So $x = y = 57$.

4. **E** As 95% of the download is complete, 5% of it remains to be downloaded. As a fraction, $5\% = \frac{5}{100} = \frac{1}{20}$.

5. **C** $201 \times 7 - 7 \times 102 = 7(201 - 102) = 7 \times 99 = 7(100 - 1) = 700 - 7 = 693$.

6. **D** Let the total of each row, column and both diagonals be T. Note that $2 + 3 + 4 + 5 + 6 + 7 + 8 + 9 + 10 = 54$. Therefore $3T = 54$, that is $T = 18$. It is clear that option D is the only option which makes each row, each column and both diagonals sum to 18.

x	10	5
8	y	4
7	2	z

7. **A** The values of the options are: A $\frac{22}{15} = 1\frac{7}{15}$; B $\frac{8}{15}$; C $\frac{11}{4} = 2\frac{3}{4}$; D $\frac{5}{6}$; E $\frac{15}{8} = 1\frac{7}{8}$. In ascending order these are: $\frac{8}{15}$; $\frac{5}{6}$; $1\frac{7}{15}$; $1\frac{7}{8}$; $2\frac{3}{4}$.

8. **B** In the diagram, U is the foot of the perpendicular from T to QR. The area of rectangle $PQRS = QR \times TU$. The area of triangle QTR is $\frac{1}{2} \times QR \times TU$. So the area of rectangle $PQRS$ is equal to $2 \times$ area of triangle $QTR = 2 \times \left(\frac{1}{2} \times 2 \times 4\right) \text{cm}^2 = 8 \text{cm}^2$.

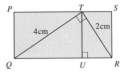

9. **D** There are 60 seconds in one minute. So the number of seconds in one thousandth of one minute is $60 \div 1000 = 0.06$.

10. **E** Note that $45 = 5 \times 9$. As 5 and 9 are coprime, a positive integer is a multiple of 45 if and only if it is a multiple of both 5 and 9. The units digit of all five options is 5, so they are all multiples of 5. An integer is a multiple of 9 if and only if the sum of its digits is also a multiple of 9. The sums of the digits of the five options is 18, 18, 18, 18 and 8. So 305 is the only one of the options which is not a multiple of 9 and hence is not a multiple of 45.

11. **B** In the diagram, each of the seven vertices of the heptagon has four angles meeting at it. This makes 28 angles in total. These comprise the seven marked angles, fourteen right angles and the seven interior angles of the heptagon. The sum of the angles meeting at a point is $360°$ and the sum of the interior angles of the heptagon is $(7 - 2) \times 180° = 5 \times 180°$. Therefore, (the sum of the seven marked angles) $+ 14 \times 90° + 5 \times 180° = 7 \times 360°$. So the sum of the seven marked angles is $(28 - 14 - 10) \times 90° = 4 \times 90° = 360°$.

12. **D** Last year, the fraction of girls at the school was $\frac{315}{600} = \frac{63}{120} = \frac{21}{40}$. This year, there are 40 more pupils at the school, but the proportion of girls has remained the same. So there are 21 more girls at the school this year, making a total of $315 + 21 = 336$.

13. **C** Statement (i) is true since $2x > x$ for all $x > 0$.
Statement (ii) is not true. For example, $\left(\frac{1}{2}\right)^2 = \frac{1}{4}$, which is not larger than $\frac{1}{2}$.
Statement (iii) is also not true. For example, $\sqrt{\frac{1}{9}} = \frac{1}{3}$, which is not smaller than $\frac{1}{9}$.

14. **B** If any corner square is shaded, then they all must be, and this gives one possible grid. Similarly if any one of b, c, j, k is shaded then so too are the others. That leaves only all four squares in the middle row, which provides the third and final possible grid.

a	b	c	d
e	f	g	h
i	j	k	l

15. **A** The square root of 49 is 7. As 7 is factor of 49, it will also be a factor of the square of 49. So the required remainder is 0.

16. **D** Since neither 13 nor 19 is a multiple of 3, one couldn't possibly use three copies of a single coin in either case. If two of the extra coins are used, that would be even, so the third coin would need to be the 5p. That would imply the extra coin would have to be a 4p or a 7p to get 13p or 19p respectively. So two of the extra coin are not used. If only one of the extra coin is used, then it would come in addition to 2p + 2p or 2p + 5p or 5p + 5p. To get 13p, you would need 9p or 6p or 3p respectively; and to get 19p you would need 15p or 12p or 9p respectively. Hence 9p is the only possible extra coin which makes both 13p and 19p possible.

17. **B** Let the required result be S. Then
$$S = (2 + 4 + 6 + \ldots + 100) - (1 + 3 + 5 + \ldots + 99)$$
$$= (2 - 1) + (4 - 3) + (6 - 5) + \ldots + (100 - 99)$$
$$= 50 \times 1 = 50.$$

18. **A** The first five positive powers of 11 are $11^1 = 11$; $11^2 = 121$; $11^3 = 1331$; $11^4 = 14641$; $11^5 = 161051$. So 3 across is 14641, since this is the only five-digit power of 11. Therefore the solution to 2 down is a two-digit square with units digit 4 and so is $8^2 = 64$, as the only other two-digit squares are 16, 25, 36, 49, 81. Hence 1 across is a three-digit cube with units digit 6 and so is $6^3 = 216$, as the only other three-digit cubes are $5^3 = 125$, $7^3 = 343$, $8^3 = 512$, $9^3 = 729$. So the sum of the digits in the completed crossnumber is $2 + 1 + 6 + 1 + 4 + 6 + 4 + 1 = 25$.

19. **A** Note that the interior angles of an equilateral triangle, a square and and a regular hexagon are $60°$, $90°$ and $120°$ respectively. The angles at a point sum to $360°$, so $\angle TUV = 360° - \left(60° + 90° + 120°\right) = 90°$
As WU is common to both equilateral triangle UVW and square $PUWX$, the lengths of the sides of UVW and $PUWX$ are equal. Similarly, UP is common to both square $PUWX$ and regular hexagon $PQRSTU$, so the lengths of the sides of $PUWX$ and $PQRSTU$ are also equal. So $UV = UP = UT$ and hence triangle UTV is a right-angled isosceles triangle with $\angle TVU = \angle VTU$. Therefore $\angle TVU = \left(180° - 90°\right) \div 2 = 45°$.

20. **B** Since the range is 20 there must be more than one integer in the list. Could we manage with just two integers? If so one would need to be 10 greater than the median of 17 and the other 10 less than 17. This is indeed possible with the list 7, 27. So two is the smallest possible number of integers.

21. **C** The diagram shows that the small trapezium may be divided into three congruent equilateral triangles. Let the length of each side of the triangles be x cm. Then the base of the small trapezium is $2x$ cm.

The perimeter of the larger trapezium is made up of five equal line segments each of length $(2x + x)$ cm. So $15x = 18$. The perimeter of the smaller trapezium is $(x + x + x + 2x)$ cm $= 5x$ cm $= 5 \times \frac{18}{15}$ cm $= 6$ cm.

{*It is left as an exercise for the reader to prove that the small trapezium may be divided into three congruent equilateral triangles.*}

22. **B** Let the number of unicycles, bicycles and tricycles be u, b and t respectively. Then $u + b + t = 7...$ (1); $u + 2b + 3t = 13...$ (2); also $b > t$. (2) − (1): $b + 2t = 6...$ (3). As b and t are both positive integers, the only values of b and t which satisfy equation (3) are $b = 2, t = 2$ and $b = 4, t = 1$. However, $b > t$ so the only solution is $b = 4, t = 1$. Substituting in (1): $u + 4 + 1 = 7$. So $u = 2$.

23. **E** As 3 and 5 are coprime, the squares that have more than one mark are multiples of both 3 and 5, (multiples of 15); or multiples of both 3 and 7, (multiples of 21); or multiples of 5 and 7, (multiples of 35); or multiples of 3, 5 and 7, (multiples of 105). However, the latter will be included in all of the first three categories. Between 1 and 150 inclusive, there are ten multiples of 15, seven multiples of 21 and four multiples of 35, making a total of 21 multiples. However, there is one multiple of 3, 5 and 7 between 1 and 150, namely 105. So 105 has been counted three times in those 21 multiples, but corresponds to exactly one marked square. Therefore the total number of marked squares is $21 − 2 = 19$.

24. **E** The diagrams below show that all four cross-sections of cut are possible.

25. **E** Sam left Exeter three hours before Morgan left London, and travelled 3×25 miles = 75 miles in the three hours to 13:00. So at 13:00, the distance between Sam and Morgan was $(175 − 75)$ miles = 100 miles.

Let the time in hours between 13:00 and the time at which Sam and Morgan met be t.

Then $25t + 35t = 100$. So $t = \frac{100}{60}$ hours = 100 minutes = 1 hour 40 minutes.

So Sam and Morgan met at 14:40.

The JMC answers

The table below shows the proportion of pupils' choices. The correct answer is shown in bold. [The percentages are rounded to the nearest whole number.]

Qn	A	B	C	D	E	Blank
1	1	0	0	0	**98**	1
2	7	1	3	**88**	1	1
3	1	2	2	**91**	2	2
4	1	11	4	3	**80**	2
5	28	3	**61**	2	4	2
6	3	4	4	**79**	8	2
7	**33**	15	20	12	12	8
8	6	**41**	13	18	13	8
9	1	4	3	**57**	33	2
10	9	5	5	7	**71**	3
11	11	**38**	17	10	15	9
12	6	8	9	**28**	40	7
13	39	9	**24**	21	4	3
14	20	**32**	18	9	16	5
15	**54**	7	9	7	18	5
16	2	16	6	**51**	7	17
17	29	**19**	7	8	3	34
18	**8**	6	10	6	4	66
19	**23**	6	3	5	3	60
20	6	**10**	22	5	4	53
21	23	4	**10**	3	4	56
22	14	**25**	8	5	2	46
23	4	6	9	6	**6**	69
24	14	8	10	7	**3**	58
25	13	5	6	6	**10**	60

JMC 2017: Some comments on the pupils' choices of answers as expressed in the feedback letter to schools

The average score this year of around 50 was similar to last year. The excellent performance of pupils on many of the early questions is encouraging. However, there were two exceptions. As these are questions dealing with basic numeracy, this is a concern.

The idea behind Question 5 was the hope that many students would use the common factor 7 to simplify their working to give $201 \times 7 - 7 \times 102 = 7 \times 201 - 7 \times 102 = 7 \times (201 - 102) = 7 \times 99 = 693$, rather than working out the products separately and then subtracting. We did not expect that so many pupils would use an incorrect method which leads to a wrong answer.

It is a standard convention that to work out the value of the expression $201 \times 7 - 7 \times 102$, the two multiplications should be carried out first, and then the subtraction. This is the method used by almost all calculators and computer programming languages. So it is worrying to see from the responses to Question 5 that a quarter of all pupils nationally seem to have chosen the left-to-right method and evaluated this expression as $((201 \times 7) - 7) \times 102$ to obtain the incorrect option 142 800.

From the table enclosed with the results a teacher will be able to judge the performance of their own pupils. If many of them gave the wrong answer to Question 5, we hope you will find the time to put them right on this important matter.

We don't know whether use of the left-to-right method of evaluating expressions is a legacy of bad habits acquired at primary school or the influence of some mobile phones which have dodgy calculators. It would be a good exercise for your pupils to evaluate $201 \times 7 - 7 \times 102$ on their calculators. This might help to convince them of the correctness of doing multiplications before additions and subtractions. As well as being fundamental to arithmetic, the use of the multiplication-first convention helps to pave the way for algebra where the multiplication signs are often not even written down. One way to see the advantage of the convention is to compare the expression $(5x + 3)(4x + 7)$ with $((5 \times x) + 3) \times ((4 \times x) + 7)$, which is what we would need to write without the use of standard conventions.

The other early question with a disappointing outcome is Question 7 on fractions. Only a third of the pupils got this question right, but it is less easy to understand where the others went wrong, as each of the incorrect options was fairly popular. Maybe "in the middle" was misunderstood, or faced with a good deal of arithmetic with fractions, many pupils just guessed, or made lots of mistakes.

On the bright side, it was good to see the number of pupils who answered the harder questions correctly and who obtained very good scores. We hope that their excellent achievement in the Junior Mathematical Challenge will gain them appropriate recognition and congratulations in your school.

The profile of marks obtained is shown below.

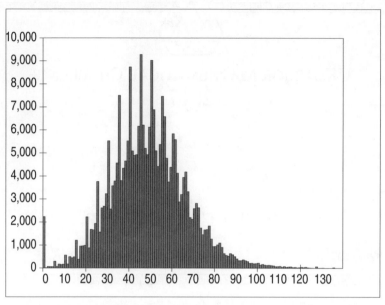

Bar chart showing the actual frequencies in the 2017 JMC

On the basis of the standard proportions used by the UKMT, the cut-off marks were set at

GOLD – 77 or over   SILVER – 63 to 76   BRONZE – 52 to 62

A sample of one of the certificates is shown on the next page.

The follow-up round to the Junior Challenge consists of the Junior Olympiad and Kangaroo (JMOK).

Candidates who scored 107 or more in the Junior Challenge automatically qualified for the Olympiad, and 1024 were invited via this route. As with our other Olympiads, schools were allowed to enter non-automatic candidates on payment of a fee. The number who entered by this route was 172.

Candidates who scored 86 to 106 were invited to sit the multiple-choice Junior Kangaroo. There were 5,708 automatic entries; we do not accept discretionary (paid-for) entries for Kangaroo competitions.

UK JUNIOR MATHEMATICAL CHALLENGE
2017

of

received a

SILVER CERTIFICATE

Institute
and Faculty
of Actuaries

Professor Chris Budd, OBE
Chairman, United Kingdom Mathematics Trust

THE UNITED KINGDOM JUNIOR MATHEMATICAL CHALLENGE

The Junior Mathematical Challenge (JMC) is run by the UK Mathematics Trust. The JMC encourages mathematical reasoning, precision of thought, and fluency in using basic mathematical techniques to solve interesting problems. It is aimed at pupils in years 7 and 8 in England and Wales, S1 and S2 in Scotland and years 8 and 9 in Northern Ireland. The problems on the JMC are designed to make students think. Most are accessible, yet challenge those with more experience; they are also meant to be memorable and enjoyable.

Mathematics controls more aspects of the modern world than most people realise – from iPods, cash machines, telecommunications and airline booking systems to production processes in engineering, efficient distribution and stock-holding, investment strategies and 'whispering' jet engines. The scientific and industrial revolutions flowed from the realisation that mathematics was both the language of nature, and also a way of analysing – and hence controlling – our environment. In the last fifty years, old and new applications of mathematical ideas have transformed the way we live.

All of these developments depend on mathematical thinking – a mode of thought whose essential style is far more permanent than the wave of technological change which it has made possible. The problems on the JMC reflect this style, which pervades all mathematics, by encouraging students to think clearly about challenging problems.

The UK JMC has grown out of a national challenge first run in 1988. In recent years over 250,000 pupils have taken part from around 3,700 schools. Certificates are awarded to the highest scoring 40% of candidates (Gold : Silver : Bronze 1 : 2 : 3). From 2014, Certificates of Participation were awarded to all participants.

There is an Intermediate and Senior version for older pupils. All three events are organised by the United Kingdom Mathematics Trust and are administered from the School of Mathematics at the University of Leeds.

The UKMT is a registered charity. For more information about us please visit our website at www.ukmt.org.uk

Donations to support our work would be gratefully received and can be made at www.donate.ukmt.org.uk

The JMC follow-on events

The Junior Kangaroo is a one-hour multiple-choice paper with 25 questions for the UK and by invitation only. It was offered to around 5,700 UK candidates who scored just below the Junior Olympiad qualifying score. The qualification mark was 86 to 106.

Junior Kangaroo Mathematical Challenge

Tuesday 13th June 2017

Organised by the United Kingdom Mathematics Trust

The Junior Kangaroo allows students in the UK to test themselves on questions set for young mathematicians from across Europe and beyond.

RULES AND GUIDELINES (to be read before starting):

1. Do not open the paper until the Invigilator tells you to do so.

2. Time allowed: **1 hour**.
   No answers, or personal details, may be entered after the allowed hour is over.

3. The use of rough paper is allowed; **calculators** and measuring instruments are **forbidden**.

4. Candidates in England and Wales must be in School Year 8 or below.
   Candidates in Scotland must be in S2 or below.
   Candidates in Northern Ireland must be in School Year 9 or below.

5. **Use B or HB pencil only**. For each question mark *at most one* of the options A, B, C, D, E on the Answer Sheet. Do not mark more than one option.

6. Five marks will be awarded for each correct answer to Questions 1 - 15.
   Six marks will be awarded for each correct answer to Questions 16 - 25.

7. *Do not expect to finish the whole paper in 1 hour*. Concentrate first on Questions 1-15. When you have checked your answers to these, have a go at some of the later questions.

8. The questions on this paper challenge you **to think**, not to guess. Though you will not lose marks for getting answers wrong, you will undoubtedly get more marks, and more satisfaction, by doing a few questions carefully than by guessing lots of answers.

Enquiries about the Junior Kangaroo should be sent to: Maths Challenges Office,
School of Mathematics, University of Leeds, Leeds, LS2 9JT.
(Tel. 0113 343 2339)
http://www.ukmt.org.uk

1. Kieran the Kangaroo takes 6 seconds to make 4 jumps. How long does it take him to make 30 jumps?

   A 30 seconds   B 36 seconds   C 42 seconds   D 45 seconds   E 48 seconds

2. Sophie wants to complete the grid shown so that each row and each column of the grid contains the digits 1, 2 and 3 exactly once. What is the sum of the digits she will write in the shaded cells?

   A 2   B 3   C 4   D 5   E 6

3. Ben has exactly the right number of cubes, each of side 5 cm, to make a solid cube of side 1 m. He places the smaller cubes side by side to form a single row. How long is this row?

   A 5 km   B 400 m   C 300 m   D 20 m   E 1 m

4. Beattie wants to walk from P to Q along the paths shown, always moving in the direction from P to Q.

   She will add the numbers on the paths she walks along. How many different totals could she obtain?

   A 3   B 4   C 5   D 6   E 8

5. Anna is 13 years old. Her mother Annie is three times as old as Anna. How old will Annie be when Anna is three times as old as she is now?

   A 13   B 26   C 39   D 52   E 65

6. Hasan writes down a two-digit number. He then writes the same two-digit number next to his original number to form a four-digit number. What is the ratio of his four-digit number to his two-digit number ?

   A 2 : 1   B 100 : 1   C 101 : 1   D 1001 : 1   E It depends on his number

7. A square piece of card has perimeter 20 cm. Charlie cuts the card into two rectangles. The perimeter of one of the rectangles is 16 cm. What is the perimeter of the other rectangle?

   A 4 cm   B 8 cm   C 10 cm   D 12 cm   E 14 cm

8. Niko counted a total of 60 birds perching in three trees. Five minutes later, 6 birds had flown away from the first tree, 8 birds had flown away from the second tree and 4 birds had flown away from the third tree. He noticed that there was now the same number of birds in each tree. How many birds were originally perched in the second tree?

   A 14   B 18   C 20   D 21   E 22

9. Alex colours all the small squares that lie on the two longest diagonals of a square grid. She colours 2017 small squares. What is the size of the square grid?

   A 1009 × 1009   B 1008 × 1008   C 2017 × 2017   D 2016 × 2016   E 2015 × 2015

10. In the sequence of letters KANGAROOKANGAROOKANG... the word KANGAROO is repeated indefinitely. What is the 2017th letter in this sequence?

    A K   B N   C G   D R   E O

11. A cube has diagonals drawn on three adjacent faces as shown in the diagram. Which of the following nets could Usman use to make the cube shown?

A   B   C   D   E none of those shown

12. Maddie has a paper ribbon of length 36 cm. She divides it into four rectangles of different lengths. She draws two lines joining the centres of two adjacent rectangles as shown.

What is the sum of the lengths of the lines that she draws?

A 18 cm   B 17 cm   C 20 cm   D 19 cm   E It depends upon the sizes of the rectangles

13. In trapezium $PQRS$, $\angle RSP = 2 \times \angle SPQ$ and $\angle SPQ = 2 \times \angle PQR$. Also $\angle QRS = k \times \angle PQR$. What is the value of k?

A 2   B 3   C 4   D 5   E 6

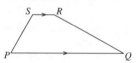

14. Taran thought of a whole number and then multiplied it by either 5 or 6. Krishna added 5 or 6 to Taran's answer. Finally Eshan subtracted either 5 or 6 from Krishna's answer. The final result was 73. What number did Taran choose?

A 10   B 11   C 12   D 13   E 14

15. In the diagram, $PRSV$ is a rectangle with $PR = 20$ cm and $PV = 12$ cm. Jeffrey marks points U and T on VS and Q on PR as shown. What is the shaded area?

A More information needed   B 60 cm^2
C 100 cm^2 D 110 cm^2 E 120 cm^2

16. The line PQ is divided into six parts by the points V, W, X, Y and Z. Squares are drawn on PV, VW, WX, XY, YZ and ZQ as shown in the diagram. The length of line PQ is 24 cm. What is the length of the path from P to Q indicated by the arrows?

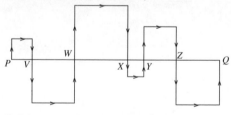

A 48 cm   B 60 cm   C 66 cm   D 72 cm   E 96 cm

17. Henna has four hair ribbons of width 10 cm. When she measures them, she finds that each ribbon is 25 cm longer than the next smallest ribbon. She then arranges the ribbons to form two different shapes as shown in the diagram.

How much longer is the perimeter of the second shape than the perimeter of the first shape?

A 75 cm   B 50 cm   C 25 cm   D 20 cm   E 0 cm

18. In the diagram, *PQRS* is a square of side 10 cm. *T* is a point inside the square so that $\angle SPT = 75°$ and $\angle TSP = 30°$. What is the length of *TR*?

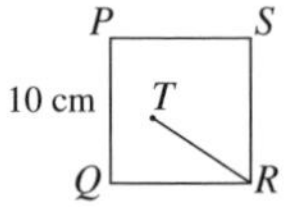

    A 8 cm   B 8.5 cm   C 9 cm   D 9.5 cm   E 10 cm

19. In the diagram, *PQRS* and *WXYZ* are congruent squares. The sides *PS* and *WZ* are parallel. The shaded area is equal to 1 cm².
    What is the area of square *PQRS*?

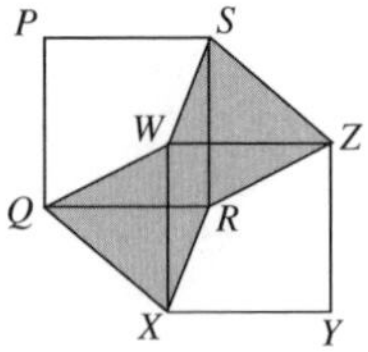

    A 1 cm²   B 2 cm²   C $\frac{1}{2}$ cm²   D $1\frac{1}{2}$ cm²   E $\frac{3}{4}$ cm²

20. The multiplication $abc \times de = 7632$ uses each of the digits 1 to 9 exactly once. What is the value of *b*?

    A 1   B 4   C 5   D 8   E 9

21. Rory uses four identical standard dice to build the solid shown in the diagram.
    Whenever two dice touch, the numbers on the touching faces are the same. The numbers on some of the faces of the solid are shown. What number is written on the face marked with question mark?
    (On a standard die, the numbers on opposite faces add to 7.)

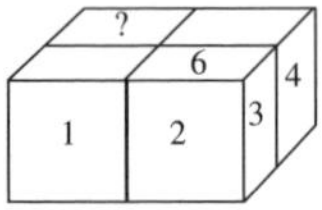

    A 6   B 5   C 4   D 3   E 2

22. Harriet tells Topaz that she is thinking of three positive integers, not necessarily all different. She tells her that the product of her three integers is 36. She also tells her the sum of her three integers. However, Topaz still cannot work out what the three integers are.
    What is the sum of Harriet's three integers?

    A 10   B 11   C 13   D 14   E 16

23. Three congruent isosceles trapeziums are assembled to form an equilateral triangle with a hole in the middle, as shown in the diagram.

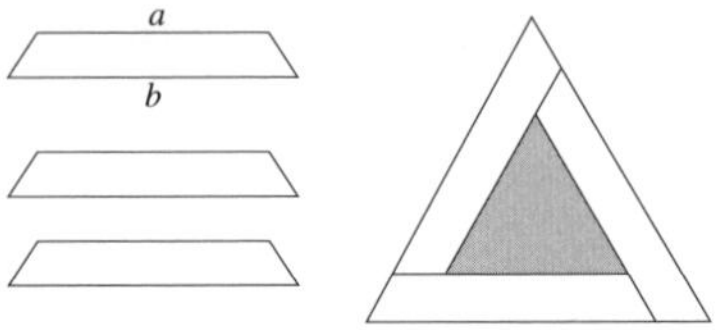

    What is the perimeter of the hole?

    A $3a + 6b$ B $3b - 6a$ C $6b - 3a$ D $6a + 3b$ E $6a - 3b$

24. Jacob and Zain take pencils from a box of 21 pencils without replacing them. On Monday Jacob takes $\frac{2}{3}$ of the number of pencils that Zain takes. On Tuesday Jacob takes $\frac{1}{2}$ of the number of pencils that Zain takes. On Wednesday morning the box is empty. How many pencils does Jacob take?

    A 8   B 7   C 6   D 5   E 4

25. How many three-digit numbers are equal to 34 times the sum of their digits?

    A 0   B 1   C 2   D 3   E 4

Solutions were provided.

Solutions to 2017 Junior Kangaroo

1. **D** Kieran makes 4 jumps in 6 seconds so makes 2 jumps in 3 seconds. Therefore it will take him $(30 \div 2) \times 3$ seconds $= 45$ seconds to make 30 jumps.

2. **C** Label the numbers to be written in the cells of the grid as shown.

1	a	b
2	1	c
d	e	f

Each row and column contains the digits 1, 2 and 3 exactly once. Hence $c = d = 3$. Therefore $b = e = 2$ (and $a = 3$ and $f = 1$ for completeness). Hence the sum of the digits in the shaded cells is $2 + 2 = 4$.

3. **B** The number of small cubes along each edge of the large cube is $100 \div 5 = 20$. Therefore Ben has $20 \times 20 \times 20 = 8000$ small cubes in total. Hence the row he forms is 8000×5 cm $= 40\,000$ cm long. Since there are 100 cm in 1 m, his row is 400 m long.

4. **B** The smallest and largest totals Beattie can obtain are $1 + 3 + 5 = 9$ and $2 + 4 + 6 = 12$ respectively. Totals of 10 and 11 can also be obtained, for example from $2 + 3 + 5 = 10$ and $1 + 4 + 6 = 11$. Therefore, since all Beattie's totals will be integers, she can obtain four different totals.

5. **E** When Anna is 13, Annie is $3 \times 13 = 39$ and so Annie is 26 years older than Anna. When Anna is three times as old as she is now, she will be 39 and Annie will still be 26 years older. Therefore Annie will be 65.

6. **C** Let Hasan's two-digit number be 'ab', which is equal to $10a + b$. The four-digit number he forms is therefore '$abab$', which is equal to $1000a + 100b + 10a + b$ and hence to $100(10a + b) + 10a + b = 101 \times (10a + b)$. Therefore the ratio of his four-digit number to his two-digit number is $101 : 1$.

7. **E** The length of the edge of Charlie's original square is $(20 \div 4)$ cm $= 5$ cm. Since he cuts his square into two rectangles, he cuts parallel to one side of the square to create two rectangles each with two sides 5 cm long as shown in the diagram.

5 cm
5 cm
5 cm
5 cm

Hence the total perimeter of his two rectangles is 2×5 cm $= 10$ cm longer than the perimeter of his square. Since the perimeter of one of the rectangles is 16 cm, the perimeter of the other rectangle is $(20 + 10 - 16)$ cm $= 14$ cm.

8. **E** Let the number of birds remaining in each tree be x. Therefore $x + 6 + x + 8 + x + 4 = 60$, which has solution $x = 14$. Hence the number of birds originally perched in the second tree is $14 + 8 = 22$.

9. **A** The two longest diagonals of an $n \times n$ square grid each contain n squares. When n is an odd number, the two diagonals meet at the square in the centre of the grid and hence there are $2n - 1$ squares in total on the diagonals. Alex coloured 2017 squares and hence $2n - 1 = 2017$, which has solution $n = 1009$. Therefore the size of the square grid is 1009×1009.

10. A The sequence KANGAROOKANGAROOKANG... repeats every 8 letters. Since $2017 = 8 \times 252 + 1$, the 2017th letter in the sequence is the first of the repeating sequence and hence is K.

11. D On each net, label the four vertices of the right-hand square 1, 2, 3 and 4 as shown. Also label any vertex on any of the other squares that will meet vertices 1, 2, 3 or 4 when the net of the cube is assembled into a cube with the corresponding value.

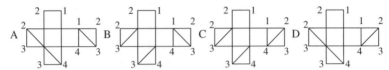

Since there are three vertices of the original cube at which two diagonals meet, to be a suitable net for the cube shown, any diagonal drawn meets another diagonal at a vertex with the same label. As can be seen, only in net D are the ends of the diagonals at vertices with the same label. Therefore Usman could only use net D to make the cube shown.

12. A Let the lengths of the four rectangles be p cm, q cm, r cm and s cm with $p + q + r + s = 36$. The lines Maddie draws join the centres of two pairs of rectangles and hence have total length $\left(\frac{1}{2}p + \frac{1}{2}q\right)$ cm $+ \left(\frac{1}{2}r + \frac{1}{2}s\right)$ cm $= \frac{1}{2}(p + q + r + s)$ cm. Therefore the sum of the lengths of the lines she draws is $\frac{1}{2} \times 36$ cm $= 18$ cm.

13. D Let the size in degrees of $\angle PQR$ and of $\angle QRS$ be x and kx. Therefore the size of $\angle SPQ$ and of $\angle RSP$ are $2x$ and $2 \times 2x = 4x$ respectively. Since the angles between parallel lines (sometimes called co-interior or allied angles) add to 180°, we have $2x + 4x = 180$. This has solution $x = 30$. Similarly $x + kx = 180$ and hence $30k = 150$. Therefore the value of k is 5.

14. C Let Taran's original number be x. When he multiplied it, he obtained either $5x$ or $6x$. When Krishna added 5 or 6, his answer was one of $5x + 5$, $5x + 6$, $6x + 5$ or $6x + 6$. Finally, when Eshan subtracted 5 or 6, his answer was one of $5x$, $5x + 1$, $6x$, $6x + 1$, $5x - 1$, $5x$, $6x - 1$ or $6x$. Since the final result was 73 and since 73 is neither a multiple of 5 or 6, nor 1 less than a multiple of 5 or 6, nor 1 more than a multiple of 5, the only suitable expression for the answer is $6x + 1$. The equation $6x + 1 = 73$ has solution $x = 12$. Hence the number Taran chose is 12.

15. E Consider the two unshaded triangles. Each has height equal to 12 cm and hence their total area is $\left(\frac{1}{2} \times PQ \times 12 + \frac{1}{2} \times QR \times 12\right)$ cm^2 $= 6 \times (PQ + QR)$ cm^2 $= 6 \times 20$ cm^2 $= 120$ cm^2. Therefore the shaded area is $(20 \times 12 - 120)$ cm^2 $= 120$ cm^2.

16. D The path indicated follows three sides of each of the squares shown. The sum of the lengths of one side of each square is equal to the length of PQ, which is 24 cm. Therefore the length of the path is 3×24 cm $= 72$ cm.

17. B Let the length of the shortest ribbon be x cm. Therefore the lengths of the other ribbons are $(x + 25)$ cm, $(x + 50)$ cm and $(x + 75)$ cm. The perimeter of the first shape (starting from the lower left corner and working clockwise) is $(x + 10 + 25 + 10 + 25 + 10 + 25 + 10 + x + 75 + 40)$ cm $= (2x + 230)$ cm while the perimeter of the second shape (again starting from the lower left corner) is $(x + 50 + 10 + 25 + 10 + 50 + 10 + 75 + 10 + x + 40)$ cm $= (2x + 280)$ cm. Hence the difference between the two perimeters is $(2x + 280)$ cm $- (2x + 230)$ cm $= 50$ cm.

18. E Draw in lines PT and TS as shown. Since angles in a triangle add to $180°$ and we are given $\angle SPT = 75°$ and $\angle TSP = 30°$, we obtain $\angle PTS = 75°$. Therefore $\triangle PTS$ is isosceles and hence $TS = PS = 10$ cm. Therefore, since $RS = 10$ cm as it is a side of the square, $\triangle RST$ is also isosceles. Since $\angle RSP = 90°$ and $\angle TSP = 30°$, we have $\angle RST = 60°$. Therefore $\triangle RST$ is isosceles with one angle equal to $60°$. Hence $\triangle RST$ is equilateral and therefore the length of TR is 10 cm.

19. A Let the length of a side of $PQRS$ and of $WXYZ$ be x cm. Consider quadrilateral $QXRW$.

The diagonals QR and WX are perpendicular and of length x cm. Therefore the area of $QXRW$ is half the area of a rectangle with sides equal in length to QR and WX and hence is equal to $\frac{1}{2} \times QR \times WX = \frac{1}{2}x^2$ cm^2. Similarly, the area of quadrilateral $SWRZ$ is also $\frac{1}{2}x^2$ cm^2. Therefore the total shaded area is x^2 cm^2. However, the question tells us that the shaded area is equal to 1 cm^2. Therefore $x^2 = 1$. Hence the area of $PQRS$ is 1 cm^2.

20. C Note first that $7632 = 2 \times 2 \times 2 \times 2 \times 3 \times 3 \times 53$. Therefore either the two-digit number $de = 53$ or the three-digit number abc is a multiple of 53. Since the multiplication uses each of the digits 1 to 9 once and 7632 contains a 3, the option $de = 53$ is not allowable. Hence we need to find a three-digit multiple of 53 that does not share any digits with 7632 and divides into 7632 leaving an answer that also does not share any digits with 7632. We can reject $2 \times 53 = 106$ since it contains a 6 but $3 \times 53 = 159$ is a possibility. The value of $7632 \div 159$ is $2 \times 2 \times 2 \times 2 \times 3 = 48$ which does not have any digits in common with 7632 nor with 159. We can also check that no other multiple of 53 will work. Therefore the required multiplication is $159 \times 48 = 7632$ and hence the value of b is 5.

21. B The information in the question tells us that the numbers on touching faces of the solid are the same and that numbers on opposite faces of a die add to 7.

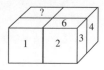

Since the number 4 is visible on the rear of the right-hand side of the solid, there is a 3 on the left-hand face of the rear right die and hence a 3 and a 4 on the right- and left-hand faces of the rear left die. Similarly, since the number 1 is visible on the left-hand side of the front of the solid, there is a 6 and a 1 on the front and back faces of the rear left die. Therefore the top and bottom faces of the rear left die have a 2 and a 5 written on them. Since the four dice are identical, comparison with the front right die of the solid tells us that a die with a 6 on its front face and a 3 on its right-hand face has a 2 on its lower face and hence a 5 on its upper face.

22. C The possible groups of three integers with product 36 are $(1, 1, 36)$, $(1, 2, 18)$, $(1, 3, 12)$, $(1, 4, 9)$, $(1, 6, 6)$, $(2, 2, 9)$, $(2, 3, 6)$ and $(3, 3, 4)$ with sums 38, 21, 16, 14, 13, 13, 11 and 10 respectively. The only value for the sum that occurs twice is 13. Hence, since Topaz does not know what the three integers chosen are, the sum of Harriet's three integers is 13.

23. E Since the triangle formed when the trapeziums are put together is equilateral, the smaller angles in the isosceles trapeziums are both 60°. Consider one trapezium split into a parallelogram and a triangle as shown.

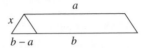

Since the original trapezium contains two base angles of 60°, the triangle also contains two base angles of 60°. Hence the triangle is equilateral and has side length $(b - a)$. Now consider the large equilateral triangle with the hole. The perimeter of the hole is $3(a - x)$ where x is the length of the shortest sides of the trapezium. Therefore the perimeter of the hole is $3(a - (b - a)) = 3(2a - b) = 6a - 3b$.

24. A Let the number of pencils Zain takes on Monday and Tuesday be x and y respectively. Therefore $x + \frac{2}{3}x + y + \frac{1}{2}y = 21$. Hence, when we multiply the equation through by 6 to eliminate the fractions and simplify, we obtain $10x + 9y = 126$. Since x and y are both positive integers and since the units digit of $10x$ is 0, the units digit of $9y$ is 6 and hence $y = 4$. Therefore $x = 9$ and hence the number of pencils Zain takes is $9 + 4 = 13$. Therefore the number of pencils Jacob takes is $21 - 13 = 8$.

25. E Let the three-digit number be $100a + 10b + c$. Since each suitable number is 34 times the sum of its digits, we have $100a + 10b + c = 34(a + b + c)$. Therefore $66a - 33c = 24b$. Since the left-hand side of this equation is a multiple of 11, the right-hand side is also a multiple of 11 and hence $b = 0$. Therefore $66a - 33c = 0$ and hence $c = 2a$. Therefore the three-digit numbers with the required property are 102, 204, 306 and 408 and hence there are four three-digit numbers with the required property.

The Junior Mathematical Olympiad

UK Junior Mathematical Olympiad 2017

Organised by The United Kingdom Mathematics Trust

Tuesday 13th June 2017

RULES AND GUIDELINES :
READ THESE INSTRUCTIONS CAREFULLY BEFORE STARTING

1. Time allowed: 2 hours.

2. **The use of calculators, measuring instruments and squared paper is forbidden.**

3. All candidates must be in *School Year 8 or below* (England and Wales), *S2 or below* (Scotland), *School Year 9 or below* (Northern Ireland).

4. **Write in blue or black pen or pencil.**
    For questions in Section A *only the answer is required*. Enter each answer neatly in the relevant box on the Front Sheet. Do not hand in rough work.
    For questions in Section B you must give *full written solutions*, including clear mathematical explanations as to why your method is correct.
    Solutions must be written neatly on A4 paper. Sheets must be STAPLED together in the top left corner with the Front Sheet on top.
    Do not hand in rough work.

5. Questions A1-A10 are relatively short questions. Try to complete Section A within the first 30 minutes so as to allow well over an hour for Section B.

6. Questions B1-B6 are longer questions requiring *full written solutions*.
    This means that each answer must be accompanied by clear explanations and proofs.
    Work in rough first, then set out your final solution with clear explanations of each step.

7. These problems are meant to be challenging! Do not hurry. Try the earlier questions in each section first (they tend to be easier). Try to finish whole questions even if you are not able to do many. A good candidate will have done most of Section A and given solutions to at least two questions in Section B.

8. Answers must be FULLY SIMPLIFIED, and EXACT using symbols like π, fractions, or square roots if appropriate, but NOT decimal approximations.

DO NOT OPEN THE PAPER UNTIL INSTRUCTED BY THE INVIGILATOR TO DO SO!

Section A

Try to complete Section A within 30 minutes or so. Only answers are required.

A1. How many centimetres are there in 1 km 2 m 3 cm 4 mm?

A2. The solid shown is formed by taking a 3 cm × 3 cm × 3 cm cube and drilling a 1 cm × 1 cm square hole from the centre of each face to the centre of the opposite face.
What is the volume in cm^3 of the solid?

A3. Howard is out running. He is now $\frac{3}{5}$ of the way through the second half of his run. What fraction of the whole run has he completed?

A4. A bookmark-maker sells bookmarks for £1 each or 7 for £6. What is the smallest amount you could pay for 2017 of her bookmarks?

A5. In 1866, the yacht *Henrietta* – with Gordon Bennett aboard – won the Great Ocean Yacht Race, travelling a distance of approximately 3000 nautical miles. The winning time was 13 days and 22 hours, to the nearest hour.
What was the yacht's average speed in nautical miles per hour, to the nearest integer?

A6. The diagram shows six identical squares arranged symmetrically.
What fraction of the diagram is shaded?

A7. A fully-grown long-tailed tit – *Aegithalos caudatus* – weighs only 9 g, whereas a £1 coin weighs 9.5 g.
To the nearest 1 %, what percentage of the weight of a £1 coin is the weight of a fully-grown long-tailed tit?

A8. A jar contains red and white marbles in the ratio 1 : 4. When Jenny replaces 2 of the white marbles with 7 red marbles, the ratio becomes 2 : 3.
What is the ratio of the total number of marbles in the jar now to the total number in the jar before?

A9. How many multiples of 3 that are less than 1000 are not divisible either by 9 or by 10?

A10. Two concentric circles are drawn, as shown in the diagram. Concentric circles share the same point as their centre. The radius of the smaller circle is a third of the radius of the larger circle. The top half of the larger circle which is outside the smaller circle, is shaded in grey.
The ratio of the grey shaded area to the area of the smaller circle in its simplest form is $a : b$. What are the values of a and b?

Section B

Your solutions to Section B will have a major effect on your JMO result. Concentrate on one or two questions first and then **write out full solutions** (not just brief 'answers').

B1. An amount of money is to be divided equally between a group of children. If there was 20p more than this amount, then there would be enough for each child to receive 70p. However, if each child was to receive 60p, then £2.10 would be left over.

How many children are there in the group?

B2. A 3-digit integer is called a 'V-number' if the digits go 'high-low-high' – that is, if the tens digit is smaller than both the hundreds digit and the units (or 'ones') digit.

How many 3-digit 'V-numbers' are there?

B3. Two identical rectangles overlap in such a way that a rhombus is formed, as indicated in the diagram. The area of the rhombus is five-eighths of the area of each rectangle.

What is the ratio of the length of the longer side of the rectangle to the length of the shorter side?

B4. My uncle lives a long way away and his letters always contain puzzles. His three local teams are the Ants (A), the Bees (B), and the Cats (C), who play each other once a year.

My uncle claimed that the league table part way through the year looked like this:

	Played	Won	Drawn	Lost	Goals for	Goals against
A	1	0	0	1	4	2
B	2	1	1	0	2	2
C	2	1	0	1	3	1

When we complained that this is impossible, he admitted that every single number was wrong but he excused himself because every number was exactly '1 out'.

Find the correct table, explaining clearly how you deduced the corrections.

B5. The diagram shows a square whose vertices touch the sides of a regular pentagon. Each vertex of the pentagon touches a side of a regular hexagon.

Find the value of $a + b + c + d$.

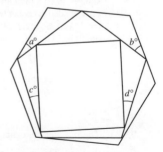

B6. The 9-digit positive integer N with digit pattern $ABCABCBBB$ is divisible by every integer from 1 to 17 inclusive.

The digits A, B and C are distinct. What are the values of A, B and C?

UK Junior Mathematical Olympiad 2017 Solutions

A1. **100203.4** When you convert all the distances to cm, you obtain 1 km = 100000 cm, 2 m = 200 cm and 4 mm = 0.4 cm. Therefore 1 km 2 m 3 cm 4 mm is equal to 100203.4 cm.

A2. **20** The volume of the large cube is 27 cm^3. To make the hole, one small cube is removed from the centre of each face and one from the centre of the large cube. Each small cube has a volume of 1 cm^3. Hence seven small cubes are removed and the remaining volume is 20 cm^3.

A3. $\frac{4}{5}$ Howard has completed $\frac{1}{2}$ of the run. He is now $\frac{3}{5}$ of the way through the second half. Hence he has completed $\frac{1}{2} + \frac{3}{5} \times \frac{1}{2} = \frac{1}{2} + \frac{3}{10} = \frac{4}{5}$ of the whole run.

A4. £1729 Since 2017 = 288 × 7 + 1, you can buy 288 lots of 7 bookmarks at £6 each. Hence the smallest amount you could pay for 2017 of the bookmarks is £6 × 288 + £1 × 1 = £1729.

A5. **9** Since 13 days and 22 hours are equivalent to 334 hours, the yacht travels 3000 nautical miles in 334 hours. Therefore the yacht travels $\frac{3000}{334}$ nautical miles in 1 hour. Hence the yacht's average speed in nautical miles per hour is 9 (to the nearest integer).

A6. $\frac{11}{24}$ There are several ways to solve this problem. This solution is just one example. Without loss of generality, let each square have a side length of 2 units. Hence the six identical squares have a total area of $6 \times 2^2 = 24$ square units. The grey shaded area can be thought of as consisting of two triangles, one rectangle and one square, as shown on the diagram. Therefore the grey shaded area is

$$\tfrac{1}{2} \times 1 \times 4 + \tfrac{1}{2} \times 3 \times 2 + 1 \times 2 + 2^2 = 11 \text{ square units.}$$

Hence $\frac{11}{24}$ of the diagram is shaded.

A7. 95% The required percentage is $\dfrac{9}{9.5} \times 100 = \dfrac{18}{19} \times 100 = \dfrac{1800}{19} \approx 94.7$ by long division. This is 95% to the nearest 1%.

A8. 6 : 5 Let m be the original number of marbles in the jar. Therefore, as Jenny replaces 2 of the white marbles with 7 red marbles, there are now $m + 5$ marbles in the jar. We know that $\frac{4}{5}$ of the original number of marbles were white, that 2 white marbles were removed and that now $\frac{3}{5}$ of the jar's marbles are white. Hence $\frac{4}{5}m - 2 = \frac{3}{5}(m + 5)$.

Solving this equation, gives $m = 25$. Therefore the ratio of the total number of marbles in the jar now to the number in the jar before is $30 : 25 = 6 : 5$.

A9. 200 There are 333 multiples of 3 less than 1000, and there are 111 multiples of 9 less than 1000. As numbers that are multiples of both 3 and 10 are multiples of 30, consider the 33 multiples of 30 that are less than 1000. The lowest common multiple of 9 and 30 is 90 and there are 11 multiples of 90 less than 1000. Hence the number of multiples of 3 that are less than 1000 but not divisible by either 9 or by 10 is $333 - 111 - 33 + 11 = 200$.

A10. 4, 1 Let the radius of the smaller circle be r, so the radius of the larger circle is $3r$.

The area of the smaller circle is πr^2 and the grey shaded area is $\frac{1}{2}\pi(3r)^2 - \frac{1}{2}\pi r^2 = 4\pi r^2$.

Therefore the ratio of the grey shaded area to the area of the smaller circle is $4\pi r^2 : \pi r^2 = 4 : 1$, and hence $a = 4$ and $b = 1$.

B1. An amount of money is to be divided equally between a group of children. If there was 20p more than this amount, then there would be enough for each child to receive 70p. However, if each child was to receive 60p, then £2.10 would be left over.

How many children are there in the group?

Solution

Let C be the number of children in the group and let A be the total amount of money in pence to be divided between the children.

Then $\dfrac{A + 20}{C} = 70$, so that $A + 20 = 70C$ and therefore $A = 70C - 20$.

Also $A = 60C + 210$.

Hence $70C - 20 = 60C + 210$.

Solving this last equation we obtain $C = 23$. Therefore there are 23 children in the group.

It is good practice to check the solution works. The total amount of money is £15.90, and $(£15.90 + £0.20) ÷ 23 = £0.70$; $£0.60 × 23 = £13.80$, and $£13.80 + £2.10 = £15.90$.

B2. A 3-digit integer is called a 'V-number' if the digits go 'high-low-high' – that is, if the tens digit is smaller than both the hundreds digit and the units (or 'ones') digit.

How many 3-digit 'V-numbers' are there?

Solution

The smallest 'V-number' is 101 and the largest 'V-number' is 989.

Consider the tens digits. The smallest tens digit is 0 and the largest tens digit is 8.

If the tens digit is 0, the hundreds digit can be 1 to 9, and the units digit can be 1 to 9, giving $9 × 9$ possible 'V-numbers'.

If the tens digit is 1, then the hundreds digit can be 2 to 9 and the units digit can be 2 to 9, giving $8 × 8$ possible 'V-numbers'.

If the tens digit is d, where d can be any digit from 0 to 8, the hundreds digit can be $(d + 1)$ to 9 and the units digit can be $(d + 1)$ to 9, giving $(9 - d) × (9 - d)$ possible 'V-numbers'.

The greatest value of d is 8. In this case, the hundreds digit can only be 9 and the units digit can only be 9, which gives just $1 × 1$ possibilities.

This gives the total number of possible 'V-numbers' to be $9 × 9 + 8 × 8 + \ldots + 1 × 1 = 285$, which is the sum of the squares from 1 to 9 inclusive.

B3. Two identical rectangles overlap in such a way that a rhombus is formed, as indicated in the diagram. The area of the rhombus is five-eighths of the area of each rectangle.

What is the ratio of the length of the longer side of the rectangle to the length of the shorter side?

Solution

Let the length of the longer side and of the shorter side of the rectangle be L and W respectively.

Since the area of the rhombus is $\frac{5}{8}$ of the area of each rectangle, the area of the rhombus is $\frac{5}{8}LW$. Also, since the area of a rhombus is equal to base × perpendicular height and the perpendicular height of the shaded rhombus is W, the length of each side of the rhombus is $\frac{5}{8}L$.

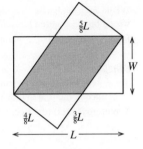

Consider one of the white right-angled triangles. The length of the hypotenuse is $\frac{5}{8}L$ and the length of one other side is $L - \frac{5}{8}L = \frac{3}{8}L$. Therefore, using Pythagoras' Theorem, we can find the length of the third side in terms of L since the triangle is a 3: 4: 5 triangle. Hence $W = \frac{4}{8}L$ and the ratio of the length of the longer side of the rectangle to the length of the shorter side of the rectangle is $L : \frac{4}{8}L = 2 : 1$.

B4. My uncle lives a long way away and his letters always contain puzzles. His three local teams are the Ants (A), the Bees (B), and the Cats (C), who play each other once a year. My uncle claimed that the league table part way through the year looked like this:

	Played	Won	Drawn	Lost	Goals for	Goals against
A	1	0	0	1	4	2
B	2	1	1	0	2	2
C	2	1	0	1	3	1

When we complained that this is impossible, he admitted that every single number was wrong but he excused himself because every number was exactly '1 out'.

Find the correct table, explaining clearly how you deduced the corrections.

Solution

The maximum number of games any team can play is 2, as each team only plays another team once in the year and there are only 3 teams.

Therefore team B (the Bees) and team C (the Cats) played 1 game each.

Team A (the Ants) played 2 games (because if they had played 0 games they would have 0 goals for). Since each figure is '1 out', team A won 1, drew 1 and lost 0 (so that the total number of matches played is 2).

Since team A won 1 match, team B lost 1 match (since team B had lost 0 games originally and team C cannot have lost 2 games). Therefore, team B won 0 games and drew 0 games.

So team A drew against team C. Therefore the number of games resulting in a draw for team C is 1 and, as they only played 1 match, they won and lost 0 games.

Since team C's only game resulted in a draw, team C's goals for and against are equal. Therefore, team C's goals for and against are 2 each.

Team B's only match resulted in a loss, so team B's goals against are greater than its goals for. Therefore, the number of team B's goals for is 1 and the number of its goals against is 3.

Because team B and team C both only played team A, the number of team A's goals for is equal to the sum of the number of team B's goals against and the number of team C's goals against. Hence the number of team A's goals for is 5. Similarly, the number of team A's goals against is the sum of the number of team B's goals for and the number of team C's goals for. Therefore the number of team A's goals against is 3.

So the correct table is:

Team	Played	Won	Drawn	Lost	Goals for	Goals against
A	2	1	1	0	5	3
B	1	0	0	1	1	3
C	1	0	1	0	2	2

B5. The diagram shows a square whose vertices touch the sides of a regular pentagon. Each vertex of the pentagon touches a side of a regular hexagon.

Find the value of $a + b + c + d$.

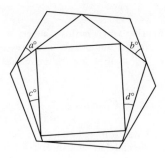

Solution

Each interior angle of a regular pentagon is 108° and each interior angle of a regular hexagon is 120°.

Consider the two shaded triangles in the diagram alongside, which contain the angles $a°$ and $b°$ and the side of the hexagon that these triangles have in common.

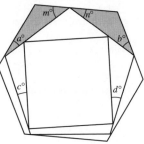

Let the two angles shown be $m°$ and $n°$. Since the sum of the interior angles in a triangle is 180°, we have $120 + a + m = 180$ and $120 + b + n = 180$. Therefore, $m = 60 - a$ and $n = 60 - b$. Now, since the sum of the angles on a straight line is 180°, we have $m + 108 + n = 180$. Hence $60 - a + 108 + 60 - b = 180$. Therefore $a + b = 48$.

The region outside the square but inside the pentagon consists of a quadrilateral, shown shaded in the diagram alongside, and three triangles. We now consider the quadrilateral.

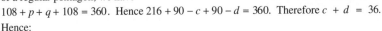

Let the two angles shown be $p°$ and $q°$. Since the interior angles of a square are 90° and the sum of the angles on a straight line is 180°, we have $c + 90 + p = 180$ and $d + 90 + q = 180$. Therefore $p = 90 - c$ and $q = 90 - d$. Now, since the sum of the angles in a quadrilateral is 360° and two of these angles are interior angles of a regular pentagon, we have $108 + p + q + 108 = 360$. Hence $216 + 90 - c + 90 - d = 360$. Therefore $c + d = 36$.

Hence:

$$a + b + c + d = 48 + 36$$

$$= 84.$$

B6. The 9-digit positive integer N with digit pattern *ABCABCBBB* is divisible by every integer from 1 to 17 inclusive.

The digits A, B and C are distinct. What are the values of A, B and C?

Solution

Since N is divisible by both 2 and 5, N is divisible by 10 and hence $B = 0$. Therefore N is of the form *A0CA0C000* = $A0C \times 1001 \times 1000$.

Now $1001 = 7 \times 11 \times 13$ and $1000 = 2 \times 2 \times 2 \times 5 \times 5 \times 5$. Hence *A0CA0C000* is certainly divisible by 1, 2, 4, 5, 7, 8, 11, 13 and 14.

We are told that N is divisible by every integer from 1 to 17. Hence, in particular, N is divisible by 9. Therefore, since the rule for divisibility by 9 is that the sum of the digits of the number is also divisible by 9, we have $2A + 2C$ is a multiple of 9 and hence $A + C$ is a multiple of 9. Also, since A and C are distinct, $A + C = 9$.

Once A and C are chosen so that N is divisible by 9, N will also be divisible by 3, 6, 12 and 15.

Since $N = A0C \times 1001 \times 1000$ is divisible by 16, *A0C* is divisible by 2 and hence C is even. Therefore, the only options for A and C (in that order) are 1 and 8, 3 and 6, 5 and 4, or 7 and 2.

To ensure N is divisible by 17, we must now ensure that A and C are chosen so that *A0C* is divisible by 17. When we look at each case in turn, we find that $108 = 6 \times 17 + 6$, $306 = 18 \times 17$, $504 = 29 \times 17 + 11$ and $702 = 41 \times 17 + 5$. Therefore $A = 3$, $B = 0$ and $C = 6$.

The marking and results

The pupils' scripts began arriving very rapidly and the marking took place in Leeds on the weekend of 24th and 25th June 2017. The discussions as to how marks should be given and for what were ably led by Andrew Jobbings. A full list of markers appears in the Volunteers section.

As has been stated, the object of the JMO is for pupils to be *challenged*, possibly in ways they have not been before. Some participants may find all of Section B rather beyond them, but it is hoped that they achieve a degree of satisfaction from Section A. Satisfaction is an important aspect of this level of paper; nevertheless, those who do succeed in tackling Section B deserve credit for that and such credit is mainly dependent on getting solutions to questions in Section B which are 'perfect' or very nearly so.

Based on the total of both A and B sections, book prizes and certificates are awarded. The top scoring 25% of all candidates receive a Certificate of Distinction. Of those scoring below this, candidates who make a good attempt at the paper (usually a score of 8+, but may be moderated based on the score distribution) will receive a Certificate of Merit. Of the remaining candidates, those who qualified automatically for the JMO via the JMC receive a Certificate of Qualification. Other candidates (discretionary) are only eligible for Distinction and Merit certificates. The top 50 scorers will be awarded a book prize; in 2017 this was *Whoever thought of that?* by Jenny Ramsden.

Medals are awarded on a different basis to certificates and prizes. The medal-awarding total will be the Section A mark + Section B marks that are 5 or more. The top 210 will receive a medal; gold: silver: bronze 30:60:120.

Average marks were slightly higher than in 2016. The numbers of medals awarded were: 35 Gold, 69 Silver and 123 Bronze.

The list below includes all the medal winners in the 2017 JMO. Within each category, the names are in alphabetical order.

Special mention should be made of David Han, Tom Harvey, Avish Kumar and Ilya Misyura who now have two JMO gold medals each and Robin Bradfield who has three.

The results and all the extras (books, book plates, certificates and medals) were posted to schools by the middle of July.

GOLD MEDALS

Bhavan Aulakh	King Edward's School, Birmingham
Ewan Azlan-Luk	Reading School
Ravi Bahukhandi	British School Manila, Philippines
Oliver Beeby	Westminster Under School, London
Robin Bradfield	Cargilfield Preparatory, Edinburgh
Helen Choi	Surbiton High Sch., Kingston-upon-Thames
Isaac Cumberlidge	Congleton High School, Cheshire
Francesca Di Cecio	St Paul's Girls' School, Hammersmith
Patrick Garman	Westminster Under School, London
Rebekah Glaze	West Kirby Grammar School, Wirral
Ojas Gulati	Tiffin School, Kingston-upon-Thames
Aditya Gupta	Westminster Under School, London
David Han	King George V School, Hong Kong
Tom Harvey	Bottisham Village College, Cambridgeshire
Tian Hsu	St Paul's Girls' School, Hammersmith
Nathaniel Johnson	Tiffin School, Kingston-upon-Thames
Avish Kumar	Westminster Under School, London
Albet Kwok	Haberdashers' Aske's School for Boys, Herts
Hieronim Lecybyl	St Olave's Grammar School, Kent
Sanghyung Lee	British School of Brussels
Arunav Maheshwari	UWCSEA East Campus, Singapore
Ilya Misyura	Westminster Under School, London
Moses Ng	Merchant Taylors' School, Middlesex
Tobin Payne	Chesham Grammar School, Buckinghamshire
Max Peel	Westminster Under School, London
Beni Prapashtica	Westminster Academy
Juneyoun Seo	The British International Sch. Jakarta, Indonesia
Kiran Shiatis	Judd School, Tonbridge, Kent
Theo Sinclair	King's College School, London
Dan Suciu	Queen Elizabeth's School, Barnet
Niklas Vainio	Westminster Under School, London

Ryan Voecks	University College School, London
Henry Wilson	Latymer School, London
Alan Xu	Crosfields School, Reading
George Zhou	Westminster Under School, London

SILVER MEDALS

Shivan Aggarwal	Bancroft's School, Essex
Tommy Ayling	The Costello School, Basingstoke
Benjamin Bishop	King Edward VI Grammar Sch., Chelmsford
Finlay Bowler	Denbigh School, Milton Keynes
Vaibhav Chaganti	King Edward's School, Birmingham
Raka Chattopadhyay	Queen's School, Chester
Sungxon Cho	The British International Sch. Jakarta, Indonesia
Micah Chote	City of London School
Connor Cusins	Aldwickbury School, Harpenden, Herts
Joseph Daly	The Purbeck School, Dorset
John Davie	Aylesbury Grammar School
Maxwell De Lorenzo	Westminster Under School, London
Finley Easton	Huntcliff School, Cleveland
Jack Finnis	Aldro School, Surrey
George Genever	Tapton School, Sheffield
Freddie Goodfellow	Sevenoaks School, Kent
Oliver Gunton	Aylesbury Grammar School
Gauri Gupta	Garden International School, Malaysia
Lorin Hallam	Matthew Arnold School, Oxford
Emma Harris	The Perse School, Cambridge
Anna Hawkins	Newstead Wood School, Kent
Ben Hermanns	The Forest School, Horsham
Cameron Hudson	Caterham School, Surrey
Theodore Jacques	Horsforth School, Leeds
Anirudh Khaitan	Reading School
Annant Khullar	Westminster Under School, London
Yeonung Kim	Hall School Wimbledon
Hyunggyu Kim	Glyn School, Ewell, Surrey

Isaac King	Hilden Grange School, Tonbridge, Kent
Peter Kippax	King Edward VI Camp Hill Sch. for Boys, Birmingham
Sasha Korovkina	Godstowe School, High Wycombe
Mansa Kumar	St Paul's Girls' School, Hammersmith
Kai Lam	Whitgift School, Surrey
Angelina (Seo Yeon) Lee	North London Collegiate Sch. Jeju, South Korea
Jiawen Li	St Paul's Girls' School, Hammersmith
Sida Li	Reading School
Michael Lin	The Perse School, Cambridge
Kai Matsumoto	Kingston Grammar School, Surrey
Sheikh Mohiddin	Queen Elizabeth's School, Barnet
Daniel Myers	Pate's Grammar School, Cheltenham
Samvit Nagpal	Westminster Under School, London
Nakul Nataraj	The Royal Grammar School, High Wycombe
Joseph Nogbou	Bacup & Rawtenstall Grammar Sch., Lancs
Ben Norman	The Perse School, Cambridge
Lydia Nottingham	Chatham & Clarendon Grammar Sch., Ramsgate
Jacob Oxtoby	King Henry VIII School, Coventry
Dectot Phileas	Loretto School, Musselburgh, Lothian
Juan Rajagopal	Rydal Penrhos School, Colwyn Bay, Conwy
Augustus Redding	St Bede's Prep School, Eastbourne
Jake Sandland	Harrogate Grammar School, N. Yorks
Abhinav Santhiramohan	Queen Elizabeth's School, Barnet
James Sarkies	Lawrence Sheriff School, Rugby
Jihwan Shin	UWCSEA Dover Campus, Singapore
Ethan Sosin	The West Bridgford School, Nottingham
Leo Takishige	Westminster Under School, London
Arun Tandon	Dr Challoner's Grammar School, Amersham
Weizhe Tao	Windlesham House School, W. Sussex
William Thomson	Pilgrims School, Winchester
Vaclav Trpisovsky	Open Gates Boarding Sch., Czech Republic
Anish Vaddiraju	Dr Challoner's Grammar School, Amersham
Jessica Wang	The Tiffin Girls' Sch., Kingston-upon-Thames

Mia Williams	Highgate School, London
Aidan Wong	The Perse School, Cambridge
James Wu	Magdalen College School, Oxford
Daniel Yap	Westminster Under School, London
Victor Yin	Beijing Dulwich International School
Jack Yu	Tiffin School, Kingston-upon-Thames
Haolin Zhao	Robin Hood Junior School, Surrey
Aaron Zheng	Renaissance College, Hong Kong

BRONZE MEDALS

Bakri Abubakar	Queen Elizabeth's School, Barnet
Jonathan Ambler	Clifton College Prep School, Bristol
Aron Arnason	Colyton Grammar School, Devon
Vedant Bahadur	UWCSEA Dover Campus, Singapore
Joshua Bannisterly	Poole Grammar School, Dorset
Jake Barry	Dr Challoner's Grammar School, Amersham
Tabitha Bates	Liverpool Blue Coat School
Brendan Bethlehem	Westminster Under School, London
Jakub Biszozanik	City of London School
Jack Burton	The Fernwood School, Nottingham
Fraser Buxton	Titus Salt School, West Yorkshire
Lorna Campbell	Newstead Wood School, Kent
Sambhav Chadha	Glasgow Academy
Thomas Chamberlain	Tapton School, Sheffield
Anoushka Chawla	North London Collegiate School
Matthew Chua	British School Manila, Philippines
Ben Chung	Comberton Village College, Cambridgeshire
Elliot Clarkson	King Edward's School, Birmingham
Conor Collins	Solihull School
Connor Compton	Pate's Grammar School, Cheltenham
Dylan Cook	Highdown S. & Sixth Form Centre, Reading
Peter Cook	Durham Johnston School
Eva Cooper	Rodillian Academy, Wakefield
Johnny Cubbon	Colet Court School, London
Nathan Curry	Aylesbury Grammar School

Raphaello de la Cruz	Reading School
Akash Dubb	King Edward's School, Birmingham
Lewis Edmond	Sawston Village College, Cambridgeshire
Oliver Gibson	Howard of Effingham School, Surrey
Sophie Goodman	Monkton Prep School, Bath
Benjamin Gray	Colyton Grammar School, Devon
Charlie Griffith	Ashfold School, Buckinghamshire
Maksym Grykshtas	King Edward VI Grammar Sch., Chelmsford
Kush Gupta	Colet Court School, London
Varun Gupta	King Edward's School, Birmingham
Vass Hadjiemmanuil	The Academy School, London
Moonis Haider	Bishop Vesey's Grammar S., Sutton Coldfield
Yueyang Han	Watford Grammar School for Boys
Ben Handley	St Aidan's Church of England H.S., Harrogate
Benedict Harvey	Elstree School, Reading
William Hodi	Nairn Academy
Hongli Hu	The Perse School, Cambridge
Ali Imam-Sadeque	Colet Court School, London
Saami Jaffer	Haberdashers' Aske's School for Boys, Herts
Dhruv Jajodia	Westminster Under School, London
Yuxuan Jiang	Eltham College Senior School, London
Jason Jiang	Queen Elizabeth's Hospital, Bristol
Barack Jin	Brockhurst and Marlston House S., Berkshire
Thomas Kan	Oundle School, Northants
Thomas Kavanagh	Reigate Grammar School, Surrey
Leona Kelly	St Bernard's Prep, Slough
Taeun Kim	Ibstock Place School, Roehampton, Surrey
Jenna Kim	North London Collegiate S. Jeju, South Korea
Katrina Kirby	The Cherwell School, Oxford
Atara Klein	Menorah High School, London
Yonni Kobrin	The Hall School, Hampstead
Adithya Kunigiri	Loughborough Grammar School
Arsen Lam	German Swiss International S., Hong Kong
Dimitri Lang	Ralph Allen School, Bath

Fred Lang	Florence Melly Community Primary S., Liverpool
Fran Lee	North London Collegiate School
Jangju Lee	North London Collegiate S. Jeju, South Korea
Chan-min Lee	North London Collegiate S. Jeju, South Korea
Charlie Lowman	Christleton High School, Chester
Leo Luo	St Olave's Grammar School, Kent
Sophie Lyne	Chesterton Community College, Cambridge
Eleanor MacGillivray	King's School Ely, Cambridgeshire
Owen Mackenzie	Glyn School, Ewell, Surrey
Louis Macro	Bristol Grammar School
Aditya Mahesh	The High School of Glasgow
Alex Mann	Highgate School, London
Sithika Medagedara	Ruthin School, Denbighshire
Patrick Meehan	Trinity School Lewisham
Sai Mehta	Reddiford School, Middlesex
Purav Menon	Westminster Under School, London
Alexander Middleton	Kingston Grammar School, Surrey
Saad Mohamed	Queen Mary's Grammar School, Walsall
Phoenix Mombru	St Paul's Girls' School, Hammersmith
Daniel Morgan	The Mall School, Twickenham
Aaditya Nagarajan	The Perse School, Cambridge
Rudra Nakade	The Royal Latin School, Buckingham
Alexander Nelson	Loughborough Grammar School
James Painter	Bell Baxter High School, Fife
Maxime Pesenti	Eltham College Senior School, London
Georgina Pilz	St Paul's Girls' School, Hammersmith
James Radford	St George's School, Windsor
Reon Raju	The Trinity Catholic School , Nottingham
Abhinav Ramisetty	Yarm School, nr Stockton-on-Tees
Freddie Reid	Skinners' School, Tunbridge Wells
Jacob Roberts	Sheldon School, Chippenham, Wiltshire
Matthew Roberts	Bishop Vesey's Grammar S., Sutton Coldfield
Jago Rowe	Parmiter's School, Watford
Grace Ruddick	Ralph Allen School, Bath

Amrit Sahu	George Abbot School, Guildford
Johnny Sammon	Reading School
Shaunak Satish	Reading School
Anisha Sawhney	North London Collegiate School
Robert Seabourne	Lavington School, Wiltshire
Abhishek Sen	The King's School, Peterborough
Shonit Sharma	Aylesbury Grammar School
Varun Sharma	Ipswich School
Matthew Smith	Haberdashers' Aske's School for Boys, Herts
Mukund Soni	Queen Elizabeth's School, Barnet
Ellis Speight	Heckmondwike Grammar S., West Yorkshire
Elliot Staniford	Bournemouth School
Anujayan Sugirtharan	City of London School
Kai Sun	Comberton Village College, Cambridgeshire
Benedek Szilvasy	Tiffin School, Kingston-upon-Thames
Miranda Thomas	The Tiffin Girls' Sch., Kingston-upon-Thames
William Trice	Court Moor School, Hampshire
Toan Truong	St Olave's Grammar School, Kent
Liam Turner	Colyton Grammar School, Devon
Orca Vanichjakvong	Shrewsbury International School, Thailand
Eunyul Wang	North London Collegiate S. Jeju, South Korea
Romeo Wang	Handcross Park School, West Sussex
Alex Williamson	Robert Bloomfield Academy, Bedfordshire
Adrian Wu	King George V School, Hong Kong
Ruixuan Wu	Queen Elizabeth's School, Barnet
Yicheng Xia	Stockport Grammar School
Seungwon Yoo	North London Collegiate S. Jeju, South Korea
Seonghyu Yoon	North London Collegiate S. Jeju, South Korea
Richard Yu	Jordanhill School, Glasgow
Ruiqi Zhang	St Olave's Grammar School, Kent

The Intermediate Mathematical Challenge and its follow-up events

The Intermediate Mathematical Challenge (IMC) was held on Thursday 2nd February 2017, and over 219,000 pupils took part. There were several different Intermediate Mathematical Olympiad and Kangaroo (IMOK) follow-up competitions and pupils were invited to the one appropriate to their school year and mark in the IMC. Around 500 candidates in each of Years 9, 10 and 11 sat the Olympiad papers (Cayley, Hamilton and Maclaurin respectively) and approximately 4000 more in each year group took a Kangaroo paper. We start with the IMC paper.

UK INTERMEDIATE MATHEMATICAL CHALLENGE

THURSDAY 2ND FEBRUARY 2017

Organised by the **United Kingdom Mathematics Trust**

and supported by

Institute
and Faculty
of Actuaries

RULES AND GUIDELINES (to be read before starting)

1. Do not open the paper until the Invigilator tells you to do so.

2. Time allowed: **1 hour**.
   No answers, or personal details, may be entered after the allowed hour is over.

3. The use of rough paper is allowed; **calculators** and measuring instruments are **forbidden**.

4. Candidates in England and Wales must be in School Year 11 or below.
   Candidates in Scotland must be in S4 or below.
   Candidates in Northern Ireland must be in School Year 12 or below.

5. **Use B or HB pencil only**. Mark *at most one* of the options A, B, C, D, E on the Answer Sheet for each question. Do not mark more than one option.

6. *Do not expect to finish the whole paper in 1 hour.* Concentrate first on Questions 1-15. When you have checked your answers to these, have a go at some of the later questions.

7. Five marks are awarded for each correct answer to Questions 1-15.
   Six marks are awarded for each correct answer to Questions 16-25.
   Each incorrect answer to Questions 16-20 loses 1 mark.
   Each incorrect answer to Questions 21-25 loses 2 marks.

8. Your Answer Sheet will be read only by a *dumb machine*. **Do not write or doodle on the sheet except to mark your chosen options**. The machine 'sees' all black pencil markings even if they are in the wrong places. If you mark the sheet in the wrong place, or leave bits of rubber stuck to the page, the machine will 'see' a mark and interpret this mark in its own way.

9. The questions on this paper challenge you to **think**, not to guess. You get more marks, and more satisfaction, by doing one question carefully than by guessing lots of answers. The UK IMC is about solving interesting problems, not about lucky guessing.

The UKMT is a registered charity
http://www.ukmt.org.uk

1. What is the value of $\dfrac{2}{5} + \dfrac{2}{50} + \dfrac{2}{500}$?

   A 0.111   B 0.222   C 0.333   D 0.444   E 0.555

2. Each of the diagrams below shows a circle and four small squares. In each case, the centre of the circle is the point where all four squares meet.

   In one of the diagrams, exactly one third of the circle is shaded. Which one?

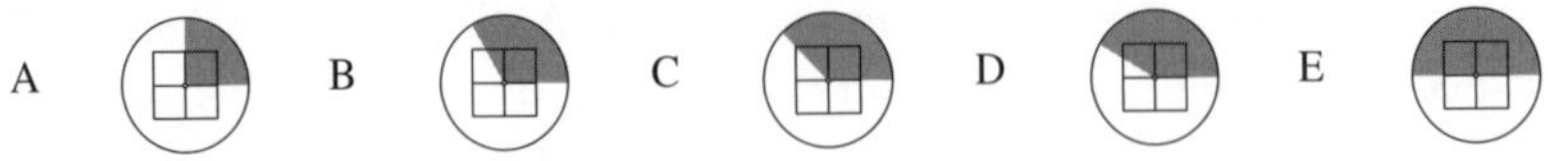

   A B C D E

3. How many squares have 7 as their units digit?

   A 0   B 1   C 2   D 3   E 4

4. Which of the following is *not* the sum of two primes?

   A 5   B 7   C 9   D 11   E 13

5. The diagram shows two circles with the same centre. The radius of the outer circle is twice the radius of the inner circle. The region between the inner circle and the outer circle is divided into six equal segments as shown.

   What fraction of the area of the outer circle is shaded?

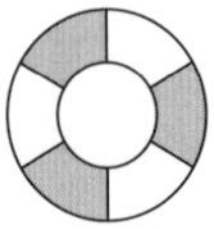

   A $\dfrac{3}{7}$ B $\dfrac{3}{8}$ C $\dfrac{3}{9}$ D $\dfrac{3}{10}$ E $\dfrac{3}{11}$

6. The angles of a quadrilateral are in the ratio $3 : 4 : 5 : 6$.

   What is the difference between the largest angle and the smallest angle?

   A 30°   B 40°   C 50°   D 60°   E 70°

7. Four different positive integers are to be chosen so that they have a mean of 2017.
   What is the smallest possible range of the chosen integers?

   A 2   B 3   C 4   D 5   E 6

8. Which of the following numbers is the largest?

   A 1.3542   B 1.354$\dot{2}$ C 1.35$\dot{4}\dot{2}$ D 1.3$\dot{5}4\dot{2}$ E 1.$\dot{3}54\dot{2}$

9. The number 'tu' is the two-digit number with units digit u and tens digit t. The digits a and b are distinct, and non-zero. What is the largest possible value of 'ab' − 'ba' ?

   A 81   B 72   C 63   D 54   E 45

10. The diagram shows three rectangles.
    What is the value of x?

    A 108   B 104   C 100   D 96   E 92

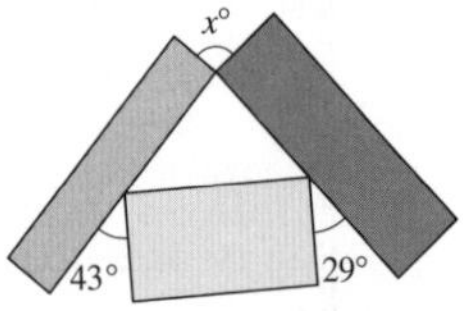

11. The diagram shows four equilateral triangles with sides of lengths 1, 2, 3 and 4. The area of the shaded region is equal to n times the area of the unshaded triangle of side-length 1.
What is the value of n?

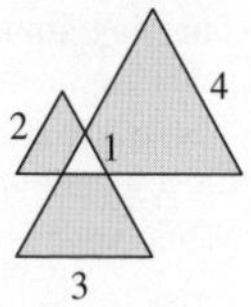

A 8   B 11   C 18   D 23   E 26

12. The combined age of Alice and Bob is 39. The combined age of Bob and Clare is 40. The combined age of Clare and Dan is 38. The combined age of Dan and Eve is 44. The total of all five ages is 105.
Which of the five is the youngest?

A Alice   B Bob   C Clare   D Dan   E Eve

13. The diagram shows a quadrilateral $PQRS$ made from two similar right-angled triangles, PQR and PRS. The length of PQ is 3, the length of QR is 4 and $\angle PRQ = \angle PSR$.
What is the perimeter of $PQRS$?

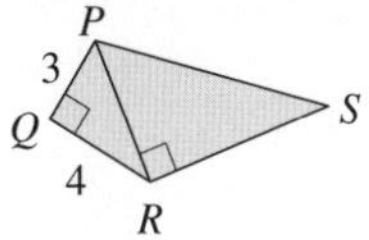

A 22   B $22\frac{5}{6}$ C 27   D 32   E $45\frac{1}{3}$

14. For what value of x is 64^x equal to 512^5 ?

A 6   B 7.5   C 8   D 16   E 40

15. In the diagram shown, $PQ = SQ = QR$ and $\angle SPQ = 2 \times \angle RSQ$.
What is the size of angle QRS?

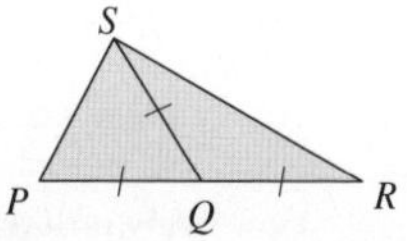

A 20°   B 25°   C 30°   D 35°   E 40°

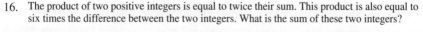

16. The product of two positive integers is equal to twice their sum. This product is also equal to six times the difference between the two integers. What is the sum of these two integers?

A 6   B 7   C 8   D 9   E 10

17. The diagram shows two rectangles and a regular pentagon. One side of each rectangle has been extended to meet at X.
What is the value of x?

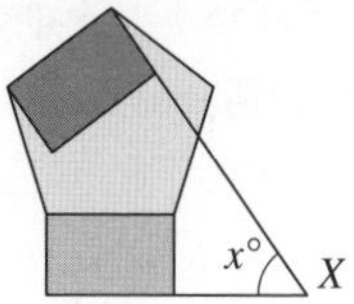

A 52   B 54   C 56   D 58   E 60

18. A water tank is $\frac{5}{6}$ full. When 30 litres of water are removed from the tank, the tank is $\frac{4}{5}$ full.
How much water does the tank hold when full?

A 180 litres   B 360 litres   C 540 litres   D 720 litres   E 900 litres

19. $PQRS$ is a square. Point T lies on PQ so that $PT : TQ = 1:2$. Point U lies on SR so that $SU : UR = 1 : 2$. The perimeter of $PTUS$ is 40 cm.
What is the area of $PTUS$?

A 40 cm²   B 45 cm²   C 48 cm²   D 60 cm²   E 75 cm²

20. The diagram shows seven circular arcs and a heptagon with equal sides but unequal angles. The sides of the heptagon have length 4. The centre of each arc is a vertex of the heptagon, and the ends of the arc are the midpoints of the two adjacent sides.

What is the total shaded area?

A 12π   B 14π   C 16π   D 18π   E 20π

---

21. *Brachycephalus* frogs are tiny – less than 1 cm long – and have three toes on each foot and two fingers on each 'hand', whereas the common frog has five toes on each foot and four fingers on each 'hand'.

Some *Brachycephalus* and common frogs are in a bucket. Each frog has all its fingers and toes. Between them they have 122 toes and 92 fingers.

How many frogs are in the bucket?

A 15   B 17   C 19   D 21   E 23

22. The diagram shows an arc PQ of a circle with centre O and radius 8. Angle QOP is a right angle, the point M is the midpoint of OP and N lies on the arc PQ so that MN is perpendicular to OP.

Which of the following is closest to the length of the perimeter of triangle PNM ?

A 17   B 18   C 19   D 20   E 21

23. Two brothers and three sisters form a single line for a photograph. The two boys refuse to stand next to each other.

How many different line-ups are possible?

A 24   B 36   C 60   D 72   E 120

24. The nth term in a certain sequence is calculated by multiplying together all the numbers $\sqrt{1 + \frac{1}{k}}$, where k takes all the integer values from 2 to $n + 1$ inclusive. For example, the third term in the sequence is $\sqrt{1 + \frac{1}{2}} \times \sqrt{1 + \frac{1}{3}} \times \sqrt{1 + \frac{1}{4}}$.

Which is the smallest value of n for which the nth term of the sequence is an integer?

A 3   B 5   C 6   D 7   E more than 7

25. The diagram shows a circle with radius 2 and a square with sides of length 2. The centre of the circle lies on the perpendicular bisector of a side of the square, at a distance x from the side, as shown. The shaded region – inside the square but outside the circle – has area 2.

What is the value of x?

A $\frac{\pi}{3} + \frac{\sqrt{3}}{2} - 1$ B $\frac{\pi}{3} + \frac{\sqrt{3}}{4} - 1$ C $\frac{\pi}{3} + \frac{1}{2}$

D $\frac{\pi}{3} + 1$ E $\frac{\pi}{3}$

The IMC solutions

As with the Junior Challenge, a solutions leaflet was sent out.

Institute
and Faculty
of Actuaries

UK INTERMEDIATE MATHEMATICAL CHALLENGE

THURSDAY 2ND FEBRUARY 2017

Organised by the **United Kingdom Mathematics Trust**
from the School of Mathematics, University of Leeds

SOLUTIONS LEAFLET

This solutions leaflet for the IMC is sent in the hope that it might provide all concerned with some alternative solutions to the ones they have obtained. It is not intended to be definitive. The organisers would be very pleased to receive alternatives created by candidates.

For reasons of space, these solutions are necessarily brief. Extended solutions, and some exercises for further investigation, can be found at:

http://www.ukmt.org.uk/

The UKMT is a registered charity

1. **D** $\dfrac{2}{5} + \dfrac{2}{50} + \dfrac{2}{500} = \dfrac{200 + 20 + 2}{500} = \dfrac{222}{500} = \dfrac{444}{1000} = 0.444.$

2. **B** When one third of the circle is shaded, the angle at the centre of the shaded sector is $360° \div 3 = 120°$. In diagram A, the sector angle is $90°$. In diagram C, the sector angle is $90° + 90° \div 2 = 135°$. So the correct diagram has a sector angle greater than that shown in A, but smaller than that shown in C. The only such sector angle is that in B.

3. **A** Consider the units digits of the squares of the integers 0, 1, 2, 3, ..., 9. These are 0, 1, 4, 9, 6, 5, 6, 9, 4, 1. Note that none of these is 7, so no square ends in a 7.

4. **D** All primes except 2 are odd. So the sum of a pair of primes cannot be odd, and so cannot be prime, unless one of the pair is 2. We note that $5 = 2 + 3$; $7 = 2 + 5$; $9 = 2 + 7$; $13 = 2 + 11$. However, $11 = 2 + 9$ and so it is not the sum of two primes, as 9 is not prime.

5. B Let the area of the inner circle be A. The radius of the outer circle is twice that of the inner circle, so its area is four times that of the inner circle, that is $4A$. Therefore the region between the two circles has area $3A$. As three of the six equal segments are shaded, the total shaded area is $3A \div 2$. So the required fraction is $\frac{3}{2}A \div 4A = \frac{3}{8}$.

6. D The sum of the interior angles of a quadrilateral is $360°$. So the smallest angle in the quadrilateral is $3 \times \frac{360°}{3+4+5+6} = 60°$ and the largest angle is $6 \times \frac{360°}{3+4+5+6} = 120°$. Hence the required difference is $60°$.

7. C The smallest possible range of four positive integers is 3. Let these integers be n, $n+1, n+2, n+3$. For the mean of these four integers to equal 2017, we have $\frac{n+n+1+n+2+n+3}{4} = 2017$, that is $n = 2015\frac{1}{2}$. So the smallest possible range is not 3. However, note that the integers 2015, 2016, 2018 and 2019 have mean 2017 and range 4. So the smallest possible range of the integers is 4.

8. D Consider options B to E: $1.354\dot{2} = 1.354222\ldots$; $1.35\dot{4}\dot{2} = 1.35424242\ldots$; $1.3\dot{5}4\dot{2} = 1.3542542\ldots$; $1.\dot{3}54\dot{2} = 1.35423542\ldots$. These are all greater than 1.3542, so option A is not correct. The other four options have the same units digit and the first four digits after the decimal point are the same in all. So the largest option is that which has the largest digit five places after the decimal point and this is $1.35\dot{4}\dot{2}$.

9. B First note that as 'ab' and 'ba' are two digit numbers, neither a nor b is equal to zero. Now 'ab' $-$ 'ba' $= (10a+b) - (10b+a) = 9a - 9b = 9(a-b)$. So for the difference to be as large as possible, a must be as large as possible, that is 9, and b must be as small as possible, that is 1.
So the required difference is $91 - 19 = 72$.

10. A As shown in the diagram, the perpendicular from A to BC meets BC at D. Because AD is parallel to two sides of the lower rectangle, $\angle BAD = 43°$ and $\angle DAC = 29°$ (corresponding angles in both cases). The angles at point A sum to $360°$, so $43 + 29 + 90 + x + 90 = 360$ and hence $x = 108$.

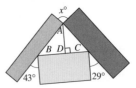

11. E Let the area of the equilateral triangle of side 1 be A. If similar figures have sides which are in the ratio $k : 1$, then the ratio of their areas is $k^2 : 1$. So the areas of the triangles with sides 2, 3, 4 are $4A$, $9A$, $16A$ respectively.
So, as shown in the diagram, the total shaded area is $3A + 8A + 15A = 26A$. Therefore $n = 26$.

12. D Let the ages of Alice, Bob, Clare, Dan and Eve be a, b, c, d, e respectively. So, for example, $b + c = 40$ and $d + e = 44$. Adding these gives $b + c + d + e = 84$. We are also told that $a + b + c + d + e = 105$. The difference between these equations shows that $a = 105 - 84 = 21$. Hence $b = 39 - 21 = 18$ and, similarly, $c = 40 - 18 = 22$, $d = 38 - 22 = 16$ and $e = 44 - 16 = 28$. So Dan is the youngest.

13. A   Pythagoras' Theorem shows that $PR = \sqrt{3^2 + 4^2} = 5$. So the perimeter of triangle PQR is 12. Since the triangles are similar and $PR : PQ = 5 : 3$ we see that the perimeter of triangle PRS is 20. Hence the perimeter of $PQRS$ is $12 + 20 - 2 \times PR = 32 - 10 = 22$.

14. B   Note that $64 = 2^6$ and $512 = 2^9$. Therefore $(2^6)^x = (2^9)^5$. So $2^{6x} = 2^{45}$. Hence $6x = 45$, that is $x = 7.5$.

15. C   Let $\angle QRS = x°$. Then, as $SQ = QR$, $\angle RSQ = x°$ also. Now $\angle SPQ = 2 \times \angle RSQ = 2x°$. In triangle PQS, $PQ = SQ$, so $\angle PSQ = \angle SPQ = 2x°$. Therefore $\angle PSR = \angle PSQ + \angle RSQ = 2x° + x° = 3x°$. The sum of the interior angles of a triangle is $180°$. So, considering triangle PSR, $\angle SPR + \angle PSR + \angle PRS = 180°$. Therefore $2x° + 3x° + x° = 180°$. So $6x = 180$, that is $x = 30$.

16. D   Let the two positive integers be m and n. Then $mn = 2(m + n) = 6(m - n)$. So $2m + 2n = 6m - 6n$, that is $8n = 4m$. Therefore $m = 2n$. Substituting for m gives: $(2n)n = 2(2n + n)$. So $2n^2 = 6n$, that is $2n(n - 3) = 0$. Therefore $n = 0$ or 3. However, n is positive so the only solution is $n = 3$. Therefore $m = 2 \times 3 = 6$ and $m + n = 6 + 3 = 9$.

17. B   Since $VWXYZ$ is a pentagon, the sum of its interior angles is $540°$. Now $\angle ZVW$ is an interior angle of a regular pentagon and so is $108°$. Both $\angle VWX$ and $\angle XYZ$ are $90°$; and the reflex angle $\angle YZV = 90° + 108°$. Therefore $540° = 108° + 90° + 90° + 90° + 108° + x°$. Hence $x = 540 - 486 = 54$.

18. E   Let the capacity of the tank be x litres. Then $30 = \frac{5x}{6} - \frac{4x}{5} = \frac{25x - 24x}{30} = \frac{x}{30}$. So $x = 30 \times 30 = 900$.

19. E   Let square $PQRS$ have side $3x$ cm. Then, as $PT : TQ = 1 : 2$, $PT = x$ cm. Similarly, $US = x$ cm. In triangles PTS and UST, $PT = US$, $\angle PTS = \angle UST$ (alternate angles) and TS is common to both. So the triangles are congruent (SAS). Therefore $UT = PS = 3x$ cm and $\angle TUS = \angle SPT = 90°$. Hence $PTUS$ is a rectangle, which has perimeter 40 cm. So $40 = 2(3x + x) = 8x$. Therefore $x = 5$ and the area of $PTUS$, in cm², is $15 \times 5 = 75$.

20. D   First note that as the length of each side of the heptagon is 4, the radius of each of the seven arcs is 2. The sum of the interior angles of a heptagon is $(7 - 2) \times 180° = 900°$. So the sum of the angles subtended by the circular arcs at the centres of the circles of radius 2 cm is $7 \times 360° - 900° = \left(7 - \frac{5}{2}\right) \times 360° = \frac{9}{2} \times 360°$. Therefore the total shaded area is equal to the total area of $\frac{9}{2}$ circles of radius 2. So the total shaded area is $\frac{9}{2} \times \pi \times 2^2 = 18\pi$.

21. A   Let the number of Brachycephalus frogs and common frogs in the bucket be b and c respectively. Note that each Brachycephalus frog has 6 toes and 4 fingers, while a common frog has 10 toes and 8 fingers. Therefore, $6b + 10c = 122$ (1); $4b + 8c = 92$ (2). Subtracting (2) from (1) gives $2b + 2c = 30$, so $b + c = 15$.

22. C Consider triangles MON and MPN. Note that $MO = MP = 4$ because M is the midpoint of OP; $\angle OMN = \angle PMN = 90°$ because MN is perpendicular to OP; side NM is common to both triangles. So triangles MON and MPN are congruent (SAS). Therefore $PN = ON = 8$ because ON is a radius of the circle. By Pythagoras' Theorem in triangle OMN, $ON^2 = OM^2 + MN^2$, so $8^2 = 4^2 + MN^2$. Therefore $MN^2 = 8^2 - 4^2 = 48$. So $MN = \sqrt{48}$. The perimeter of triangle PNM is $PN + NM + MP = 8 + \sqrt{48} + 4 = 12 + \sqrt{48}$. Now $6.5 < \sqrt{48} < 7$, since $\sqrt{42.25} < \sqrt{48} < \sqrt{49}$. So $\sqrt{48}$ is closer in value to 7 than it is to 6. So $12 + \sqrt{48}$ is nearer to 19 than it is to 18.

23. D Let the five positions in the photograph be numbered 1, 2, 3, 4, 5. Then the boys may occupy a total of six positions: 1 and 3; 1 and 4; 1 and 5; 2 and 4; 2 and 5; 3 and 5. For each of these positions, the boys may be arranged in two ways as they can interchange places. So there are 12 ways of positioning the boys. For each of these, the girls must be placed in three positions. In each case, the first girl may choose any one of three positions, the second girl may choose either of two positions and then there is just one place remaining for the third girl. So for each arrangement of the two boys there are $3 \times 2 \times 1$ different ways of arranging the three girls. Therefore the total number of line-ups is $12 \times 6 = 72$.

24. C The product may be written $\sqrt{\frac{3}{2}} \times \sqrt{\frac{4}{3}} \times \sqrt{\frac{5}{4}} \times \sqrt{\frac{6}{5}} \times \ldots = \frac{\sqrt{3}}{\sqrt{2}} \times \frac{\sqrt{4}}{\sqrt{3}} \times \frac{\sqrt{5}}{\sqrt{4}} \times \frac{\sqrt{6}}{\sqrt{5}} \times \ldots$ Notice that the numerator of each fraction is cancelled out by the denominator of the following fraction and the only terms which are not cancelled are the denominator of the first fraction and the numerator of the last fraction. So the n th term of the sequence is $\frac{\sqrt{n+2}}{\sqrt{2}} = \sqrt{\frac{n+2}{2}}$. As $n \geqslant 1$ the product is not equal to 1. The product increases with n. So the next possible integer value to consider is 2 and this does occur when $n = 6$ as $\sqrt{\frac{6+2}{2}} = \sqrt{4} = 2$.
So the smallest number of terms required for the product to be an integer is 6.

25. A The diagram shows part of the diagram in the question. Point O is the centre of the circle and points A, B, C, D, E, F, are as shown. Consider triangle BOF: BF is equal in length to the side of the square so $BF = 2$. Also $OB = OF = 2$ as they are both radii of the circle. So triangle BOF is equilateral. Therefore $\angle BOF = 60°$, so the area of sector $OBF = \frac{60}{360} \times \pi \times 2^2 = \frac{2\pi}{3}$.

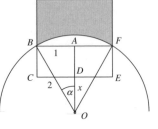

By Pythagoras' Theorem: $OA = \sqrt{2^2 - 1^2} = \sqrt{3}$. So the area of triangle $OBF = \frac{1}{2} \times 2 \times \sqrt{3} = \sqrt{3}$. Therefore the area of the segment bounded by arc BF and line segment $BF = \frac{2\pi}{3} - \sqrt{3}$. The area of rectangle $BFEC = BF \times AD = 2 \times (\sqrt{3} - x)$.

The shaded region has area 2, so the area of the above segment + area of rectangle $BFEC$ = area of the given square minus $2 = 4 - 2 = 2$.
Hence $\frac{2\pi}{3} - \sqrt{3} + 2\sqrt{3} - 2x = 2$. So $x = \frac{\pi}{3} + \frac{\sqrt{3}}{2} - 1$.

The answers

The table below shows the proportion of pupils' choices. The correct answer is shown in bold. [The percentages are rounded to the nearest whole number.]

Qn	A	B	C	D	E	Blank
1	4	16	3	**69**	7	2
2	1	**72**	23	3	0	1
3	**66**	8	10	6	4	6
4	5	6	13	**62**	10	2
5	20	**25**	36	5	6	7
6	19	5	4	**66**	2	3
7	13	18	**36**	13	12	8
8	6	1	2	**67**	21	2
9	13	**48**	13	8	9	9
10	**73**	4	2	7	10	3
11	11	16	18	11	**34**	9
12	16	7	16	**51**	4	5
13	**29**	19	20	13	7	11
14	8	**16**	23	20	24	8
15	8	12	**45**	11	14	9
16	6	3	8	**29**	3	51
17	4	**17**	5	4	6	65
18	8	5	3	3	**40**	40
19	3	4	5	5	**15**	68
20	3	8	5	**6**	3	75
21	**9**	4	4	4	6	73
22	3	4	**6**	3	3	80
23	10	9	5	**5**	2	69
24	3	3	**4**	3	3	85
25	**3**	3	3	2	2	86

IMC 2017: Some comments on the pupils' choice of answers as sent to schools in the letter with the results

With your results you will find tables showing the distribution of the responses of your pupils to the individual questions, and the national distribution of answers. It is pleasing to note that the mean score is 45, considerably higher than last year. However, you will see that, despite the higher mean score, there wasn't a single question that more than 80% of all the entrants answered correctly.

When pupils give wrong answers to the Challenge questions, this may be the result of a wild guess, or carelessness, or a basic mathematical misconception. We can only conjecture the reasons why some questions were not answered as well as we might have expected. We hope that you will be able to talk to your pupils to learn more, and that you will then be able to put right any misunderstandings that led to wrong answers.

Question 1 was intended to be a straightforward first question about converting fractions into decimals, but only 70% of all the pupils chose the right option. The existence of three 2s in the question seems to have led one in six of the pupils to choose the wrong option 0.222 because it also contains three 2s.

The poor response to Question 5 was also surprising. The popularity of the wrong answer $\frac{3}{9}$ is a puzzle. This would be the correct option only if the area of the inner circle were one-third of the area of the outer circle. If many of your pupils chose this option, please discuss this question with them, and try to find the source of their mistake. We would be interested to hear explanations of why only a quarter of all pupils nationally chose the correct option for this question.

Although no question was answered correctly by more than 80% of the pupils, it is good to see that more questions than usual were answered correctly by more than half of the pupils, and this includes some of the later questions.

The Problems Group aims to arrange the questions in order of difficulty, but often does not succeed. Therefore all your pupils should be encouraged to look at the later questions. This year Question 18 turned out to be easier than we had judged. It was attempted by 60% of all the pupils, and 70% of the pupils who answered it gave the correct answer. Did the 40% who left their answer to this question blank not know how to attempt it, or did they just assume that a question so late in the paper would be beyond them?

Pupils who did well enough to gain a certificate should be congratulated. We hope that their achievement will gain recognition throughout your school.

The profile of marks obtained is shown below.

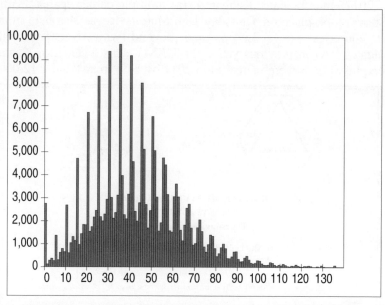

Bar chart showing the actual frequencies in the 2017 IMC

On the basis of the standard proportions used by the UKMT, the cut-off marks were set at

GOLD – 78 or over   SILVER – 61 to 77   BRONZE – 47 to 60

The certificates were virtually identical in design to those used for the JMC.

The cut-off scores for the follow-up competitions were

Year (E&W)	Minimum mark	Event	Minimum mark	Event
11	112	Maclaurin	81	Kangaroo Pink
10	106	Hamilton	81	Kangaroo Pink
9	97	Cayley	72	Kangaroo Grey

The Intermediate Mathematical Olympiad and Kangaroo

(a) *Kangaroo*

The 2017 Intermediate Kangaroo (a multiple-choice paper with 25 questions) took place on Thursday 16th March. It was also held in many other countries across Europe and beyond with over five million candidates. As in previous years, the UKMT constructed two Kangaroo papers. Invitations were increased in 2017 by 14% to just under 12,000.

EUROPEAN 'KANGAROO' MATHEMATICAL CHALLENGE
'GREY' and 'PINK'
Thursday 16th March 2017

Organised by the United Kingdom Mathematics Trust and the
Association Kangourou Sans Frontières

This competition is being taken by 6 million students in over 60 countries worldwide.

RULES AND GUIDELINES (to be read before starting):

1. Do not open the paper until the Invigilator tells you to do so.

2. Time allowed: **1 hour.**
   No answers, or personal details, may be entered after the allowed hour is over.

3. The use of rough paper is allowed; **calculators** and measuring instruments are **forbidden.**

4. Candidates in England and Wales must be in School Year 9 or below.
   Candidates in Scotland must be in S2 or below.
   Candidates in Northern Ireland must be in School Year 10 or below.

5. **Use B or HB non-propelling pencil only**. For each question mark *at most one* of the options A, B, C, D, E on the Answer Sheet. Do not mark more than one option.

6. Five marks will be awarded for each correct answer to Questions 1 - 15.
   Six marks will be awarded for each correct answer to Questions 16 - 25.

7. *Do not expect to finish the whole paper in 1 hour.* Concentrate first on Questions 1-15. When you have checked your answers to these, have a go at some of the later questions.

8. The questions on this paper challenge you **to think**, not to guess. Though you will not lose marks for getting answers wrong, you will undoubtedly get more marks, and more satisfaction, by doing a few questions carefully than by guessing lots of answers.

Enquiries about the European Kangaroo should be sent to:
UKMT, School of Mathematics, University of Leeds, Leeds, LS2 9JT.
(Tel. 0113 343 2339)
http://www.ukmt.org.uk

2017 European Grey Kangaroo Questions

1. A group of girls stands in a circle. Florence is the fourth on the left from Jess and the seventh on the right from Jess. How many girls are in the group?

   A 9   B 10   C 11   D 12   E 13

2. Which of the following equalities is true?

   A $\frac{4}{1} = 1.4$ B $\frac{5}{2} = 2.5$ C $\frac{6}{3} = 3.6$ D $\frac{7}{4} = 4.7$ E $\frac{8}{5} = 5.8$

3. The diagram shows two rectangles whose corresponding sides are parallel as shown. What is the difference between the lengths of the perimeters of the two rectangles?

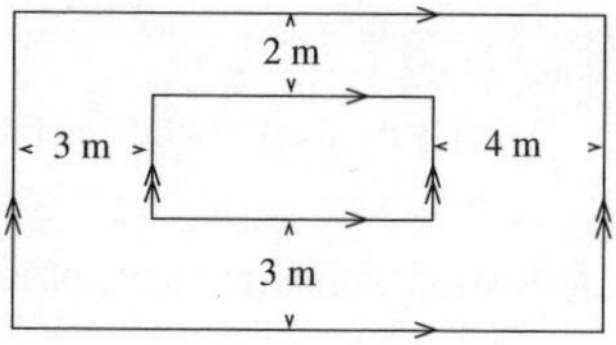

   A 12 m   B 16 m   C 20 m D 22 m   E 24 m

4. The sum of three different positive integers is 7. What is the product of these three integers?

   A 12   B 10   C 9   D 8   E 5

5. The diagram shows four overlapping hearts. The areas of the hearts are 1 cm^2, 4 cm^2, 9 cm^2 and 16 cm^2. What is the total shaded area?

   A 9 cm^2 B 10 cm^2 C 11 cm^2 D 12 cm^2 E 13 cm^2

6. What time is it 2017 minutes after 20:17?

   A 05:54   B 09:54   C 16:34   D 20:34   E 23:34

7. Olivia has 20 euros. Each of her four sisters has 10 euros. How many euros does Olivia need to give to each of her sisters so that each of the five girls has the same amount of money?

   A 2   B 4   C 5   D 8   E 10

8. Adam the Ant started at the left-hand end of a pole and crawled $\frac{2}{3}$ of its length. Benny the Beetle started at the right-hand end of the same pole and crawled $\frac{3}{4}$ of its length. What fraction of the length of the pole are Adam and Benny now apart?

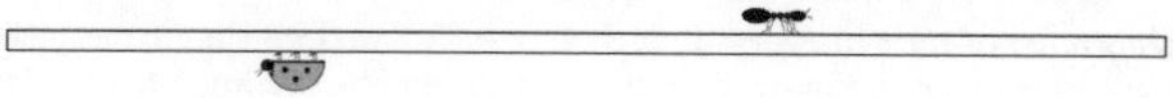

   A $\frac{3}{8}$ B $\frac{1}{12}$ C $\frac{5}{7}$ D $\frac{1}{2}$ E $\frac{5}{12}$

9. Four cousins Alan, Bob, Carl and Dan are 3, 8, 12 and 14 years old, although not necessarily in that order. Alan is younger than Carl. The sum of the ages of Alan and Dan is divisible by 5. The sum of the ages of Carl and Dan is divisible by 5. What is the sum of the ages of Alan and Bob?

   A 26   B 22   C 17   D 15   E 11

10. One sixth of an audience in a children's theatre are adults. Two fifths of the children are boys. What fraction of the audience are girls?

    A $\frac{1}{2}$ B $\frac{1}{3}$ C $\frac{1}{4}$ D $\frac{1}{5}$ E $\frac{2}{5}$

11. This year there were more than 800 entrants in the Kangaroo Hop race. Exactly 35% of the entrants were female and there were 252 more males than females. How many entrants were there in total?

   A 802   B 810   C 822   D 824   E 840

12. Ellie wants to write a number in each box of the diagram shown. She has already written in two of the numbers. She wants the sum of all the numbers to be 35, the sum of the numbers in the first three boxes to be 22, and the sum of the numbers in the last three boxes to be 25.

What is the product of the numbers she writes in the shaded boxes?

   A 0   B 39   C 48   D 63   E 108

13. Rohan wants to cut a piece of string into nine pieces of equal length. He marks his cutting points on the string. Jai wants to cut the same piece of string into only eight pieces of equal length. He marks his cutting points on the string. Yuvraj then cuts the string at all the cutting points that are marked. How many pieces of string does Yuvraj obtain?

   A 15   B 16   C 17   D 18   E 19

14. Two segments, each 1 cm long, are marked on opposite sides of a square of side 8 cm. The ends of the segments are joined as shown in the diagram. What is the total shaded area?

   A $2\,cm^2$ B $4\,cm^2$ C $6.4\,cm^2$ D $8\,cm^2$ E $10\,cm^2$

15. Margot wants to prepare a jogging timetable. She wants to jog exactly twice a week, and on the same days every week. She does not want to jog on two consecutive days. How many different timetables could Margot prepare?

   A 18   B 16   C 14   D 12   E 10

16. Ella wants to write a number into each cell of a 3 × 3 grid so that the sum of the numbers in any two cells that share an edge is the same. She has already written two numbers, as shown in the diagram.

When Ella has completed the grid, what will be the sum of all the numbers in the grid?

   A 18   B 20   C 21   D 22   E 23

17. Tom has a list of nine integers: 1, 2, 3, 4, 5, 6, 7, 8 and 9. He creates a second list by adding 2 to some of the integers in the first list and by adding 5 to all of the other integers in the first list. What is the smallest number of different integers he can obtain in the second list?

   A 5   B 6   C 7   D 8   E 9

18. Ten kangaroos stood in a line as shown in the diagram.

At a particular moment, two kangaroos standing nose-to-nose exchanged places by jumping past each other. Each of the two kangaroos involved in an exchange continued to face the same way as it did before the exchange. This was repeated until no further exchanges were possible. How many exchanges were made?

   A 15   B 16   C 18   D 20   E 21

19. Buses leave the airport every 3 minutes to travel to the city centre. A car leaves the airport at the same time as one bus and travels to the city centre by the same route. It takes each bus 60 minutes and the car 35 minutes to travel from the airport to the city centre. How many of these airport buses does the car overtake on its way to the city centre, excluding the bus it left with?

    A 8   B 9   C 10   D 11   E 13

20. Anastasia's tablecloth has a regular pattern, as shown in the diagram. What percentage of her tablecloth is black?

    A 16   B 24   C 25   D 32   E 36

21. Each number in the sequence starting 2, 3, 6, 8, 8, 4, ... is obtained in the following way. The first two numbers are 2 and 3 and afterwards each number is the last digit of the product of the two preceding numbers in the sequence. What is the 2017th number in the sequence?

    A 8   B 6   C 4   D 3   E 2

22. Stan had 125 small cubes. He glued some of them together to form a large cube with nine tunnels, each perpendicular to two opposite faces and passing through the cube, as shown in the diagram.

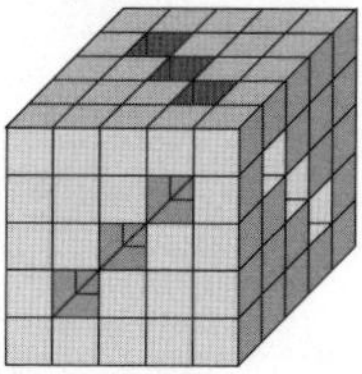

    How many of the small cubes did he not use?

    A 52   B 45   C 42   D 39   E 36

23. Eric and Eleanor are training on a 720 metre circular track. They run in opposite directions, each at a constant speed. Eric takes four minutes to complete the full circuit and Eleanor takes five minutes. How far does Eleanor run between consecutive meetings of the two runners?

    A 355 m   B 350 m   C 340 m   D 330 m   E 320 m

24. Ellen wants to colour some of the cells of a 4 × 4 grid. She wants to do this so that each coloured cell shares at least one side with an uncoloured cell and each uncoloured cell shares at least one side with a coloured cell.

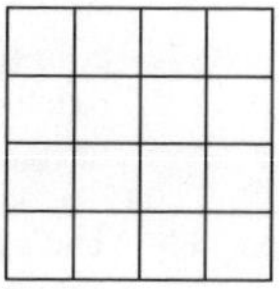

    What is the largest number of cells she can colour?

    A 12   B 11   C 10   D 9   E 8

25. The diagram shows a parallelogram $WXYZ$ with area S. The diagonals of the parallelogram meet at the point O. The point M is on the edge ZY. The lines WM and ZX meet at N. The lines MX and WY meet at P. The sum of the areas of triangles WNZ and XYP is $\frac{1}{3}S$. What is the area of quadrilateral $MNOP$?

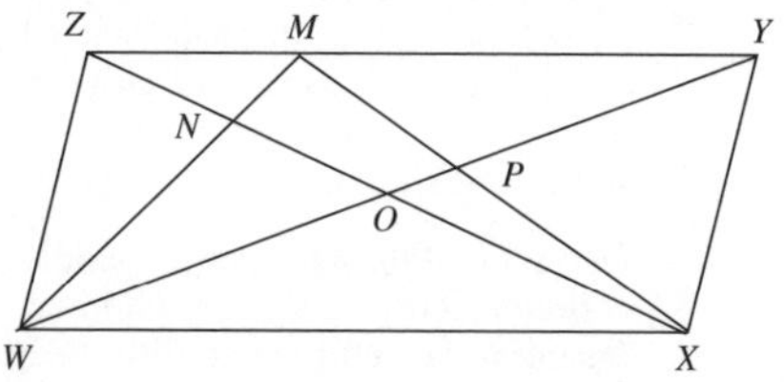

    A $\frac{1}{6}S$ B $\frac{1}{8}S$ C $\frac{1}{10}S$ D $\frac{1}{12}S$ E $\frac{1}{14}S$

Solutions to the 2017 European Grey Kangaroo

1. C   Since Florence is the fourth on the left from Jess, there are three girls between them going left round the circle. Similarly, since Florence is the seventh on the right from Jess, there are six girls between them going right. Therefore there are nine other girls in the circle apart from Florence and Jess. Hence there are 11 girls in total.

2. B   When you evaluate correctly the left-hand side of each proposed equality in turn, you obtain 4, 2.5, 2, 1.75 and 1.6. Hence the only true equality is $\frac{5}{2} = 2.5$.

3. E   The length of the outer rectangle is $(3 + 4)$ m = 7 m longer than the length of the inner rectangle. The height of the outer rectangle is $(2 + 3)$ m = 5 m longer than the height of the inner rectangle. Hence the length of the perimeter of the outer rectangle is $(2 \times 7 + 2 \times 5)$ m = 24 m longer than the length of the perimeter of the inner rectangle.

4. D   The sum of the three smallest positive integers is $1 + 2 + 3 = 6$. Hence the only way to add three different positive integers to obtain a total of 7 is $1 + 2 + 4$. Therefore the product of the three integers is $1 \times 2 \times 4 = 8$.

5. B   Since the areas of the four hearts are 1 cm^2, 4 cm^2, 9 cm^2 and 16 cm^2, the outer and inner shaded regions have areas $16\,\text{cm}^2 - 9\,\text{cm}^2 = 7\,\text{cm}^2$ and $4\,\text{cm}^2 - 1\,\text{cm}^2 = 3\,\text{cm}^2$ respectively. Therefore the total shaded area is $7\text{ cm}^2 + 3\text{ cm}^2 = 10\text{ cm}^2$.

6. A   Since $2017 = 33 \times 60 + 37$, a period of 2017 minutes is equivalent to 33 hours and 37 minutes or 1 day, 9 hours and 37 minutes. Hence the time 2017 minutes after 20:17 will be the time 9 hours and 37 minutes after 20:17, which is 05:54.

7. A   The total amount of the money the five girls have is $(20 + 4 \times 10)$ euros = 60 euros. Therefore, if all five girls are to have the same amount, they need to have $(60 \div 5)$ euros = 12 euros each. Since each of Olivia's sisters currently has 10 euros, Olivia would need to give each of them $(12 - 10)$ euros = 2 euros.

8. E   Adam the Ant has crawled $\frac{2}{3}$ of the length of the pole and so is $\frac{1}{3}$ of the length of the pole from the right-hand end. Benny the Beetle has crawled $\frac{3}{4}$ of the length of the pole and so is $\frac{1}{4}$ of the length of the pole from the left-hand end. Hence the fraction of the length of the pole that Adam and Benny are apart is $\left(1 - \frac{1}{3} - \frac{1}{4}\right) = \frac{5}{12}$.

9. C   The ages of the four cousins are 3, 8, 12 and 14. When these are added in pairs, we obtain $3 + 8 = 11$, $3 + 12 = 15$, $3 + 14 = 17$, $8 + 12 = 20$, $8 + 14 = 22$ and $12 + 14 = 26$. Only two of these, 15 and 20, are divisible by 5. However, we are told that the sum of the ages of Alan and Dan and the sum of the ages of Carl and Dan are both divisible by 5. Hence, since Dan's age appears in both sums that are divisible by 5, his age is 12. Since Alan is younger than Carl, Alan's age is 3 and Carl's age is 8. Hence Bob's age is 14. Therefore the sum of the ages of Alan and Bob is $3 + 14 = 17$.

10. A   One sixth of the audience are adults. Therefore five sixths of the audience are children. Two fifths of the children are boys and hence three fifths of the children are girls. Therefore three fifths of five sixths of the audience are girls. Now $\frac{3}{5} \times \frac{5}{6} = \frac{1}{2}$. Hence the fraction of the audience who are girls is $\frac{1}{2}$.

11. E   Since 35% of the entrants were female, 65% of the entrants were male. Hence, since there were 252 more males than females, 252 people represent $(65 - 35)\% = 30\%$ of the total number of entrants. Therefore the total number of entrants was $(252 \div 30) \times 100 = 840$.

12. D Since the sum of the numbers in the first three boxes is to be 22, the sum of the numbers in the last three boxes is to be 25 and the sum of the numbers in all five boxes is to be 35, Ellie will write $(22 + 25 - 35) = 12$ in the middle box. Therefore she will write $(22 - 3 - 12) = 7$ in the second box and $(25 - 12 - 4) = 9$ in the fourth box. Hence the product of the numbers in the shaded boxes is $7 \times 9 = 63$.

13. B Rohan wants to obtain 9 equal pieces and so makes eight marks. Jai wants to obtain 8 equal pieces and so makes seven marks. Since 9 and 8 have no common factors (9 and 8 are co-prime), none of the marks made by either boy coincide. Therefore Yuvraj will cut at 15 marked points and hence will obtain 16 pieces of string.

14. B Let the height of the lower triangle be h cm. Therefore the height of the upper triangle is $(8 - h)$ cm. Hence the shaded area in cm^2 is $\frac{1}{2} \times 1 \times h + \frac{1}{2} \times 1 \times (8 - h) = \frac{1}{2} \times (h + 8 - h) = 4$.

15. C Whichever day of the week Margot chooses for her first jogging day, there are four other days she can choose for her second day since she does not want to jog on either the day before or the day after her first chosen day. Therefore there are $7 \times 4 = 28$ ordered choices of days. However, the order of days does not matter when forming the timetable, only the two days chosen. Hence Margot can prepare $28 \div 2 = 14$ different timetables.

16. D Label the numbers Ella writes down as shown in the diagram.

2	a	b
c	d	3
e	f	g

Since the sum of the numbers in any two adjacent cells is the same, $2 + a = a + b$ and hence $b = 2$. Therefore $b + 3 = 2 + 3 = 5$. Hence the sum of the numbers in any two adjacent cells is 5. It is now straightforward to see that $a = c = f = 3$ and that $b = d = e = g = 2$. Therefore the sum of all the numbers in the grid is $5 \times 2 + 4 \times 3 = 22$.

17. B Since 5 and 2 differ by 3, Tom can obtain the same integer from two different integers in the first list that also differ by 3 by adding 5 to the smaller integer and adding 2 to the larger integer. In the first list there are six pairs of integers that differ by 3, namely 1 and 4, 2 and 5, 3 and 6, 4 and 7, 5 and 8 and 6 and 9. However, the integers 4, 5 and 6 appear in two of these pairs and hence the same integer in the second list can be obtained from only three pairs of integers from the first list leaving three integers in the first list unpaired. Therefore, the smallest number of different integers Tom can obtain in the second list is six.

18. C Label the kangaroos facing right as K1, K2, K3, K4, K5 and K6 as shown in the diagram.

No further exchanges will be possible only when the kangaroos facing right have moved past all the kangaroos facing left. Kangaroos K1, K2 and K3 each have four left-facing kangaroos to move past while kangaroos K4, K5 and K6 each have two left-facing kangaroos to move past. Hence there will be $(3 \times 4 + 3 \times 2) = 18$ exchanges made before no further exchanges are possible.

19. A Since the car takes 35 minutes to travel from the airport to the city centre and the buses all take 60 minutes, the car will arrive 25 minutes before the bus it left with. Since buses leave the airport every 3 minutes, they will also arrive at the city centre every 3 minutes. Since $25 = 8 \times 3 + 1$, in the 25 minute spell between the car arriving and the bus it left with arriving eight other buses will arrive. Therefore the car overtook eight airport buses on its way to the city centre.

20. D Divide the tablecloth into 25 equal squares as shown. Half of each of the 16 outer squares is coloured black which is equivalent to 8 complete squares. Therefore the percentage of the tablecloth that is coloured black is

$$\frac{8}{25} \times 100 = 32.$$

21. E Continue the sequence as described to obtain 2, 3, 6, 8, 8, 4, 2, 8, 6, 8, 8, 4, 2, 8, 6, 8 and so on. Since the value of each term depends only on the preceding two terms, it can be seen that, after the first two terms, the sequence 6, 8, 8, 4, 2, 8 repeats for ever. Now $2017 - 2 = 335 \times 6 + 5$. Therefore the 2017th number in the sequence is the fifth number of the repeating sequence 6, 8, 8, 4, 2, 8. Hence the required number is 2.

22. D Each of the nine tunnels in Stan's cube is five cubes long. However, the three tunnels starting nearest to the top front vertex of the cube all intersect one cube in. Similarly, the three tunnels starting at the centres of the faces all intersect at the centre of the large cube and the final three tunnels all intersect one cube in from the other end to that shown. Hence the number of small cubes not used is $9 \times 5 - 3 \times 2 = 45 - 6 = 39.$

23. E The ratio of the times taken to complete a circuit by Eric and Eleanor is 4:5. Therefore, since distance = speed × time and they both complete the same circuit, the ratio of their speeds is 5:4. Hence, since the total distance Eric and Eleanor cover between consecutive meetings is a complete circuit, Eleanor will run $\frac{4}{4+5}$ of a circuit between each meeting. Therefore Eleanor will run $\frac{4}{9}$ of 720 m which is 320 m between each meeting.

24. A Consider the four cells in the top left corner. It is not possible for all four cells to be coloured or the top left cell would not be touching an uncoloured cell and so there is at least one uncoloured cell in that group of four cells. By a similar argument, there is at least one uncoloured cell amongst the four cells in the bottom left corner, amongst the four cells in the bottom right corner and amongst the four cells in the top right corner. Therefore there are at least four uncoloured cells in the grid and hence at most twelve coloured cells. The diagram above shows that an acceptable arrangement is possible with twelve coloured cells.

Hence the largest number of cells Ellen can colour is twelve.

25. D The area of parallelogram $WXYZ$ is S. Therefore the area of triangle WXM, which has the same base and height, is $\frac{1}{2}S$. Hence the sum of the areas of triangle WMZ and triangle XYM is also $\frac{1}{2}S$. The sum of the areas of triangle WNZ and triangle XYP is given as $\frac{1}{3}S$ and therefore the sum of the areas of triangle ZNM and triangle MPY is $\frac{1}{2}S - \frac{1}{3}S = \frac{1}{6}S$. The area of triangle ZOY, which has the same base as the parallelogram but only half the height is $\frac{1}{2} \times \frac{1}{2}S = \frac{1}{4}S$. Therefore the area of quadrilateral $MNOP$ is $\frac{1}{4}S - \frac{1}{6}S = \frac{1}{12}S.$

2017 European Pink Kangaroo Questions

1. In the number pyramid shown each number is the sum of the two numbers immediately below. What number should appear in the left-hand cell of the bottom row?

		2039
	2020	
?		2017

   A 15   B 16   C 17   D 18   E 19

2. Which of the following diagrams shows the locus of the midpoint of the wheel when the wheel rolls along the zig-zag curve shown?

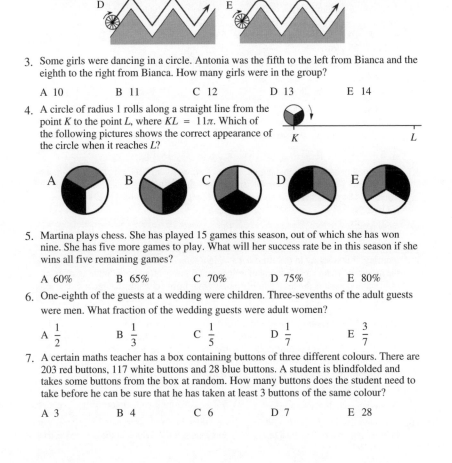

3. Some girls were dancing in a circle. Antonia was the fifth to the left from Bianca and the eighth to the right from Bianca. How many girls were in the group?

   A 10   B 11   C 12   D 13   E 14

4. A circle of radius 1 rolls along a straight line from the point K to the point L, where $KL = 11\pi$. Which of the following pictures shows the correct appearance of the circle when it reaches L?

   A   B   C   D   E

5. Martina plays chess. She has played 15 games this season, out of which she has won nine. She has five more games to play. What will her success rate be in this season if she wins all five remaining games?

   A 60%   B 65%   C 70%   D 75%   E 80%

6. One-eighth of the guests at a wedding were children. Three-sevenths of the adult guests were men. What fraction of the wedding guests were adult women?

   A $\dfrac{1}{2}$ B $\dfrac{1}{3}$ C $\dfrac{1}{5}$ D $\dfrac{1}{7}$ E $\dfrac{3}{7}$

7. A certain maths teacher has a box containing buttons of three different colours. There are 203 red buttons, 117 white buttons and 28 blue buttons. A student is blindfolded and takes some buttons from the box at random. How many buttons does the student need to take before he can be sure that he has taken at least 3 buttons of the same colour?

   A 3   B 4   C 6   D 7   E 28

8. As shown in the diagram, *FGHI* is a trapezium with side *GF* parallel to *HI*. The lengths of *FG* and *HI* are 50 and 20 respectively. The point *J* is on the side *FG* such that the segment *IJ* divides the trapezium into two parts of equal area. What is the length of *FJ*?

   A 25   B 30   C 35   D 40   E 45

9. How many positive integers *N* possess the property that exactly one of the numbers *N* and $(N + 20)$ is a 4-digit number?

   A 19   B 20   C 38   D 39   E 40

10. The sum of the squares of three consecutive positive integers is 770. What is the largest of these integers?

    A 15   B 16   C 17   D 18   E 19

11. A belt drive system consists of the wheels *K*, *L* and *M*, which rotate without any slippage. The wheel *L* makes 4 full turns when *K* makes 5 full turns; also *L* makes 6 full turns when *M* makes 7 full turns.

    The perimeter of wheel *M* is 30 cm. What is the perimeter of wheel *K*?

    A 27 cm   B 28 cm   C 29 cm   D 30 cm   E 31 cm

12. Tycho wants to prepare a schedule for his jogging for the next few months. He wants to jog three times per week. Every week, he wants to jog on the same days of the week. He never wants to jog on two consecutive days. How many schedules can he choose from?

    A 6   B 7   C 9   D 10   E 35

13. Four brothers have different heights. Tobias is shorter than Victor by the same amount by which he is taller than Peter. Oscar is shorter than Peter by the same amount as well. Tobias is 184 cm tall and the average height of all the four brothers is 178 cm. How tall is Oscar?

    A 160 cm   B 166 cm   C 172 cm   D 184 cm   E 190 cm

14. Johannes told me that it rained seven times during his holiday. When it rained in the morning, it was sunny in the afternoon; when it rained in the afternoon, it was sunny in the morning. There were 5 sunny mornings and 6 sunny afternoons. Without more information, what is the least number of days that I can conclude that the holiday lasted?

    A 7   B 8   C 9   D 10   E 11

15. Maja decided to enter numbers into the cells of a 3 × 3 grid. She wanted to do this in such a way that the numbers in each of the four 2 × 2 grids that form part of the 3 × 3 grid have the same totals. She has already written numbers in three of the corner cells, as shown in the diagram. Which number does she need to write in the bottom right corner?

    A 0   B 1   C 4   D 5   E impossible to determine

16. Seven positive integers *a*, *b*, *c*, *d*, *e*, *f*, *g* are written in a row. Every number differs by one from its neighbours. The total of the seven numbers is 2017. Which of the numbers can be equal to 286?

    A only *a* or *g*   B only *b* or *f*   C only *c* or *e*   D only *d*   E any of them

17. Niall's four children have different integer ages under 18. The product of their ages is 882. What is the sum of their ages?

    A 23   B 25   C 27   D 31   E 33

18. Ivana has two identical dice and on the faces of each are the numbers $-3, -2, -1, 0, 1, 2$. If she throws her dice and multiplies the results, what is the probability that their product is negative?

    A $\dfrac{1}{4}$ B $\dfrac{11}{36}$ C $\dfrac{1}{3}$ D $\dfrac{13}{36}$ E $\dfrac{1}{2}$

19. Maria chooses two digits a and b and uses them to make a six-digit number $ababab$. Which of the following is always a factor of numbers formed in this way?

    A 2   B 5   C 7   D 9   E 11

20. Frederik wants to make a special seven-digit password. Each digit of his password occurs exactly as many times as its digit value. The digits with equal values always occur consecutively, e.g. 4444333 or 1666666. How many possible passwords can he make?

    A 6   B 7   C 10   D 12   E 13

21. Carlos wants to put numbers in the number pyramid shown in such a way that each number above the bottom row is the sum of the two numbers immediately below it. What is the largest number of *odd* numbers that Carlos could put in the pyramid?

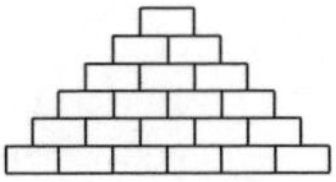

    A 13   B 14   C 15   D 16   E 17

22. Liza found the total of the interior angles of a convex polygon. She missed one of the angles and obtained the result $2017°$. Which of the following was the angle she missed?

    A $37°$ B $53°$ C $97°$ D $127°$ E $143°$

23. On a balance scale, three different masses were put at random on each pan and the result is shown in the picture. The masses are of 101, 102, 103, 104, 105 and 106 grams. What is the probability that the 106 gram mass stands on the heavier pan?

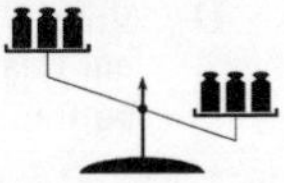

    A 75%   B 80%   C 90%   D 95%   E 100%

24. The points G and I are on the circle with centre H, and FI is tangent to the circle at I. The distances FG and HI are integers, and $FI = FG + 6$. The point G lies on the straight line through F and H. How many possible values are there for HI?

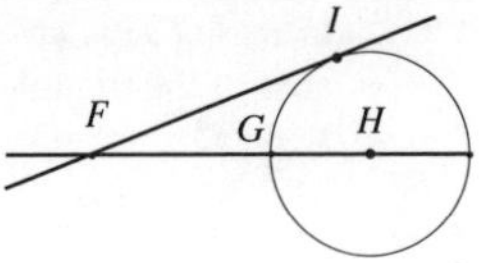

    A 0   B 2   C 4   D 6   E 8

25. The diagram shows a triangle FHI, and a point G on FH such that $GH = FI$. The points M and N are the midpoints of FG and HI respectively. Angle $NMH = \alpha°$. Which of the following gives an expression for $\angle IFH$?

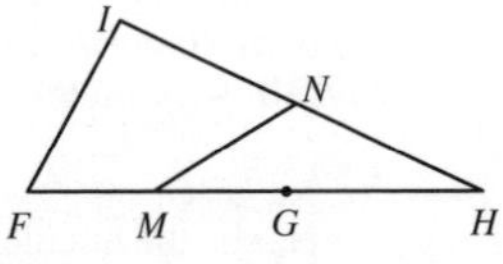

    A $2\alpha°$ B $(90 - \alpha)°$ C $45 + \alpha°$ D $(90 - \tfrac{1}{2}\alpha)°$ E $60°$

Solutions to the 2017 European Pink Kangaroo

1. **B** The left-hand cell in the middle row is $2039 - 2020 = 19$. The middle cell in the bottom row is $2020 - 2017 = 3$, so the left-hand cell in the bottom row is $19 - 3 = 16$.

2. **E** As the wheel goes over the top it pivots around the peak so the midpoint travels through a circular arc. At the troughs the wheel changes directions in an instant from down-right to up-right, so the midpoint undergoes a sharp change of direction. This gives the locus in diagram E.

3. **D** Antonia is fifth to the left of Bianca, so there are four girls in between. Similarly there are seven between them to the right. Hence there are $4 + 7 + 1 + 1 = 13$ girls.

4. **D** The circumference is 2π, so every time the circle rolls 2π it has turned $360°$ and looks the same as it did at K. After 11π, it has turned $5\frac{1}{2}$ turns, which is picture D.

5. **C** If Martina wins five more games, then she will have won 14 out of 20, which is equivalent to $\frac{7}{10}$ or 70%.

6. **A** Seven-eighths of all the guests were adults, of which three-sevenths were men, so the fraction of guests who were adult women equals $\frac{4}{7} \times \frac{7}{8} = \frac{1}{2}$.

7. **D** If the student has taken six buttons, he may already have three of the same colour, but it is possible that he has exactly two of each. However, if he takes a seventh button, he is guaranteed to have three of the same colour.

8. **C** Let x be the length of FJ, and h be the height of the trapezium. Then the area of triangle FJI is $\frac{1}{2}xh$ and the area of trapezium $FGHI$ is $\frac{1}{2}h(20 + 50) = 35h$. The area of the triangle is half the area of the trapezium, so $\frac{1}{2}xh = \frac{1}{2} \times 35h$, so $x = 35$.

9. **E** If exactly one of N and $N + 20$ has four digits, then the other has either three or five digits. If N has three digits and $N + 20$ has four digits, then $980 \leqslant N \leqslant 999$, giving 20 possibilities. If N has four digits and $N + 20$ has five digits, then $9980 \leqslant N \leqslant 9999$, giving 20 possibilities. Overall there are 40 possibilities for N.

10. **C** Let n be the middle integer and then add the squares $(n-1)^2 + n^2 + (n+1)^2 = n^2 - 2n + 1 + n^2 + n^2 + 2n + 1 = 3n^2 + 2 = 770$. This gives $n^2 = 256$ and hence $n = 16$, so the largest integer is 17.

11. B To compare wheels K and M, we can use the lowest common multiple of 4 and 6, which is 12. When wheel L makes 12 turns, wheel K makes 15 turns and wheel M makes 14 turns. When wheel L makes 24 turns, wheel K makes 30 turns and wheel M makes 28 turns, so the ratio of the circumferences of wheel K to wheel M is 28:30.

12. B Any day when Tycho jogs is immediately followed by a day without a jog. Therefore any period of seven days has three pairs of 'jog, no-jog' days and one extra no-jog day. There are seven possibilities for this extra non-jog day, so seven distinct schedules.

13. A Let k cm be the amount by which Victor is taller than Tobias (and Tobias is taller than Peter). Then the heights in cm are: Tobias 184, Victor $184 + k$, Peter $184 - k$, and Oscar $184 - 2k$. The mean is 178 so $\frac{1}{4}(184 + 184 + k + 184 - k + 184 - 2k) = 178$. Hence $4 \times 184 - 2k = 4 \times 178$, giving $2k = 4 \times 184 - 4 \times 178 = 4 \times 6 = 24$. Hence $k = 12$.
Therefore Oscar's height in cm is $184 - 2 \times 12 = 160$ cm.

14. C Let m be the number of days with sunny mornings and wet afternoons. Let n be the number of days with sunny mornings and sunny afternoons. There were 5 sunny mornings so $m + n = 5 \dots$ (1). Since there are seven wet days, the number of days with wet mornings and sunny afternoons must be $7 - m$. There are 6 sunny afternoons so $n + (7 - m) = 6$, which rearranges to $m = n + 1 \dots$ (2).
Equations (1) and (2) together give $m = 3$, $n = 2$, so Johannes had 3 days with sunny mornings and wet afternoons, 2 days sunny all day, and 4 days with wet mornings and sunny afternoons, a total of 9 days (not counting any cloudy days he may have had!).

15. A Let the numbers around the top left cell be a, b and c as shown. Then the sum of the top left 2×2 square (and hence *all* the 2×2 squares) is $a + b + c + 3$. The top right 2×2 square already contains a and b and 1, so the middle right cell must contain $c + 2$. The bottom left 2×2 square contains b and c and 2 so the bottom middle cell is $a + 1$. The bottom right 2×2 square already contains $a + 1$ and b and $c + 2$ so the missing value is zero. There are many ways to complete the grid; one way is shown here.

3	a	1
c	b	$c+2$
2	$a+1$	?

3	7	1
4	5	6
2	8	0

16. A Each number a, b, c, d, e, f, g differs from its neighbour by one, so they alternate odd and even. To obtain an odd total, we must have an odd number of odd numbers in the list. Hence b, d, f are odd and cannot be equal to 286.
If $c = 286$, then the biggest total possible is $288 + 287 + 286 + 287 + 288 + 289 + 290 = 2015$ which is too small. By reversing this list, we can also rule out $e = 286$.
We can obtain the total 2017 if we start with $a = 286$ since $286 + 287 + 288 + 289 + 290 + 289 + 288 = 2017$. By reversing this, we could also end with $g = 286$.

17. D The prime factor decomposition of 882 is $2 \times 3^2 \times 7^2$. The ages must be under 18, so cannot be $3 \times 7 = 21$ or $7 \times 7 = 49$. Hence, the only way to create two different numbers using 7 are: 7 and $2 \times 7 = 14$. This leaves only 3^2 which can create the two ages 1 and 9. The sum of the ages is then $1 + 9 + 7 + 14 = 31$.

18. C We can get a negative product if the first die is negative and the second positive, with probability $\frac{3}{6} \times \frac{2}{6} = \frac{6}{36}$, or if the first die is positive and the second is negative, with probability $\frac{2}{6} \times \frac{3}{6} = \frac{6}{36}$. Together this gives a probability of $\frac{12}{36} = \frac{1}{3}$.

19. C Let 'ab' be the 2-digit number with digits a and b. Then the 6-digit number '$ababab$' = 'ab' $\times$ 10101 = 'ab' $\times$ 3 $\times$ 7 $\times$ 13 $\times$ 37 so is always divisible by 3, 7, 13 and 37. But it is only divisible by 2, 5, 9 or 11 if 'ab' is.

20. E The password has length 7 so the different digits making it up must add to 7. The possibilities are: {7}, {6, 1}, {5, 2}, {4, 3}, {4, 2, 1}. Using only the digit 7 produces just one password, 7777777. Using two digits gives two possibilities, depending on which digit goes first, so the three pairs give $2 \times 3 = 6$ passwords. Three different digits can be arranged in six ways. This gives $1 + 6 + 6 = 13$ possibilities.

21. B

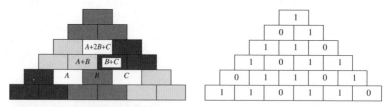

Each 'triple' consisting of a cell and the two cells immediately below can have at most two odds (for if the bottom two are both odd, the one above is even, so they cannot be all odd). The whole diagram can be dissected into six of these (shaded) triples as shown in the left-hand diagram, with three other (white) cells left over. These six triples have at most $6 \times 2 = 12$ odds between them. Moreover, the three remaining white cells cannot all be odd; if we assign the values A and C to the lowest of these white cells, and B to the cell between them, then the cells above have values $A + B$ and $B + C$. The top white cell then contains $A + 2B + C$, which is even when A and C are both odd. Hence the three white cells have at most two odds, giving the whole diagram at most $12 + 2 = 14$ odds.

The right-hand diagram shows one possible way of achieving this maximum of 14 odds.

22. E Let $x°$ be the missing angle. The correct sum of the angles is then $(2017 + x)°$. The polygon is convex so $x < 180$. Therefore $2017 < x < 2197$. The sum of the interior angles of a polygon with n sides is $180(n - 2)°$. In particular, it is a multiple of $180°$. The only multiple of 180 in the range from 2017 to 2197 is $12 \times 180 = 2160$. Therefore $2017 + x = 2160$. Hence $x = 2160 - 2017 = 143$.

23. B The total mass is 621g so the three masses in the heavier pan must have a total mass exceeding 310.5g. There are eight of these triples that include the 106g mass: (106, 105, 104), (106, 105, 103), (106, 105, 102), (106, 105, 101), (106, 104, 103), (106, 104, 102), (106, 104, 101), and (106, 103, 102).

Without 106, there are 2 ways to make a set over 310.5g: (105, 104, 103) and (105, 104, 102).

Hence the probabililty that the 106g mass is included in the heavier pan is $\frac{8}{8+2} = \frac{8}{10}$ or 80%.

24. D Let x be the length of FG and let r be the radius. Then $FI = x + 6$ and $GH = HI = r$.

Angle FIH is a right angle (the tangent and radius are perpendicular) so $FI^2 + HI^2 = FH^2$, which gives $(x + 6)^2 + r^2 = (x + r)^2$. Expanding this gives $x^2 + 12x + 36 + r^2 = x^2 + 2rx + r^2$, which simplifies to $12x + 36 = 2rx$. Halving this gives $6x + 18 = rx$, which rearranges to $r = 6 + \frac{18}{x}$. Since r is an integer, x must be a (positive) factor of 18, namely 1, 2, 3, 6, 9, 18; each of these six factors gives a different value of r (or HI) as required.

25. A We start by drawing the line segment IG. Let P be the point on IG such that PN is parallel to FH. The angle PNM is alternate to NMH so $\angle PNM = \alpha$. Also, the triangle PNI is similar to the triangle GHI (the angles of each triangle are clearly the same); moreover since N is the midpoint of HI, $PN = \frac{1}{2}GH$. Also $IP = \frac{1}{2}IG$,

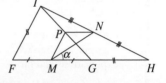

so $PG = \frac{1}{2}IG$. Since $MG = \frac{1}{2}FG$, the triangle PMG is similar to IFG, and in particular, $PM = \frac{1}{2}IF$. However, we know IF is equal in length to GH so we have $PN = \frac{1}{2}GH = \frac{1}{2}IF = PM$, so triangle MNP is isosceles and $\angle PMN = \angle PNM = \alpha$. Since triangles PMG and IFG are similar, we have $\angle IFG = \angle PMG = \alpha + \alpha = 2\alpha$.

Alternative:

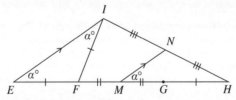

Extend the line HF to the point E so that $EF = GH$. Then, because $FM = MG$, M is the midpoint of EH. Therefore, since N is the midpoint of IH, the triangles IHE and NHM are similar. Hence $\angle IEH = \angle NMH = \alpha°$. Because $EF = GH = FI$, the triangle EFI is isosceles. Therefore, $\angle FIE = \angle IEF = \alpha°$. Therefore, by the external angle theorem, $\angle IFG = \angle IEF + \angle FIE = \alpha° + \alpha° = 2\alpha°$.

74

(b) *The IMOK Olympiad*

 The United Kingdom Mathematics Trust

Intermediate Mathematical Olympiad and Kangaroo (IMOK)

Olympiad Cayley/Hamilton/Maclaurin Papers

Thursday 16th March 2017

READ THESE INSTRUCTIONS CAREFULLY BEFORE STARTING

1. Time allowed: 2 hours.

2. **The use of calculators, protractors and squared paper is forbidden.**
   Rulers and compasses may be used.

3. Solutions must be written neatly on A4 paper. Sheets must be STAPLED together in the top left corner with the Cover Sheet on top.

4. Start each question on a fresh A4 sheet.
   You may wish to work in rough first, then set out your final solution with clear explanations and proofs. *Do not hand in rough work.*

5. Answers must be FULLY SIMPLIFIED, and EXACT. They may contain symbols such as π, fractions, or square roots, if appropriate, but NOT decimal approximations.

6. Give full written solutions, including mathematical reasons as to why your method is correct.
   Just stating an answer, even a correct one, will earn you very few marks; also, incomplete or poorly presented solutions will not receive full marks.

7. **These problems are meant to be challenging!** The earlier questions tend to be easier; the last two questions are the most demanding.
   Do not hurry, but spend time working carefully on one question before attempting another. Try to finish whole questions even if you cannot do many; you will have done well if you hand in full solutions to two or more questions.

DO NOT OPEN THE PAPER UNTIL INSTRUCTED BY THE INVIGILATOR TO DO SO!

The United Kingdom Mathematics Trust is a Registered Charity.
Enquiries should be sent to: Maths Challenges Office,
School of Mathematics Satellite, University of Leeds, Leeds, LS2 9JT.
(Tel. 0113 343 2339)
http://www.ukmt.org.uk

2017 Olympiad Cayley Paper

> **All candidates must be in** *School Year 9 or below* **(England and Wales),** *S2 or below* **(Scotland), or** *School Year 10 or below* **(Northern Ireland).**

C1. Four times the average of two different positive numbers is equal to three times the greater one. The difference between the numbers is three less than the average.

What are the two numbers?

C2.

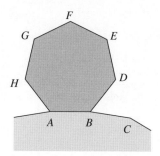

The diagram shows three adjacent vertices A, B and C of a regular polygon with forty-two sides, and a regular heptagon $ABDEFGH$. The polygons are placed together edge-to-edge.

Prove that triangle BCD is equilateral.

C3. Peaches spends exactly £3.92 on some fruit, choosing from apples costing 20p each and pears costing 28p each.

How many of each type of fruit might she have bought?

C4. The point X lies inside the square $ABCD$ and the point Y lies outside the square, in such a way that triangles XAB and YAD are both equilateral.

Prove that $XY = AC$.

C5. In a sports league there are four teams and every team plays every other team once. A team scores 3 points for a win, 1 point for a draw, and 0 points for a loss.

What is the smallest number of points that a team could have at the end of the league and still score more points than each of the other teams?

C6. We write 'pq' to denote the two-digit integer with tens digit p and units digit q.

For which values of a, b and c are the two fractions $\dfrac{`ab`}{`ba`}$ and $\dfrac{`bc`}{`cb`}$ equal and different from 1?

2017 Olympiad Hamilton Paper

All candidates must be in *School Year 10* (England and Wales), *S3* (Scotland), or *School Year 11* (Northern Ireland).

H1. The diagram shows four equal arcs placed on the sides of a square. Each arc is a major arc of a circle with radius 1 cm, and each side of the square has length $\sqrt{2}$ cm.

What is the area of the shaded region?

H2. A ladybird walks from A to B along the edges of the network shown. She never walks along the same edge twice. However, she may pass through the same point more than once, though she stops the first time she reaches B.

How many different routes can she take?

H3. The diagram shows squares $ABCD$ and $EFGD$. The length of BF is 10 cm. The area of trapezium $BCGF$ is 35 cm^2.

What is the length of AB?

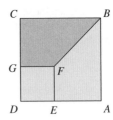

H4. The largest of four different real numbers is d. When the numbers are summed in pairs, the four largest sums are 9, 10, 12 and 13.

What are the possible values of d?

H5. In the trapezium $ABCD$, the lines AB and DC are parallel, $BC = AD$, $DC = 2AD$ and $AB = 3AD$.
The angle bisectors of $\angle DAB$ and $\angle CBA$ intersect at the point E.

What fraction of the area of the trapezium $ABCD$ is the area of the triangle ABE?

H6. Solve the pair of simultaneous equations

$$x^2 + 3y = 10 \quad \text{and}$$

$$3 + y = \frac{10}{x}.$$

2017 Olympiad Maclaurin Paper

All candidates must be in *School Year 11* (England and Wales), *S4* (Scotland), or *School Year 12* (Northern Ireland).

M1. The diagram shows a semicircle of radius r inside a right-angled triangle. The shorter edges of the triangle are tangents to the semicircle, and have lengths a and b. The diameter of the semicircle lies on the hypotenuse of the triangle.

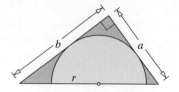

Prove that

$$\frac{1}{r} = \frac{1}{a} + \frac{1}{b}.$$

M2. How many triangles (with non-zero area) are there with each of the three vertices at one of the dots in the diagram?

M3. How many solutions are there to the equation

$$m^4 + 8n^2 + 425 = n^4 + 42m^2,$$

where m and n are integers?

M4. The diagram shows a square $PQRS$ with sides of length 2. The point T is the midpoint of RS, and U lies on QR so that $\angle SPT = \angle TPU$.

What is the length of UR?

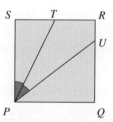

M5. Solve the pair of simultaneous equations

$$(a + b)(a^2 - b^2) = 4 \quad \text{and}$$

$$(a - b)(a^2 + b^2) = \frac{5}{2}.$$

M6. The diagram shows a 10×9 board with seven 2×1 tiles already in place.

What is the largest number of additional 2×1 tiles that can be placed on the board, so that each tile covers exactly two 1×1 cells of the board, and no tiles overlap?

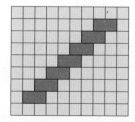

Solutions to the 2017 Olympiad Cayley Paper

C1. Four times the average of two different positive numbers is equal to three times the greater one. The difference between the numbers is three less than the average.

What are the two numbers?

Solution

It is good to give the numbers names, so let them be a and b, where b is the larger. The first fact we are given says that

$$4 \times \frac{a + b}{2} = 3b,$$

and the second says that

$$b - a = \frac{a + b}{2} - 3.$$

We may simplify the first fact to obtain $2(a + b) = 3b$, that is, $2a = b$; multiplying the second fact by two, we get $2b - 2a = a + b - 6$, that is, $b = 3a - 6$.

Equating these values of b, we get $2a = 3a - 6$, that is, $6 = a$, and hence $b = 12$.

So the two numbers are 6 and 12.

C2. The diagram shows three adjacent vertices *A*, *B* and *C* of a regular polygon with forty-two sides, and a regular heptagon *ABDEFGH*. The polygons are placed together edge-to-edge.

Prove that triangle *BCD* is equilateral.

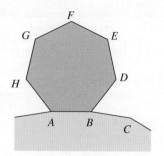

Solution

One can prove that a triangle is equilateral in several different ways, and the diagram gives a few hints about which will be easiest. Two of the sides and one of the angles look more important than the other side and the other two angles, so we'll talk about them.

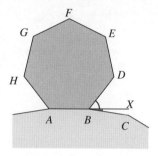

All sides of the heptagon are of equal length, so *AB* = *BD*; similarly all sides of the 42-sided polygon are of equal length, so *AB* = *BC*. Thus *BD* = *BC*, making triangle *DBC* isosceles.

We'll now compute the angle *DBC* by extending the common side of the two polygons to *X*, as shown in the diagram alongside. We see that angle *DBC* is the sum of the external angles of two regular polygons. Thus

$$\angle DBC = \angle DBX + \angle XBC$$

$$= \frac{360°}{7} + \frac{360°}{42}$$

$$= \left(\frac{1}{7} + \frac{1}{42}\right) \times 360°$$

$$= \frac{1}{6} \times 360°$$

$$= 60°.$$

Hence *DBC* is an isosceles triangle with an angle of 60°, which means that it is equilateral.

C3. Peaches spends exactly £3.92 on some fruit, choosing from apples costing 20p each and pears costing 28p each.

How many of each type of fruit might she have bought?

Solution

First we should try to translate this word problem into algebra. Let a be the number of apples and p the number of pears, then what we have is that $20a + 28p = 392$.

All these numbers are divisible by 4, so we may divide each term by 4 to obtain
$5a + 7p = 98$.

Now 98 is a multiple of 7, and $7p$ is always a multiple of 7, so $5a$ is also a multiple of 7. This means that a itself is a multiple of 7.

So we can have $a = 0$ (giving $p = 14$), or $a = 7$ (giving $p = 9$), or $a = 14$ (giving $p = 4$). We can't take a to be a higher multiple of 7, such as 21 or more, because then $5a \geqslant 105$, so that $20a \geqslant 240$, which means that Peaches would be spending more on apples than she spends altogether.

Hence the numbers of each type of fruit that Peaches might have bought are shown in the following table.

Apples	Pears
0	14
7	9
14	4

C4. The point X lies inside the square $ABCD$ and the point Y lies outside the square, in such a way that triangles XAB and YAD are both equilateral.

Prove that $XY = AC$.

Solution

See the diagram alongside.

We'll start by working out some angles at A, since that is the vertex where the most is going on.

Firstly, $\angle DAB = 90°$ since $ABCD$ is a square. Also, each of angles XAB and YAD is 60° since each of the triangles XAB and YAD is equilateral.

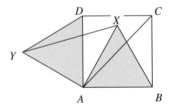

Therefore

$$\angle YAX = \angle YAD + \angle DAB - \angle XAB$$

$$= 60° + 90° - 60°$$

$$= 90°.$$

Also, since each of the equilateral triangles shares a side with the square, they have sides that are the same length as the side of the square. In particular, $YA = AB$ and $AX = BC$.

It follows that the triangles YAX and ABC are congruent (SAS), and hence $AC = XY$.

C5. In a sports league there are four teams and every team plays every other team once. A team scores 3 points for a win, 1 point for a draw, and 0 points for a loss.

What is the smallest number of points that a team could have at the end of the league and still score more points than each of the other teams?

Solution

There are six games, and each game contributes 2 or 3 points in total, depending on whether it was drawn or won, so the total number of points in the league is $12 + w$, where w is the number of won games. So the total number of points in the league is at least 12 and at most 18.

Consider the number of points at the end of the league scored by a team scoring more points than every other team.

3 points or fewer

There are at least 9 other points scored in the league, and so it's not possible for every other team to score 2 points or fewer: that makes at most 6 points.

4 points

The only way for a team to score 4 points is $3 + 1 + 0$, so there are at least two won games. That means that the total number of points is at least 14 points, so the other teams have at least 10 points between them. It is thus not possible for each of them to score 3 points or fewer: that makes at most 9 points.

5 points

This is possible: label the teams A, B, C and D; if A beats D but every other game is drawn, then A has 5 points, two of the other teams have 3 points and one has 2 points.

Hence the answer is 5.

C6. We write '*pq*' to denote the two-digit integer with tens digit p and units digit q.

For which values of a, b and c are the two fractions $\dfrac{\text{'}ab\text{'}}{\text{'}ba\text{'}}$ and $\dfrac{\text{'}bc\text{'}}{\text{'}cb\text{'}}$ equal and different from 1?

Solution

Write this using 'proper' algebra: the question asks us to find solutions to

$$\frac{10a + b}{10b + a} = \frac{10b + c}{10c + b}, \tag{1}$$

where a, b and c are integers from 1 to 9 (none of them can be 0 because 'ab' and so on are two-digit numbers).

Multiplying each side of (1) by $(10b + a)(10c + b)$, we obtain

$$(10a + b)(10c + b) = (10b + c)(10b + a),$$

that is,

$$100ac + 10(ab + bc) + b^2 = 100b^2 + 10(ab + bc) + ac,$$

so that

$$100ac + b^2 = 100b^2 + ac.$$

But a, b and c are integers between 1 and 9, hence b^2 and ac are between 1 and 81. Therefore b^2 and ac are less than 100, whereas $100ac$ and $100b^2$ are greater than 100. It follows that $b^2 = ac$.

Note that $a \neq b$ (otherwise $a = b$ and then $b = c$ too, so that $a = b = c$).

Remembering that a, b and c are integers from 1 to 9, we get the values shown in the following table.

b	a, c in either order
2	1, 4
3	1, 9
4	2, 8
6	4, 9

Solutions to the 2017 Olympiad Hamilton Paper

H1. The diagram shows four equal arcs placed on the sides of a square. Each arc is a major arc of a circle with radius 1 cm, and each side of the square has length $\sqrt{2}$ cm.

What is the area of the shaded region?

Solution

Join the centres of the circles, as shown in the diagram alongside, to form a quadrilateral whose sides have length 1 cm + 1 cm. Each angle of this quadrilateral is equal to 90° from the converse of Pythagoras' Theorem, since we are given the 'inner' square has sides of length $\sqrt{2}$ cm. Because it has equal sides. it follows that the quadrilateral is a square.

The shaded region comprises this square and four sectors of circles, each of radius 1 cm and angle 270°, thus its area is equal to $2 \times 2 + 4 \times \frac{3}{4} \times \pi \times 1^2$, in cm².

Therefore, in cm², the shaded area is equal to $4 + 3\pi$.

H2. A ladybird walks from A to B along the edges of the network shown. She never walks along the same edge twice. However, she may pass through the same point more than once, though she stops the first time she reaches B.

How many different routes can she take?

Solution

Label the centre point X, as shown in the diagram alongside.

Clearly any route that the ladybird takes from A to B passes through X, and she stops the first time she reaches B.

Therefore the number of different routes that the ladybird can take is equal to
(the number of routes from A to X) × (the number from X to B).

The number of routes from A to X is equal to
(the number of 'direct' routes from A to X) + (the number from A to X that visit X twice), which is $3 + 3 \times 2$.

However, the number of routes from X to B is just 3, since the ladybird stops the first time she reaches B, so that it is not possible for her to visit X again. Thus the total number of different routes that the ladybird can take is 9×3, which equals 27.

H3. The diagram shows squares *ABCD* and *EFGD*. The length of *BF* is 10 cm. The area of trapezium *BCGF* is 35 cm².

What is the length of *AB*?

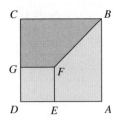

Solution

The point *F* lies on the diagonal *BD* of the square *ABCD*, so that $\angle FBC$ is equal to 45°. Let point *X* lie on *BC* so that $\angle FXB = 90°$, as shown in the diagram alongside. Then $\angle XFB = 45°$ from the angle sum of triangle *BXF*; it follows from 'sides opposite equal angles are equal' that $BX = XF$.

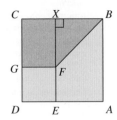

Now, using Pythagoras' Theorem in triangle *BXF*, we obtain $XF = 5\sqrt{2}$ cm. But *CGFX* is a rectangle, so that $CG = XF$.

Let the length of *AB* be *a* cm. Then

$$\tfrac{1}{2} \times 5\sqrt{2} \times \left(2a - 5\sqrt{2}\right) = 35 \text{ and so } 2a - 5\sqrt{2} = \frac{14}{\sqrt{2}}.$$

Hence $2a = 5\sqrt{2} + 14\frac{\sqrt{2}}{2}$, so that $a = 6\sqrt{2}$.

Therefore the length of *AB* is $6\sqrt{2}$ cm.

H4. The largest of four different real numbers is d. When the numbers are summed in pairs, the four largest sums are 9, 10, 12 and 13.

What are the possible values of d?

Solution

Let the other three different numbers be a, b and c, in increasing order. Then each of them is less than d, so that $c + d$ is the largest sum of a pair. The next largest is $b + d$, because it is larger than any other sum of a pair. But we do not know whether $b + c$ or $a + d$ is next (though each of these is larger than $a + c$, which in turn is larger than $a + b$). There are thus two cases to deal with, depending on whether $b + c \leqslant a + d$ or $a + d < b + c$.

$b + c \leqslant a + d$

We have

$$b + c = 9, \tag{1}$$

$$a + d = 10, \tag{2}$$

$$b + d = 12 \tag{3}$$

$$\text{and} \quad c + d = 13. \tag{4}$$

From equations (1), (3) and (4), we find that $2d = 16$, so that $d = 8$.

$a + d < b + c$

We have

$$a + d = 9, \tag{5}$$

$$b + c = 10, \tag{6}$$

$$b + d = 12 \tag{7}$$

$$\text{and} \quad c + d = 13. \tag{8}$$

From equations (6) to (8), we find that $2d = 15$, so that $d = 7.5$.

In each case, it is possible to find the values of a, b and c from the equations, and to check that these fit the conditions in the question.

Therefore the possible values of d are 7.5 and 8.

H5. In the trapezium $ABCD$, the lines AB and DC are parallel, $BC = AD$, $DC = 2AD$ and $AB = 3AD$.

The angle bisectors of $\angle DAB$ and $\angle CBA$ intersect at the point E.

What fraction of the area of the trapezium $ABCD$ is the area of the triangle ABE?

Solution

Let $BC = AD = k$, so that $DC = 2k$ and $AB = 3k$, and let the point X lie on AB so that $XBCD$ is a parallelogram, as shown in the diagram on the left below. It follows that $DX = k$ and $XB = 2k$ (opposite sides of a parallelogram), so that $AX = k$.

Hence triangle AXD has three equal sides—it is therefore an equilateral triangle. In particular, this means that angle DAX is equal to $60°$.

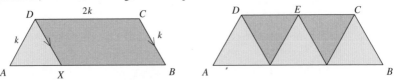

As a consequence, the trapezium $ABCD$ is actually made up from five equilateral triangles, as shown in the diagram on the right above.

Now the triangle ABE comprises one equilateral triangle and two half-rhombuses. The area of the two half-rhombuses is equal to the area of two equilateral triangles.

Therefore the area of the triangle ABE is $\frac{3}{5}$ of the area of the trapezium $ABCD$.

H6. Solve the pair of simultaneous equations

$$x^2 + 3y = 10 \qquad \text{and}$$

$$3 + y = \frac{10}{x}.$$

Solution

First, let us number the two given equations, so that it is easy to refer to them.

$$x^2 + 3y = 10 \tag{1}$$

$$3 + y = \frac{10}{x} \tag{2}$$

It is possible to eliminate one of the two unknowns by substituting from equation (2) into equation (1), but this leads to a cubic equation. We present another method that avoids this.

By subtracting $x \times$ equation (2) from equation (1), we get

$$x^2 + 3y - 3x - xy = 0$$

so that

$$(x - 3)(x - y) = 0.$$

Hence either $x = 3$ or $x = y$. We deal with each of these two cases separately.

$x = 3$

Using equation (1), say, we obtain $y = \frac{1}{3}$.

$x = y$

Using equation (1) we obtain

$$x^2 + 3x = 10$$

so that

$$x^2 + 3x - 10 = 0.$$

Hence

$$(x - 2)(x + 5) = 0,$$

and therefore either $x = 2$ or $x = -5$. When $x = 2$ then $y = 2$; when $x = -5$ then $y = -5$.

By checking in the two given equations, we find that all three solutions are valid. Thus there are three solutions of the simultaneous equations, namely

$$\text{either } x = -5 \text{ and } y = -5,$$
$$\text{or } x = 2 \text{ and } y = 2,$$
$$\text{or } x = 3 \text{ and } y = \tfrac{1}{3}.$$

Solutions to the 2017 Olympiad Maclaurin Paper

M1. The diagram shows a semicircle of radius r inside a right-angled triangle. The shorter edges of the triangle are tangents to the semicircle, and have lengths a and b. The diameter of the semicircle lies on the hypotenuse of the triangle.

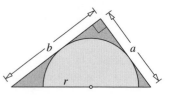

Prove that

$$\frac{1}{r} = \frac{1}{a} + \frac{1}{b}.$$

Solution

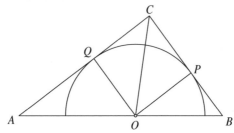

Label the points as shown above, and join O to P, Q and C.

Method 1

The area of triangle AOC is $\frac{1}{2}rb$, that of triangle BOC is $\frac{1}{2}ra$ and that of triangle ABC is $\frac{1}{2}ab$.

Hence, adding, we have

$$\tfrac{1}{2}ab = \tfrac{1}{2}rb + \tfrac{1}{2}ra.$$

Dividing each term by $\frac{1}{2}abr$, we obtain

$$\frac{1}{r} = \frac{1}{a} + \frac{1}{b}.$$

Method 2

$AQ = b - r$. The triangles AOQ and ABC are similar (AA), so that

$$\frac{r}{b - r} = \frac{a}{b}.$$

Multiplying each side by $b(b - r)$, we get

$$rb = ab - ar$$

and now, dividing each term by abr, we obtain

$$\frac{1}{r} = \frac{1}{a} + \frac{1}{b}.$$

M2. How many triangles (with non-zero area) are there with each of the three vertices at one of the dots in the diagram?

Solution

Method 1

There are 17 dots in the array, and we must choose 3 of them to obtain a triangle. This can be done in $\binom{17}{3}$ = 680 ways. However, some of these triangles have zero area.

The triangle will have zero area if we choose all three dots on the same line. Hence the number of triangles of zero area is $2 \times \binom{9}{3} = 2 \times 84 = 168$.

So there are 512 triangles of non-zero area.

Method 2

We may choose two points on the line across the page in $\binom{9}{2}$ = 36 ways, and one point on the line up the page in 8 ways. These choices give rise to $8 \times 36 = 288$ triangles of non-zero area.

Similarly we obtain another 288 triangles from two points on the line up the page and one on the line across the page.

But we have counted twice triangles with a vertex at the point where the lines meet, and there are $8 \times 8 = 64$ of these. So altogether we have $2 \times 288 - 64 = 512$ triangles.

M3. How many solutions are there to the equation

$$m^4 + 8n^2 + 425 = n^4 + 42m^2,$$

where m and n are integers?

Solution

By 'completing the square', we may rewrite the equation in the form

$$\left(m^2 - 21\right)^2 = \left(n^2 - 4\right)^2.$$

Then, taking the square root of each side, we get

$$m^2 - 21 = \pm\left(n^2 - 4\right).$$

Hence there are two cases to consider.

$m^2 - 21 = n^2 - 4$

In this case, we have

$$m^2 - n^2 = 21 - 4,$$

so that

$$(m - n)(m + n) = 17.$$

Therefore, because 17 is prime, $m - n$ and $m + n$ are equal to 1 and 17, or -1 and -17, in some order. Thus in this case there are four solutions for (m, n), namely $(\pm9, \pm8)$.

$m^2 - 21 = -\left(n^2 - 4\right)$

In this case, we have

$$m^2 + n^2 = 21 + 4.$$

Hence

$$m^2 + n^2 = 5^2.$$

Now a square is non-negative, so that $-5 \leqslant m, n \leqslant 5$.

Thus in this case there are twelve solutions for (m, n), namely $(0, \pm5), (\pm5, \ 0),$ $(\pm3, \pm4)$ and $(\pm4, \pm3)$.

Therefore altogether there are sixteen solutions to the given equation.

M4. The diagram shows a square *PQRS* with sides of length 2. The point *T* is the midpoint of *RS*, and *U* lies on *QR* so that $\angle SPT = \angle TPU$.

What is the length of *UR*?

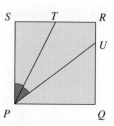

Solution

Let *F* be the point on *PU* so that $\angle TFP = 90°$ and join *T* to *F* and *U*, as shown. Then triangles *PTS* and *PTF* are congruent (AAS), so that $TF = 1$.

Hence triangles *TUR* and *TUF* are congruent (RHS), so that $\angle RTU = \angle UTF$.

Now the four angles at *T* are angles on the straight line *RTS*, so they add up to 180°. It follows that $\angle RTU = \angle SPT$.

Therefore triangles *RTU* and *SPT* are similar (AA), so that

$$\frac{UR}{RT} = \frac{TS}{SP} = \frac{1}{2}.$$

Thus $UR = \frac{1}{2}$.

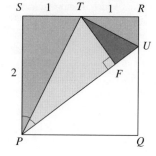

M5. Solve the pair of simultaneous equations

$$(a + b)(a^2 - b^2) = 4 \qquad \text{and}$$

$$(a - b)(a^2 + b^2) = \frac{5}{2}.$$

Solution

Since $a^2 - b^2 = (a - b)(a + b)$, we may write the first equation as
$(a + b)^2(a - b) = 4$.

Note that $a - b \neq 0$, since this would make the left-hand side of both equations zero, which is impossible. Hence we can divide the first equation by the second and cancel the term $a - b$ to produce

$$\frac{(a + b)^2}{a^2 + b^2} = \frac{8}{5}.$$

Multiplying each side by $5(a^2 + b^2)$ we get

$$5(a + b)^2 = 8(a^2 + b^2).$$

When we multiply this out and collect like terms, we obtain

$$0 = 3a^2 - 10ab + 3b^2$$

$$= (3a - b)(a - 3b),$$

so either $a = 3b$ or $b = 3a$.

We substitute each of these in turn back into the first equation.

$a = 3b$

   Then $4b \times 8b^2 = 4$, so that $b = \frac{1}{2}$ and $a = \frac{3}{2}$.

$b = 3a$

   Then $4a \times (-8a^2) = 4$, so that $a = -\frac{1}{2}$ and $b = -\frac{3}{2}$.

Hence we have two solutions $(a, b) = \left(\frac{1}{2}, \frac{3}{2}\right)$ or $(a, b) = \left(-\frac{1}{2}, -\frac{3}{2}\right)$. These solutions should be checked by substituting back into the second equation.

M6. The diagram shows a 10×9 board with seven 2×1 tiles already in place.

What is the largest number of additional 2×1 tiles that can be placed on the board, so that each tile covers exactly two 1×1 cells of the board, and no tiles overlap?

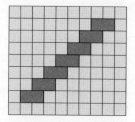

Solution

The first observation is that it is possible to add a further 36 tiles to the grid. The diagram shows one way of doing this: the additional tiles are lighter grey and the uncovered squares are indicated.

There are 36 additional tiles in the grid, and four squares are left uncovered.

We show that you cannot improve on this.

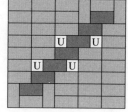

Colour the grid like a chessboard with alternating grey and white cells, as shown in Figure 1.

Notice that any tile will cover one cell of each colour.

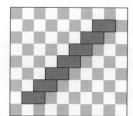
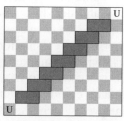
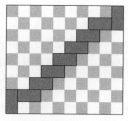

| Figure 1 | Figure 2 | Figure 3 |

Suppose that each corner is left uncovered, as shown in Figure 2. Then the remainder of the board consists of two separate 'staircases'.

The upper staircase has 17 grey and 20 white cells, so that at most seventeen 2×1 tiles may be placed here. Similarly for the lower staircase: at most seventeen 2×1 tiles may be placed there. In other words, with this arrangement, at most 34 additional tiles may be placed.

The only way to cover the corners whilst also reducing the excess in both staircases is to place tiles in the corners as shown in Figure 3. This reduces the number of white cells in the upper staircase by one, and reduces the number of grey cells in the lower staircase by one. Once again at most seventeen tiles may be placed in each staircase, achieving at most 36 additional tiles in total.

Therefore the greatest number of additional 2×1 tiles that can be placed on the board is 36.

94

Comments on the IMOK Olympiad Papers and Scripts

General comments

Both candidates and their teachers will find it helpful to know something of the general principles involved in marking Olympiad-type papers. These preliminary paragraphs therefore serve as an exposition of the 'philosophy' which has guided both the setting and marking of all such papers at all age levels, both nationally and internationally.

What we are looking for, essentially, is solutions to problems. This approach is therefore rather different from what happens in public examinations such as GCSE, AS and A level, where credit is given for the ability to carry out individual techniques regardless of how these techniques fit into a protracted argument. Such marking is cumulative; a candidate may gain 60% of the available marks without necessarily having a clue about how to solve the final problem. Indeed, the questions are generally structured in such a way as to facilitate this approach, divided into many parts and not requiring an overall strategy for tackling a multi-stage argument.

In distinction to this, Olympiad-style problems are marked by looking at each question synoptically and deciding whether the candidate has some sort of overall strategy or not. An answer which is essentially a solution, but might contain either errors of calculation, flaws in logic, omission of cases or technical faults, will be marked on a '10 minus' basis. One question we often ask is: if we were to have the benefit of a two-minute interview with this candidate, could they correct the error or fill the gap? On the other hand, an answer which shows no sign of being a genuine solution is marked on a '0 plus' basis; up to 3 marks might be awarded for particular cases or insights. It is therefore important that candidates taking these papers realise the importance of the rubric about trying to finish whole questions rather than attempting lots of disconnected parts.

Cayley (comments from Stephen Power)

This year's Cayley paper was found to be accessible by most candidates and very low scores were relatively rare. Hopefully, the students sitting the paper were pleased that they had been able to make headway on an Olympiad paper and felt at the end of the examination that they had been able to give a good account of themselves.

One difficulty that follows from this level of accessibility is that many students will feel that they have solved some of the questions asked but the marks scored by their solutions do not appear to reflect this. At Olympiad level we are looking for essentially correct solutions before we award the higher scores of 7, 8, 9 or even 10. This means that the steps involved in the solutions need to be justified properly. Large gaps in logic, missing cases or unwarranted assumptions can prove costly in terms of marks earned.

1. This question proved to be relatively straightforward and many candidates found the correct answer through algebraic methods. A few argued successfully in terms of ratios. It was noticeable that even those candidates who could handle the algebraic manipulation required to solve their equations often did not define their variables properly. In particular, it was helpful to the reader and aided the correct formation of the equations if it was clear which letter represented the greater of the two numbers.

   It is also worth pointing out to candidates that this was a question where the answers could be checked very easily and arithmetic errors leading to incorrect answers could have been spotted and remedied by unsuccessful candidates. Few candidates wrote down any form of check, although many may have undertaken one in their heads.

2. Many candidates were comfortable working with either exterior or interior angles of regular polygons and found angle *CBD* relatively easily. Candidates must, however, remember to justify each step with a reason, for example 'angles at a point add up to 360°' or 'angles on a straight line add up to 180°'. Similarly, it is crucial that rather than just asserting that *BD* = *BC*, they must specify that the two regular polygons share a side.

   Markers were relatively generous to any candidates who gave decimal approximations for angles. Clearly, approximations do not prove the required result but we hope that this will be pointed out to any candidates who made this error and that they will see how unnecessary it was to use decimal approximations in the first place.

3. A variety of successful methods were used to answer this question. The simplest involved working through all the possible numbers of apples or pears, seeing how much money was left and deciding whether a whole number of the other fruit could be bought using all the remaining money. The small numbers involved meant this method was entirely feasible and all that was needed was care in calculation.

   More sophisticated methods involved forming an equation involving the numbers of apples and pears bought and looking at the divisibility of the terms involved. This method produced answers more quickly. Many students used the fact that the cost of the apples, being a multiple of 20, would not affect the units digit of the number of pence spent in total and that the number of pears bought would have to produce the 2 pence of 392 pence.

It was pleasing to see so many different approaches being successful: candidates were thinking for themselves rather than merely applying taught methods.

4. The first step to a good solution to this question was surely to draw a good diagram. Given that candidates were allowed a ruler and a pair of compasses, this should have been entirely possible. Candidates do need to know that the square should be labelled 'around the shape' (by convention anticlockwise) otherwise the diagram will not correspond to the question. Candidates must ensure that they justify each step of their arguments and clearly stated explanations were relatively rare.

5. This question was by far the most difficult to mark as the arguments constructed by candidates were mainly word-based and involved statements that appeared obvious to the candidate but often were not helpful or even true.

   The question needs to be handled systematically, eliminating relatively easily the cases where the one winning team might score a total of 1, 2 or 3 points and then going on to show that scoring a total of 4 points and winning was impossible, and finally that scoring a total of 5 points was possible through one win and every other game ending in a draw.

6. The key first step in answering this question was to turn any two-digit number 'ab' into the actual number $10a + b$ and then form an equation from the given connection between the fractions. This led relatively easily to the connection that the square of b is equal to ac. A systematic search for integers that satisfied this connection gave eight possible sets of values.

   An alternative method, used by some, involved considering a 'scale factor' that changed the numerator and denominator of one fraction into the corresponding values for the other fraction, and then argued by considering possible unit digits. Often candidates made the mistake of assuming the scale factor had to be an integer and missed possible solutions.

   Sadly, some candidates found one set of possible values and stopped, presumably thinking that they had an answer so could stop at that point. Olympiad questions often have more than one answer and any method employed must result in finding all of them.

Hamilton (comments from James Hall)

The Hamilton paper was found to be accessible this year, with more than half of the entrants submitting responses to all six questions. Almost half of the solutions scored 7 or more marks out of 10; a pleasing proportion.

It is worth reiterating that, to score well, candidates need to produce solutions; in particular, the claims made need some justification and the methods employed need some explanation.

1. The key to answering this problem is to join the centres of each circle to the nearest vertices of the square, allowing the given figure to be split into constituent parts whose areas are straightforward to evaluate.

   The main stumbling block was failure to justify why the construction given produced right-angled triangles. Candidates who merely used this fact without explaining why it was true (for example, by using the converse of Pythagoras' Theorem) could not score more than 3 out of 10.

2. This was the most successfully answered question on the paper, with more than half of all the candidates scoring full marks. The majority of these correct solutions used an argument which involved counting the number of routes from A to the central point and then from the central point on to B before multiplying these values together.

   A small number of candidates tried to produce a complete list of routes; these were often unsuccessful, generally because their approach was not methodical (or, at least, their method was unclear) and they missed out routes.

   There was a handful of entrants who answered the (much harder!) question where the ladybird was allowed to pass through B more than once. It is important to read the question carefully!

3. This was another question where high scores were abundant, with 9 and 10 the two most common scores. There were some very eloquently explained solutions, all using Pythagoras' Theorem at some point with a variety of creative approaches. It is worth mentioning that, again, lots of marks were lost for a lack of explanation of method. In particular, several drew new points on their diagrams (for example, extending EF to meet BC), and should remember to explain how these new points are defined.

   Whilst several candidates will have experience working with surds, there was no penalty if a correct solution in an unrationalised form such as $12/\sqrt{2}$ was reached.

4. This question was found more challenging than the first three; it is, after all, at the harder end of the paper. Almost all successful solutions established that $a + b < a + c < (b + c)$ or $(a + d) < b + d < c + d$, leading to two cases which they then considered separately.

There were a fair number who did not read the question properly: some decided that a, b, c and d were all integers and therefore missed one of the cases.

It was important to check that the answers which came from each case satisfied the given conditions and the restrictions which stemmed from the cases themselves; candidates who did not do this sacrificed the tenth mark.

5. This was clearly thought to be the least accessible question on the paper, with more candidates not attempting it than for any other question. It is worth noting that all the correct solutions, without exception, contained a decent diagram.

   There were several approaches, the two most common of which involved either drawing perpendiculars from DC to AB to create some 30-60-90 triangles or by proving that the point E lies on DC.

   In the former of these approaches, there was a minor penalty for candidates who did not make it clear that they were using the fact that the trapezium given was isosceles (and therefore symmetrical). In the latter, some students just claimed that E lies on BC without justification (sometimes a 'proof by diagram'), limiting themselves to a maximum of 2 marks out of 10.

6. This was a simply-stated question, which may be why it was reasonably popular, but proved a challenge for most candidates who attempted it. A lot managed to make a little progress, and the cubic $x^3 - 19x + 30 = 0$ (or other forms) made frequent appearances, but, understandably, candidates often got stuck at this point.

   Some candidates just stated solutions to this cubic (often just one or two of them), and then limited themselves to only a few marks. Even those who found all three solutions via a cubic equation needed either to have demonstrated their method properly or somehow explained why there could be no further solutions.

   A pleasing number of candidates reached a factorised equation involving x and y—the accessible method. It was a shame when a candidate got this far and then divided by a bracket containing an unknown without considering what might happen if that bracket were equal to zero. It is really important to check that, when dividing by an expression involving an unknown, zero is considered carefully. Even better, everything to one side and factorise.

   Finally, as in question 4, it is important to check that the solutions reached do indeed satisfy the original equation; again those who did not do this lost the final mark.

Maclaurin (comments from Gerry Leversha)

1. This question was answered confidently by many candidates.

   A natural first step was to draw the radii OP and OQ to the points of tangency.

   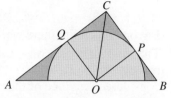

   Most successful candidates then used either areas, similar triangles or trigonometry.

   A poor strategy was that of calculating the distances AO, OB and AB using Pythagoras' and using the fact that $AO + OB = AB$; this gives rise to an unpleasant equation involving square roots which is very hard to solve. However, CO bisects the angle in the square, so it is possible to use the angle bisector theorem.

   Some candidates made the assumption that the triangle ABC was isosceles, sometimes without realising they were doing so, and this approach was not given any credit.

2. The key here was to describe a way of enumerating the triangles without omitting any of them and without counting any more than once. Most candidates attempted to do this and in general the standard of presentation was good. It was not necessary to know the formula for combinations since these could be evaluated by summing a finite sequence. The crux, however, was to avoid either including degenerate triangles (with three vertices on an 'axis') or over-counting. The former could be eliminated by counting two points on one axis and one on the other. Triangles with a vertex at the 'origin' were counted twice, but this was easy to cope with. Another method which worked was to consider three types of triangle: those with a vertex at the origin, those which used two 'half-axes' and those which used three 'half-axes'.

   All the successful attempts began by thinking about the different ways in which triangles could be constructed. Some others focused more on points, thinking about the 'left-most' and 'top-most' of the three, and enumerating ways of finding the third. These tended to run into difficulties with over-counting, particularly as concerned the origin. This is particularly an issue when the strategy employed counts some triangles once, some twice and others more than twice, since it is generally impossible to remedy this by a simple division. The lesson is that it is important to understand which triangles will be counted twice before embarking on an enumeration, and then divide the process up into cases if necessary.

3. Nearly all successful solutions began by rearranging the equation in the form

$$(m^2 - 21)^2 = (n^2 - 4)^2.$$

Beyond this point there were a number of pitfalls to be avoided.

The first of these was failing to realise that there were two cases, namely $m^2 - 21 = n^2 - 4$ and $m^2 - 21 = 4 - n^2$. Candidates who considered only one of these cases obtained a maximum of 3 marks.

The first case gives rise to the equation $m^2 - n^2 = 17$. An algebraic approach is to factorise this as $(m - n)(m + n) = 17$ and to realise that 17 can be factorised in four ways, each of which provides a solution. Many candidates forgot to consider the case where the factors were both negative. An alternative approach was to look at differences of perfect squares. It was acceptable to state that the differences between consecutive squares increased as the numbers did, so the only possibility is $m^2 = 81$ and $n^2 = 64$, but again it was necessary to note that either or both of m and n could be negative. It was also important to consider whether there were any non-consecutive squares satisfying this condition.

The second case gives rise to the equation $m^2 + n^2 = 25$ and here it is sufficient to consider perfect squares less than 36. However, many candidates failed to see that one solution was $0^2 + 5^2$, that one or both of m and n could be negative, or that the roles of m and n could be interchanged.

The lesson here is that you need to be very careful to see at each stage of this calculation that there can be more than one alternative, and also to understand that using a mantra such as 'we can swap m and n' might be valid in one situation but not in another.

4. This is an intriguing configuration. Markers were particularly concerned that candidates should not *assume* that $\angle UTP = 90°$. This *happens* to be true, and the proof that $UR = \frac{1}{2}$ is straightforward from then on, but the right-angle needs to be proved.

One useful approach was to consider congruent triangles formed by drawing a perpendicular from T to UP, after which it is possible to show that $\angle UTP = 90°$. Several candidates came up with an ingenious method which shows that the quadrilateral $PQUT$ is cyclic; others considered the effect of extending PU to meet SR at a point, and yet others began by defining a point U' on RQ with $RU' = \frac{1}{2}$ and showing that $\angle SPT = \angle TPU'$. It is also possible to solve this using the cosine rule, avoiding consideration of $\angle UTP$.

It should be emphasised that the statement

$$UR = 2 - 2 \tan\left(90° - 2 \tan^{-1}\left(\frac{1}{2}\right)\right)$$

is not regarded in this context as a 'fully simplified answer'. In this respect, candidates who knew the double angle formula for tangent had an advantage, but those who did not should have avoided a situation where they would need to use it.

5. There were two successful methods employed. The most popular was to factorise $a^2 - b^2$ as a difference of two squares and to combine the two equations into the quadratic equation $3a^2 - 10ab + 3b^2 = 0$. Depending on the method, this usually needed an observation such as $a \neq b$ or $a^2 + b^2 \neq 0$. This is trivial to show but candidates should always be careful that they are not dividing by zero. From there on it is straightforward to obtain the two solutions.

An alternative was to process the two equations to obtain the cubic $(a - b)^3 = 1$, from which we obtain the simple relationship $a = b + 1$.

Is it necessary to check solutions back in the original equations? On the whole, it is advisable to do so, particularly when working with unfamiliar simultaneous equations. It is absolutely necessary when the steps in the solution process are not reversible, and particularly when both sides of an equation have been squared, say, thereby introducing new and inappropriate solutions. However, in this case it is not necessary to check that the solutions fit the given equations, since all the derived equations are just linear combinations of the originals. Despite this, it is good advice to check solutions, if only to eliminate any minor errors in calculation.

6. This was the hardest question on the paper. There are two parts.

A candidate who showed how to fit 36 additional tiles earned one mark.

It is much more difficult to prove that no more than 36 tiles can be fitted. An argument that proceeds by saying something like 'I have placed tiles into the grid in what is clearly the best arrangement, and still I can only fit 36 of them' is unlikely to gain any credit, since the whole point is knowing what the 'best' arrangement is, and it might not be obvious at all.

In order to score beyond this, it was necessary to employ a colouring argument. It turns out that ordinary chessboard colouring is adequate. When this is done, there are the same number of black and white squares to be covered, and each tile covers one square of each colour, so in theory there is no reason why 38 tiles cannot be added. However, is it possible to do this around the seven tiles which are already in position? Experiment suggests that this is not the case.

Several candidates partitioned the remaining squares on the board into two symmetrical congruent pieces, and then argued that in each half of the partition there were unequal numbers of black and white squares, drawing the conclusion that only 18 tiles could be placed in each half of the partition and so only 36 altogether. The trouble with this argument is that it implies that the best possible tiling will 'respect' the partition. Perhaps an extra tile might be fitted in if it is allowed to cross the boundary. Arguments of this type generally earned two marks.

Only a handful of candidates managed to overcome this difficulty. The crux is to consider what happens at the two corners. If both corner squares are left uncovered, the colouring argument shows that only 34 tiles can be placed. It follows that, if the corners are then made available, the maximum is 36. It is still necessary, of course, to show that the maximum can be achieved by showing an explicit way of placing 36 tiles. There are a variety of arguments available for this question and successful candidates should be pleased at being able to solve a tricky problem.

Marking

The marking was carried out on the weekend of 24th-26th March 2017 in Leeds. There were three marking groups led by Stephen Power, James Hall and Gerry Leversha. The other markers are listed later in this book.

IMOK certificates

All participating students who qualified automatically were awarded a certificate. These came in three varieties: Qualification, Merit and Distinction.

THE UKMT INTERMEDIATE MATHEMATICAL OLYMPIAD AND KANGAROO

The IMOK is the follow-on round for the Intermediate Mathematical Challenge and is organised by the UK Mathematics Trust. For each year group, the top scoring 500 or so IMC pupils are invited to participate in the Olympiad, and the next 3000 are invited to participate in the European Kangaroo. Schools may also enter additional pupils to the Olympiad upon payment of a fee; the Kangaroo is by invitation only.

The Olympiad is a two-hour examination which includes six demanding questions requiring full written solutions. The problems are designed to include interesting and attractive mathematics and may involve knowledge or understanding beyond the range of normal school work.

The one-hour multiple choice European Kangaroo requires the use of logic as well as mathematical understanding to solve amusing and thought-provoking questions. The 'Kangourou sans Frontières' is taken by students in over forty countries in Europe and beyond.

The UKMT is a registered educational charity. See our website www.ukmt.org.uk for more information.
Donations would be gratefully received and can be made at
www.donate.ukmt.org.uk if you would like to support our work in this way.

IMOK Olympiad awards

As in recent years, medals were awarded in the Intermediate Mathematical Olympiad. Names of medal winners are listed below. Book prizes were awarded to the top 50 or so in each age group. The Cayley prize was *Alice's Adventures in Numberland* by Alex Bellos; the Hamilton prize was *The Simpsons and their Mathematical Secrets* by Simon Singh; and for Maclaurin, *17 Equations that changed the world* by Ian Stewart.

IMOK
2017

Decode:

2 50 17.
0339 03 28
92046796

IMOK medal winners

Cayley

Arlan Abzhanov	Reading School
Taha Ahmed	The Priory Academy LSST, Lincoln
Tahmeed Ali	Latymer School, London
Kiran Amin	Harrogate Grammar School, N. Yorks
Arthur Ashworth	Sutton Grammar School for Boys, Surrey
Wilfred Ashworth	Sutton Grammar School for Boys, Surrey
Christopher Austin	Hampton School, Middlesex
Fin Brickman	Dragon School, Oxford
Jacob Brown	King's School Macclesfield
Christian Cases	Tiffin School, Kingston-upon-Thames
Prompt Chotanaphuti	Shrewsbury International School, Thailand
Conor Collins	Solihull School
Matthew Cresswell	Hampton School, Middlesex
Jack Dennis	St Martin's Academy, nr Nuneaton
Kira Dhariwal	Wycombe High School, Buckinghamshire
Ben Fearnhead	Lancaster Royal Grammar School
Rish Fulmali	Pate's Grammar School, Cheltenham
Richard Gong	The Romsey School, Hampshire
Ewan Green	Debenham High School, Suffolk
Ojas Gulati	Tiffin School, Kingston-upon-Thames
Yogya Gupta	Lampton Academy, London
Anant Gupta	Whitgift School, Surrey
Aditya Gupta	Westminster Under School, London

Anthony Gutsev	Westminster School, London
Freddie Hand	Judd School, Tonbridge, Kent
Edward Hilditch	Eton College, Windsor
Rikako Hirai	St Paul's Girls' School, Hammersmith
David Kang	Bangkok Patana School
Ethan Kang	Westminster Under School, London
Otoharu Kawaguchi	Merchant Taylors' School, Middlesex
Chris Dohoo Kim	Eton College, Windsor
Yoon Jin Kim	St Paul's Girls' School, Hammersmith
Gaurav Kocher	Westminster School, London
Avish Kumar	Westminster Under School, London
Alex Kwang	St Paul's School, Barnes, London
Charlotte Lampe	Beaconsfield High Sch., Buckinghamshire
Seul Lee	North London Coll. S. Jeju, South Korea
William Leung	Winchester College
Rhys Lewis	Sir Thomas Picton Sch., Haverfordwest
Samuel Liew	The West Bridgford School, Nottingham
Harvey Lin	Eton College, Windsor
Harry List	Blundell's School, Devon
Linus Luu	St Olave's Grammar School, Kent
Yuhka Machino	Millfield School, Somerset
Ismail Mardin	St Paul's School, Barnes, London
Tanishq Mehta	Queen Elizabeth's School, Barnet
Jonah Milnes	D'Overbroeck's College, Oxford
Ilya Misyura	Westminster Under School, London
Conall Moss	Parmiter's School, Watford
Alexander Mousley	Newquay Tretherras, Cornwall
Jack Murphy	Hampton School, Middlesex
Samvit Nagpal	Westminster Under School, London
Daniel Naylor	Matthew Arnold School, Oxford
Colin (Ka Him) Ng	Winchester College
Nitya Nigam	German Swiss International S., Hong Kong
Rtvik Patel	Winchester College
Shyam Patel	King Edward VI Grammar S., Chelmsford
Ian Pebody	The Perse School, Cambridge
Vlad Penzyev	Hampton School, Middlesex
Gao Qu	The Stephen Perse Foundation, Cambridge

Kiran Raja	Manchester Grammar School
Ricky Rim	Kingston Grammar School, Surrey
Adrian Sahani	Westminster School, London
Qasim Salahuddin	Noor Ul Islam Primary School
Oscar Selby	Westminster School, London
Daniel Shapiro	Haberdashers' Aske's S. for Boys, Herts
Kishan Sharma	King Edward's School, Birmingham
Kiran Shiatis	Judd School, Tonbridge, Kent
John Skeen	Churchill Academy, North Somerset
Andrew Spielmann	St Paul's School, Barnes, London
Ben Stokes	Rutlish School, London
Paris Suksmith	Eton College, Windsor
James Tan	Queen Elizabeth's School, Barnet
Chin Wei Tang	Tiffin School, Kingston-upon-Thames
Leon Tasch	Sir William Borlase's Grammar S., Bucks
Ashwin Tennant	Abingdon School
David Teo Kai	Anglo-Chinese School, Singapore
Zach Thompson	Birkdale School, Sheffield
Vaclav Trpisovsky	Open Gates Boarding S., Czech Republic
Thien Udomsrirungruag	Shrewsbury International School, Thailand
Saanya Verma	North London Collegiate School
Jathusan Vijayakumar	Bancroft's School, Essex
Alex Walker	The Perse School, Cambridge
Tommy Walkermackay	Stretford Grammar School, Manchester
Daniel Warren	Trinity School, Croydon
Carson White	Winchester College
Henry Wilson	Latymer School, London
Wing Lam Wong	Wycombe Abbey School, High Wycombe
Elyne Wu	Cheltenham Ladies' College
Amy Xu	The Perse School, Cambridge
David Xu	Haberdashers' Aske's S. for Boys, Herts
Sam Yang	North London Coll. S. Jeju, South Korea
Zhe (Amy) Ye	Sherborne School for Girls, Dorset
Yen Li Yeap	Torquay Girls' Grammar School
Jack Yu	Tiffin School, Kingston-upon-Thames
John Yu	The Portsmouth Grammar School
Jimmy Yuan	King Edward's School, Birmingham

Nimar Zhao	Westminster School, London
Cathy Zheng	Roedean School, Brighton
George Zhou	Westminster Under School, London
Michelle Zhu	Wycombe Abbey School, High Wycombe

Hamilton

Suyash Agarwal	St John's College, Cardiff
Edward Allen	Hampton School, Middlesex
Gianfranco Ameri	Westminster School, London
Nathaniel Ang Boon Han	Anglo-Chinese School, Singapore
Gaurav Arya	King George V School, Hong Kong
Somsubhro Bagchi	Devonport High Sch. for Boys, Plymouth
Victor Baycroft	Notre Dame High School, Sheffield
Naomi Bazlov	King Edward VI HS for Girls, Birmingham
Caroline Bong	Garden International School, Malaysia
William Boyce	Hampton School, Middlesex
Imogen Breeze	Withington Girls' School, Manchester
Matthew Buckley	Eton College, Windsor
Thomas Burchell	Hethersett Academy, Norfolk
Haoran Cao	Loughborough Grammar School
Jun San Chakma	Westcliff High School for Girls, Essex
Ngo Hang Chan	Charterhouse, Godalming, Surrey
Haofei Chen	Anglo-Chinese School, Singapore
Kevin Chen	Taipei European School
Steven (Bingham) Chen	Bedstone College, Shropshire
Xue Bang Chen	King Edward VI Camp Hill S. for Boys, Birmingham
William Ching	Westminster School, London
Soren Choi	Westminster School, London
Matthew Chuang	YMCA of Hong Kong Christian College
Toby Cole	Kingston Grammar School, Surrey
Gustav Conradie	Eton College, Windsor
Brian Davies	St Edward's College, Liverpool
Tom de Csillery	Westminster School, London
Rishit Dhoot	West Hill School, Lancashire
Yuexin Ding	Badminton School, Bristol
Andrew Dubois	Wellsway School, Bristol
James Edmiston	Magdalen College School, Oxford
Hamish Elder	St Paul's School, Barnes, London

Anton Fedotov	St Paul's School, Barnes, London
Danil Filatov	Eton College, Windsor
Toby Galbraith	Eton College, Windsor
Alex Gao	Bolton School (Boys Division)
Jason (Zhijian) Gao	Bedstone College, Shropshire
Sarah Gleghorn	Skipton Girls' High School, N. Yorks
Kirpal Grewal	Westminster School, London
Tomasen Haley	Reading School
Chloe Han	North London Coll. S. Jeju, South Korea
James Hindmarch	Oxted School, Surrey
Jennifer Hu	Loughborough High School
Minjae Joh	North London Coll. S. Jeju, South Korea
Daniel Kaddaj	Westminster School, London
Rubaiyat Khondaker	Wilson's School, Surrey
Eugene Kim	Harrow School
Aiden (Nahckkyun) Kim	North London Coll. S. Jeju, South Korea
Subin Kim	North London Coll. S. Jeju, South Korea
Sungyoon Kim	North London Coll. S. Jeju, South Korea
Chuixin Kong	Jinan Foreign Language School, China
Sebastian Kreutz-Wellsted	Dame Alice Owen's School, Herts
Jonathan Lee	Queen Elizabeth's Hospital, Bristol
Kevin Lee	Tonbridge School, Kent
Kingston Lee	Harrow School
Yejin Lee	North London Coll. S. Jeju, South Korea
Weihe (Claire) Li	Ashford School, Kent
Nathan Lockwood	The Sele School, Hertford
Yikun Lu	Oundle School, Northants
Yingzi Ma	Harrow International School, Bangkok
Wenqi Min	Bullers Wood School, Kent
Kyungseo Min	North London Coll. S. Jeju, South Korea
Maddie Miyazaki	Henrietta Barnett School, London
George Monro-Davies	St Paul's School, Barnes, London
Emre Mutlu	British School of Chicago, Illinois, USA
Jason Ng	Abingdon School
Moe Okawara	The British School in Tokyo Showa
Euan Ong	Magdalen College School, Oxford
Ouw Brian Thadius Santoso	Anglo-Chinese School, Singapore
Dillon Patel	King Edward VI S., Stratford-upon-Avon

Sejal Patel	Millais School, Horsham
Benedict Place	Marlborough College, Wiltshire
Chenxin Qi	Douglas Academy, East Dunbartonshire
Benedict Randall Shaw	Westminster School, London
Luke Rasmussen	Sevenoaks School, Kent
Dhruv Rattan	Winchester College
Tom Rose	Bristol Grammar School
Tibor Rothschild	University College School, London
Anthony Shin	Eton College, Windsor
Jaehyun Shin	North London Coll. S. Jeju, South Korea
Vikram Singh	The Perse School, Cambridge
Ben Skaile	Monmouth School
Andrew Smith	Westminster School, London
Tianze Sun	Jinan Foreign Language School, China
Joseph Tapper	Abbey Grange CE Academy, Leeds
Aron Thomas	Dame Alice Owen's School, Herts
Becky Ting	Rugby School
Shashwat Tomar	Brighton College Abu Dhabi
Chi Heng (Jensen) Tong	Dulwich College
Stephon Umashangar	Hampton School, Middlesex
Amu Varma	St Paul's School, Barnes, London
Luis Wahl	Eton College, Windsor
Weixi (Selina) Wang	Burgess Hill School, West Sussex
Max (Tsz Chun) Wong	Winchester College
Ruizi Wu	Beijing New Talent Academy
Jonathan Yang	Eton College, Windsor
Norm Yeung	Westminster School, London
Zixu Zhai	Warwick School
Han Zhang	Jinan Foreign Language School, China
Helen Zhang	Clifton College Upper School, Bristol

Maclaurin

Kiran Aberdeen	Queen Elizabeth's School, Barnet
Hyunchan Ahn	North London Coll. S. Jeju, South Korea
Bashmy Basheer	Queen Elizabeth's School, Barnet
Daniel Bassett	Caistor Grammar School, Lincs
Ralph Battle	The North School, Ashford
Oliver Beken	Horndean Technology College, Hampshire

Rose Blyth	Tonbridge Grammar School, Kent
Alexander Buck	St Ninian's High School, Isle of Man
Bill Cao	Eastbourne College
Matthew Chan	Lancaster Royal Grammar School
Raghav Chandra	Newcastle under Lyme School
Richard Chappell	Aylesbury Grammar School
Ruoyan Chen	Roedean School, Brighton
Walace Chen	Leighton Park School, Reading
Jinheon Choi	The British International School, Shanghai
Jiwon Choi	North London Coll. S. Jeju, South Korea
Pino Cholsaipant	Shrewsbury International School, Thailand
Arthur Conmy	St Gregory the Great Catholic Sch., Oxford
Alex Darby	Sutton Grammar School for Boys, Surrey
Nicholas Dibbfuller	Hampton School, Middlesex
Eamon Dutta Gupta	King Edward VI Grammar S., Chelmsford
Eric Bryan	Anglo-Chinese School, Singapore
Bill Gao	Blundell's School, Devon
Edward Garemo	Brighton College Abu Dhabi
Dao Minh Hai	Anglo-Chinese School, Singapore
Zichen Han	Abbey College, Cambridge
Ella Hao	King's School Ely, Cambridgeshire
Faiz Haris Osman	British School of Brussels
Henry He	Bedford School
Robert Hillier	King Edward VI Camp Hill S. for Boys, Birmingham
Thomas Hillman	St Albans School
Yang Hsu	St Paul's School, Barnes, London
Zixiao Hu	Impington Village College, Cambridgeshire
Dion Huang	Westminster School, London
Shuqi Huang	St Swithun's School, Winchester
Kerou (Coco) Jin	Scarborough College
Matthew Jolly	St Laurence School, Wiltshire
Seou Kahng	North London Coll. S. Jeju, South Korea
Jakub Kara	Open Gates Boarding S., Czech Republic
Isaac Kaufmann	City of London School
Yoon Seo Kim	Brighton College Abu Dhabi
Sae Koyama	Rodborough Technology College, Surrey
Yao Chih Kuo	The Perse School, Cambridge
Yardley Kwan	Renaissance College, Hong Kong
Anthony (Chen Rong) Lee	Garden International School, Malaysia

Gina (Na-Kyum) Lee	Ruamrudee International School, Thailand
Sheppard Li	Ashford School, Kent
Michael Liu	Culford School, Suffolk
Amrit Lohia	Westminster School, London
Kevin Angelo Lukito	Anglo-Chinese School, Singapore
Nigel Luo	Queen Ethelburga's College, N. Yorks
Longxiao Ma	Jinan Foreign Language School, China
Scarlett Ma	Westbourne School, Vale of Glamorgan
Ma Mancheng	St George's School, Birmingham
Joe Mansley	UTC Cambridge
Fraser Mason	St Mary's Music School, Edinburgh
Moses Mayer	The British International S. Jakarta, Indonesia
Anoushka Mazumdar	Manchester High School for Girls
George Mears	George Abbot School, Guildford
Stephen Mellor	Fulford School, York
Qi Miao	Jinan Foreign Language School, China
James Morris	Beechen Cliff School, Bath
Navonil Neogi	Tiffin School, Kingston-upon-Thames
Andrew Ng	Dulwich College
Nguyen Minh Tuan	Anglo-Chinese School, Singapore
Lorcan O'Connor	University College School, London
Shou Otsuka	International School of Luxembourg
Inji Park	North London Coll. S. Jeju, South Korea
Nico Puthu	Queen Elizabeth's School, Barnet
Anqi Qiu	Bellerbys College, Brighton
David Rae	St Paul's School, Barnes, London
Nick Scott	Dame Alice Owen's School, Herts
Andrea Sendula	Kenilworth School, Warks
Claire Shen	Harrogate Ladies' College
Xin Shen	Mayfield School, East Sussex
Zikai Shen	St Julian's School, Portugal
Yigi Shi	St Mary's School, Wiltshire
Alexander Song	Westminster School, London
Xin Ran Song	International School of Luxembourg
Yuchen Sun	Jinan Foreign Language School, China
Matthew Scott Tan	Anglo-Chinese School, Singapore
Vincent Trieu	Tiffin School, Kingston-upon-Thames
Mayuran Visakan	Birkdale School, Sheffield
Douglas Wang	Harrow International School, Hong Kong

George Wang	Epsom College, Surrey
Sean White	City of London School
William Wahyudi	Anglo-Chinese School, Singapore
Heedo (Peter) Woo	Hampton School, Middlesex
Isaac Wood	Redland Green School, Bristol
Yuqing Wu	Bangkok Patana School
Bruce Xu	West Island School (ESF), Hong Kong
Gloria Xu	Westbourne School, Vale of Glamorgan
Simon Xu	Dulwich College
Ziqi Yan	The Tiffin Girls' S., Kingston-upon-Thames
Han Chieh Yang	Lansdowne College, London
Changwoo Yang	The British International School, Shanghai
Yang Shaobo	Anglo-Chinese School, Singapore
Zhengkun (Chris) Ye	Bromsgrove School, Worcestershire
Mingqi Yin	St Catherine's School, Guildford
Narinat Yongphiphatwong	Shrewsbury International School, Thailand
Mina You	North London Coll. S. Jeju, South Korea
Joanna Yu	Taunton School (Upper School)
Joy Yu	Rugby School
Julian Yu	British School Manila, Philippines
Sitong Zeng	Concord College, Shrewsbury
Baoyuan Zhang	Anglo-Chinese School, Singapore
Jichuan Zhang	Trent College, nr Nottingham
Haowen Zhao	St Bede's College, Manchester
Rudi Zhu	Culford School, Suffolk

UKMT Summer Schools 2016-2017

Introduction

The first summer school was held in Queen's College, Oxford in July 1994. Dr. Tony Gardiner organised and ran the first five events from 1994, and UKMT took over the organisation in 1998. From 1997 to 2012 the summer schools were held in Queen's College, Birmingham and for a few years the Trust organised five annual summer schools, two being held in West Yorkshire and three in Oxford. Four summer schools were held in 2016.

Summer School for Girls

The Summer School for Girls was held in Oxford between Sunday 21st and Friday 26th August 2016. The accommodation was at St Anne's College with teaching being held in the Andrew Wiles Building, at the Mathematical Institute. Somerville College provided the venue for lunch each day. There were 40 students from years 10 and 11 invited to attend, along with 5 senior students who had previously attended a summer school or other UKMT residential event. Their role was to assist the younger students throughout the week, as well as having the opportunity to attend more advanced sessions of their own. The director of the Summer School for Girls was Mrs Sue Cubbon.

National Mathematics Summer Schools (NMSS)

There were three NMSS summer schools held this year, one in Oxford during the summer of 2016 and two near Leeds in July 2017.

Oxford NMSS Summer School 2016

The National Maths Summer School in Oxford was led by Dr Dominic Rowland between Sunday 7th and Friday 12th August 2016. Accommodation for this school was also at St Anne's College, with the teaching again being at the Mathematical Institute, in the Andrew Wiles Building. Lunches were taken at Somerville College.

Once again 40 junior students from years 10 and 11 were invited to attend, with 5 senior students assisting throughout the week, and also attending their own more advanced sessions.

Leeds NMSS Summer Schools (43 and 44) 2017

The first Leeds event this year was held at Woodhouse Grove School between Sunday 9th and Friday 14th July and was led by Dorothy Winn and Catherine Ramsey. The second week was also at Woodhouse Grove School, running from Sunday 16th until Friday 21st July and was led by James Gazet.

Both these schools were attended by 48 junior students, who were guided and assisted by 8 different senior students each week. Like the seniors in Oxford, these seniors had previously attended a summer school as a junior. The Enrichment subtrust made the decision in August 2016 to invite an additional 8 students to the 2017 events to allow more students to take up the opportunity of attending a summer school.

Students attending Summer Schools in 2016-2017
Summer School for Girls, 21st - 26th August 2016
Students: Emily Carr, Jillian Cheng, Fiona Davies, Ursula Eastwood, Megan Evans, Maia Eyre Morgan, Anna Fenton Smith, Matilda Ferrand, Non Geraint, Eleanor Gwynne, Sara Ha, Cat Jackson, Rhianna Jones, Cecilia (Jee-In) Kim, Karolina Kowalczyk, Bethan Law, Eunice Lee, Ruchika Madhotra, Eleanor Medcalf, Megan Miller, Caitlin Obee, Polly Palmer-Jones, Ioana Pascariu, Charlotte Payne, Amrit Phull, Isabelle Santhiapillai, Katie Shaw, Lisa She-Yin, Freya Stancliffe, Abigail Terry, Isabelle Thomas, Anna Townsend, Rei-Lin Tran, Katherine Usherwood, Mahek Vara, Mathilda Vere, Eirlys Walters, Eleanor Washington, Abigail Wheeler, Rebecca Woodburn,
Seniors: Alice Vaughn Williams, Constance Bambridge Sutton, Elizabeth Holdcroft, Naomi Wei, Robyn Ware

Oxford NMSS, 7th - 12th August 2016
Students:, Najeeb Al-Shabibi, Helena Bayley, George Bird, Joshua Brown, Alexander Buck, Emma Campbell, Sze-Tat Cheung, John Conacher, Arianna Cox, Michael Doyle, Andrew Ejemai, Chris Finn, Alise Furse, Ben Hayward, Isabelle Humphreys, Jonathan Innes, Jaewon Jung, Nikita Kamath, Mantra Kusumgar, Rose Laurie, Megan Lear, Sarah Li, Matthew Lowry, Thomas Malloch, Izumu Mishima, Oliver Mustafa, Ella Olamona, Joshua Payne, Anna Pearse, Jonathan Ralphs, Oliver Ross, Prerak Shah, Aric Smith, Charles Stanton, August Taylor, Mayuran Visakan, Alexander Wallace, Laura Waterworth, Hanna Whydle, Esther Wiggers
Seniors: Joseph Adams, Emma Brown, Elizabeth Holdcroft, Bertie Ellison-Wright, Chris Uren

Woodhouse Grove NMSS 43, 9th and 14th July 2017
Students: Thomas Bain, Thomas Carroll, Jun San Chakma, Joey Chen, Jonathan Chen, Seo Yeon Cho, Catherine Cronin, Jonathan Fernandes, Nathan Foster, Kam'ron Galloway, Jennifer Greenfield, Arul Gupta, Matthew Hale, Seung-Ju Han, Pippy Harrison, Samuel Holt, Sho Ishikawa, Charlie Kidd, Charlotte Knight, Jing-Ting Kuo, Alex Law,

Kevin Lee, Sheppard (Jia Hao) Li, Damon Marlow, George Mears, Madoka Miyazaki, Sho Nakano, Jack Nolan, Timothy Peng, Susie Petri, Katrina Qian, Maz Rizwan, Thomas Roland, Vidhi Sharma, Matthew Shipway, James Stickland, Zebedee Summerfield, Tamas Vamos, Peter Westbrooke, Callum White, Jono Whittle, Maartje Wisse, Xiao Xiao (Carol) Yan, Yu Jui Yang, Han Chieh Yang, Joy Yu, Jichuan Zhang, Shixiao (Selena) Zhu

Seniors: Sameer Aggarwal, Anusha Ashok, Joseph Brason, Bruno Lindan, Kira Miller, Matthew Varley, Hanna Whydle, James Zhang

Woodhouse Grove NMSS 44, 16th - 21st July 2017

Students: Alex Apen, Henry Bittleston, Charlie Buckley, Aditi Chandana, Daniel Claydon, Tyler Crowley, Ben Durkan, Bjork Elezi, Daniel Farrow, Imogen Ferguson, Natalie Gass, Yana Gavrilova, Sarah Gleghorn, Ella Hao, James Hensman, Bailey Higson, Harry Hopkins, Jiahan Huang, Ben Hughes, Victoria (Xinyi) Jiang, Dariyan Khan, Jamie Lear, Audrey Lim, Clara McKee, Vishvesh Mehta, Hazel Meier, Oliver Newton-Coombs, Julianna Nowaczek, George O'Dell, Thomas Pelling, Joe Phelps, Tyler Phillips, Jake Phillips, Vickram Phull, James Rogers, Chris Sapiano, Lunzhi Shi, William Skipwith, Theo Snelson, Reemon Spector, Kapenajah Sribaskaran, Cameron Stocks, Louis Trout, Weixi (Selena) Wang, Yu Tong Wei, James Westwood, Charlie Wilson, Oksana Zimina

Seniors: John Bamford, Melissa Knapton, Sophie McInerney, Michael Ng, Patrick Ramsay, Amelia Rout, Yannis Wells, Lennie Wells

Our thanks go to everyone who made these Summer Schools such a success, in particular: Woodhouse Grove School, St Anne's College, Somerville College and the Oxford University Mathematical Institute.

We also thank all our volunteers who work tirelessly to make these weeks a success, particularly the leaders: Sue Cubbon, James Gazet, Catherine Ramsay, Dominic Rowland and Dorothy Winn. A list of all the volunteers who gave sessions and helped at the summer schools can be found at the back of this Yearbook.

Senior Mathematical Challenge and follow-on rounds

The Senior Challenge took place on Tuesday 8th November 2016, and over 83,000 pupils took part. Once again it was sponsored by the Institute and Faculty of Actuaries. Around 1000 top scorers were invited to take part in the next stage, British Mathematical Olympiad Round 1, held on Friday 2nd November 2016, with others able to enter on payment of a fee. The Senior Kangaroo was held on the same day, invitations to this were increased to around 5,000.

UK SENIOR MATHEMATICAL CHALLENGE

Tuesday 8 November 2016

Organised by the **United Kingdom Mathematics Trust**

and supported by

Institute
and Faculty
of Actuaries

RULES AND GUIDELINES (to be read before starting)

1. Do not open the question paper until the invigilator tells you to do so.

2. Time allowed: **90 minutes**.
   No answers or personal details may be entered on the Answer Sheet after the 90 minutes are over.

3. The use of rough paper is allowed.
   Calculators, measuring instruments and squared paper are forbidden.

4. Candidates must be full-time students at secondary school or FE college, and must be in Year 13 or below (England & Wales); S6 or below (Scotland); Year 14 or below (Northern Ireland).

5. **Use B or HB pencil only**. Mark *at most one* of the options A, B, C, D, E on the Answer Sheet for each question. Do not mark more than one option.

6. **Scoring rules**: all candidates start out with 25 marks;

   0 marks are awarded for each question left unanswered;

   4 marks are awarded for each correct answer;

   1 mark is deducted for each incorrect answer.

7. **Guessing**: Remember that there is a penalty for incorrect answers. Note also that later questions are deliberately intended to be harder than earlier questions. You are thus advised to concentrate first on solving as many as possible of the first 15-20 questions. Only then should you try later questions.

The United Kingdom Mathematics Trust is a Registered Charity.

http://www.ukmt.org.uk

1. How many times does the digit 9 appear in the answer to 987654321×9 ?

    A 0   B 1   C 5   D 8   E 9

2. On a Monday, all prices in Isla's shop are 10% more than normal. On Friday all prices in Isla's shop are 10% less than normal. James bought a book on Monday for £5.50. What would be the price of another copy of this book on Friday?

    A £5.50   B £5.00   C £4.95   D £4.50   E £4.40

3. The diagram shows a circle with radius 1 that rolls without slipping around the inside of a square with sides of length 5.

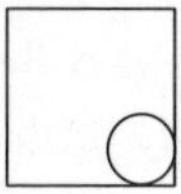

    The circle rolls once around the square, returning to its starting point.

    What distance does the centre of the circle travel?

    A $16 - 2\pi$ B 12   C $6 + \pi$ D $20 - 2\pi$ E 20

4. Alex draws a scalene triangle. One of the angles is 80°.

    Which of the following could be the difference between the other two angles in Alex's triangle?

    A 0°   B 60°   C 80°   D 100°   E 120°

5. 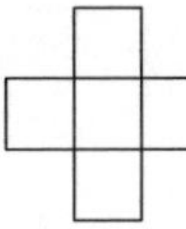 All the digits 2, 3, 4, 5 and 6 are placed in the grid, one in each cell, to form two three-digit numbers that are squares.

    Which digit is placed in the centre of the grid?

    A 2   B 3   C 4   D 5   E 6

6. The diagram shows a square $ABCD$ and a right-angled triangle ABE. The length of BC is 3. The length of BE is 4.

    What is the area of the shaded region?

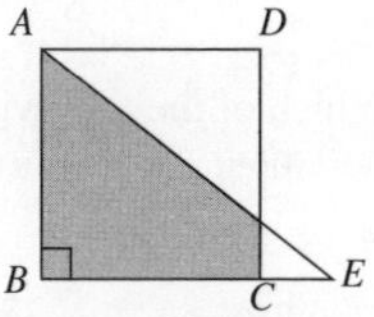

    A $5\frac{1}{4}$ B $5\frac{3}{8}$ C $5\frac{1}{2}$ D $5\frac{5}{8}$ E $5\frac{3}{4}$

7. Which of these has the smallest value?

    A 2016^{-1} B $2016^{-1/2}$ C 2016^{0} D $2016^{1/2}$ E 2016^{1}

8. Points are drawn on the sides of a square, dividing each side into n equal parts (so, in the example shown, $n = 4$).

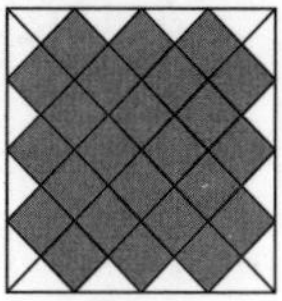

    The points are joined in the manner indicated, to form several small squares (24 in the example, shown shaded) and some triangles.

    How many small squares are formed when $n = 7$?

    A 56   B 84   C 140   D 840   E 5040

9. A square has vertices at $(0, 0)$, $(1, 0)$, $(1, 1)$ and $(0, 1)$. Graphs of the following equations are drawn on the same set of axes as the square.

    $$x^2 + y^2 = 1, \qquad y = x + 1, \qquad y = -x^2 + 1, \qquad y = x, \qquad y = \frac{1}{x}$$

    How many of the graphs pass through exactly two of the vertices of the square?

    A 1   B 2   C 3   D 4   E 5

10. The digits from 1 to 9 are to be written in the nine cells of the 3 × 3 grid shown, one digit in each cell.

The product of the three digits in the first row is 12.

The product of the three digits in the second row is 112.

The product of the three digits in the first column is 216.

The product of the three digits in the second column is 12.

What is the product of the digits in the shaded cells?

A 24   B 30   C 36   D 48   E 140

11. In the grid below each of the blank squares and the square marked X are to be filled by the mean of the two numbers in its adjacent squares. Which number should go in the square marked X?

| 10 | | X | | 25 |

A 15   B 16   C 17   D 18   E 19

12. What is the smallest square that has 2016 as a factor?

A 42^2 B 84^2 C 168^2 D 336^2 E 2016^2

13. Five square tiles are put together side by side. A quarter circle is drawn on each tile to make a continuous curve as shown. Each of the smallest squares has side-length 1.

What is the total length of the curve?

A 6π B 6.5π C 7π D 7.5π E 8π

14. Which of the following values of the positive integer n is a counterexample to the statement: "If n is not prime then $n - 2$ is not prime" ?

A 6   B 11   C 27   D 33   E 51

15. The diagram shows three rectangles and three straight lines.

What is the value of $p + q + r$?

A 135   B 180   C 210
     D 225   E 270

16. For which value of k is $\sqrt{2016} + \sqrt{56}$ equal to 14^k ?

A $\frac{1}{2}$ B $\frac{3}{4}$ C $\frac{5}{4}$ D $\frac{3}{2}$ E $\frac{5}{2}$

17. Aaron has to choose a three-digit code for his bike lock. The digits can be chosen from 1 to 9. To help him remember them, Aaron chooses three different digits in increasing order, for example 278. How many such codes can be chosen?

A 779   B 504   C 168   D 84   E 9

18. The circumference of a circle with radius 1 is divided into four equal arcs. Two of the arcs are 'turned over' as shown. What is the area of the shaded region?

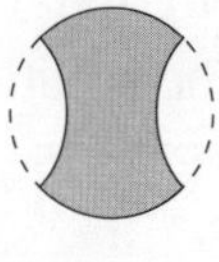

    A 1   B $\sqrt{2}$ C $\frac{1}{2}\pi$ D $\sqrt{3}$ E 2

19. Let S be a set of five different positive integers, the largest of which is m. It is impossible to construct a quadrilateral with non-zero area, whose side-lengths are all distinct elements of S. What is the smallest possible value of m?

    A 2   B 4   C 9   D 11   E 12

20. Michael was walking in Marrakesh when he saw a tiling formed by tessellating the square tile as shown.

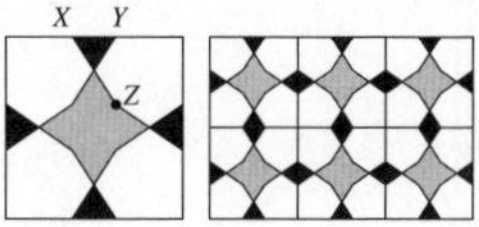

    The tile has four lines of symmetry and the length of each side is 8 cm. The length of XY is 2 cm. The point Z is such that XZ is a straight line and YZ is parallel to sides of the square. What is the area of the central grey octagon?

    A $6 \, \text{cm}^2$ B $7 \, \text{cm}^2$ C $8 \, \text{cm}^2$ D $9 \, \text{cm}^2$ E $10 \, \text{cm}^2$

21. The diagram shows ten equal discs that lie between two concentric circles – an inner circle and an outer circle. Each disc touches two neighbouring discs and both circles. The inner circle has radius 1. What is the radius of the *outer* circle?

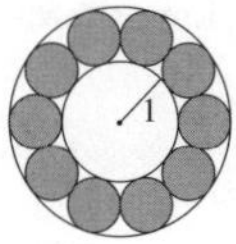

    A $2\tan 36°$ B $\dfrac{\sin 36°}{1 - \sin 36°}$ C $\dfrac{1 + \sin 18°}{1 - \sin 18°}$ D $\dfrac{2}{\cos 18°}$ E $\dfrac{9}{5}$

22. Three friends make the following statements.
    Ben says, "Exactly one of Dan and Cam is telling the truth."
    Dan says, "Exactly one of Ben and Cam is telling the truth."
    Cam says, "Neither Ben nor Dan is telling the truth."
    Which of the three friends is lying?

    A Just Ben   B Just Dan   C Just Cam   D Each of Ben and Cam
    E Each of Ben, Cam and Dan

23. A cuboid has sides of lengths 22, 2 and 10. It is contained within a sphere of the smallest possible radius. What is the side-length of the largest cube that will fit inside the same sphere?

    A 10   B 11   C 12   D 13   E 14

24. The diagram shows a square $PQRS$. The arc QS is a quarter circle. The point U is the midpoint of QR and the point T lies on SR. The line TU is a tangent to the arc QS. What is the ratio of the length of TR to the length of UR ?

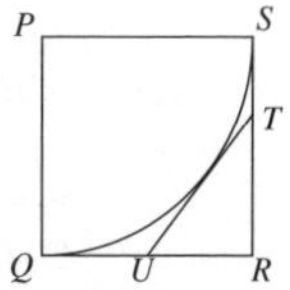

    A $3:2$ B $4:3$ C $5:4$ D $7:6$ E $9:8$

25. Let n be the smallest integer for which $7n$ has 2016 digits. What is the units digit of n?

    A 0   B 1   C 4   D 6   E 8

120

Further remarks

The solutions are provided.

UK SENIOR MATHEMATICAL CHALLENGE

Tuesday 8 November 2016

Organised by the United Kingdom Mathematics Trust
from the School of Mathematics, University of Leeds

SOLUTIONS LEAFLET

This solutions leaflet for the SMC is sent in the hope that it might provide all concerned with some alternative solutions to the ones they have obtained. It is not intended to be definitive. The organisers would be very pleased to receive alternatives created by candidates.

For reasons of space, these solutions are necessarily brief. There are more in-depth, extended solutions available on the UKMT website, which include some exercises for further investigation:

http://www.ukmt.org.uk/

The UKMT is a registered charity

---

1. **B** Since the answer to 987654321×9 is 8 888 888 889, the digit 9 appears once.

2. **D** James bought a book for £5.50, so the normal price would be £5. On Friday, another copy of this book would therefore cost £4.50.

3. **B** As the circle rolls, the centre of the circle moves along four straight lines shown as dashed lines. Each dashed line has length $5 - (1 + 1)$ so the total distance travelled is 4×3 which is 12.

4. **C** One angle in Alex's triangle is 80°. Let $\alpha°$ be the smaller of the other two angles so $(100 - \alpha)°$ is the third angle. The difference between these angles is then $(100 - 2\alpha)°$. Considering each option:
    A: $100 - 2\alpha = 0$ gives both α and $100 - \alpha$ to be 50. This triangle is therefore isosceles and not scalene.
    B: $100 - 2\alpha = 60$ gives α to be 20 and $100 - \alpha$ to be 80. This is again isosceles.
    Option D gives angles of 80, 0 and 100. Option E gives angles of 80, −10 and 110. Neither of these cases forms a triangle.
    C: $100 - 2\alpha = 80$ gives α to be 10 and $100 - \alpha$ to be 90. All three angles are different so this is the correct option.

5. **A** From the available digits the squares could be 256, 324 or 625. Since the middle digits must be the same, the centre digit must be 2.

6. **D**   Let F be the point of intersection of the lines AE and CD. Let the length of CF be h. Then, using similar triangles, $\dfrac{CF}{CE} = \dfrac{BA}{BE}$, so $\dfrac{h}{1} = \dfrac{3}{4}$ giving $h = \dfrac{3}{4}$. The shaded region $ABCF$ is a trapezium, so has area $\dfrac{1}{2}\left(3 + \dfrac{3}{4}\right) \times 3 = \dfrac{45}{8}$ which is $5\frac{5}{8}$.

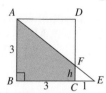

7. **A**   The number 2016^0 has value 1. As $2016 > 1, 2016^{1/2} < 2016^1$. The values of their reciprocals, $2016^{-1/2}$ and 2016^{-1} are then in the opposite order. So the five options given are in numerical order, with 2016^{-1}, or $\frac{1}{2016}$, being the smallest.

8. **B**   One way to count the number of small squares formed is to divide the large square into four quarters along its two diagonals. The number of small squares formed is $4 \times T_{n-1}$, where T_{n-1} is the $(n-1)$th triangular number. When $n = 7$, this is $4 \times \frac{1}{2}(6 \times 7)$ which is 4×21. So 84 squares are formed.

9. **C**   Let $O = (0,0), A = (1,0), B = (1,1), C = (0,1)$ be the vertices of the square. The equation $x^2 + y^2 = 1$ gives a circle passing through A and C. The equation $y = x + 1$ gives a straight line passing only through C. The equation $y = -x^2 + 1$ gives a parabola passing through A and C. The equation $y = x$ gives a straight line passing through O and B. The equation $y = \frac{1}{x}$ gives a rectangular hyperbola which has two branches and passes only through B. So, only $x^2 + y^2 = 1, y = x$ and $y = -x^2 + 1$ have graphs passing through exactly two of the vertices of the square.

10. **B**   None of the products for the first two rows and first two columns contains a factor of 5, so the bottom right cell must contain the 5. The prime factorisation of 112 is $2^4 \times 7$ and, as 7 is not a factor of 216

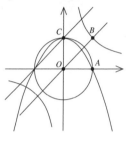

or 12, then 7 must be in the right cell of the middle row. The remaining 2^4 must be the product of two different numbers, namely 8 and 2. The 2 must be in the centre cell as 8 is not a factor of 12. The grid is now as shown above. The prime factorisation of 216 is $2^3 \times 3^3$ and the 3^3 must be the product of a 3 and a 9. The 3 must be in the top left cell as the product of the top row is 12 which is not a multiple of 9. Thus, the product of the three shaded cells is $3 \times 2 \times 5$ which is 30. The completed grid is as shown on the right.

3	1	4	12
8	2	7	112
9	6	5	

216   12

11. **E**   For each square to be filled with the mean of the numbers in the adjacent squares, the differences between all five pairs of adjacent numbers must be equal. This common difference is $\left(\dfrac{25 - 10}{5}\right)$ which is 3. The grid is then

10	13	16	**19**	22	25

and the 19 is in the desired square.

12. **C**   The prime factorisation of 2016 is $2^5 \times 3^2 \times 7$. To create the smallest square which is a multiple of 2016, the powers of each prime must be as small as possible and even, whilst also being at least as big as those in the prime factorisation of 2016. This gives $2^6 \times 3^2 \times 7^2$ which is $(2^3 \times 3 \times 7)^2$ or 168^2.

13. **A**   A quarter circle of radius r has length $\frac{2\pi r}{4}$ which is $\frac{\pi r}{2}$. The total length of the curve shown is then $\frac{\pi}{2}(1 + 1 + 2 + 3 + 5)$ which is 6π.

14. **D** The five options give the values of n to be considered. In option B, 11 is prime so that can be discounted. The options A, C and E are 6, 27 and 51 which are not prime and subtracting 2 from each of these gives 4, 25 and 49 which are also not prime. However in D, $n = 33$ which is not prime but $n - 2 = 31$ is prime.

15. **B** A non-regular hexagon can be drawn on the diagram as shown. Three of the exterior angles of the hexagon are then $55°$, $60°$ and $65°$. Since corresponding angles on parallel lines are equal, the other three exterior angles are $p°$, $q°$ and $r°$. The total of the exterior angles of any polygon is $360°$. Hence $p + q + r + 55 + 60 + 65 = 360$ and so $p + q + r = 180$.

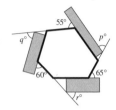

16. **D** The expression $\sqrt{2016} + \sqrt{56}$ can be written as $\sqrt{2^5 \times 3^2 \times 7} + \sqrt{2^3 \times 7}$ which is $\sqrt{4^2 \times 3^2 \times 2 \times 7} + \sqrt{2^2 \times 2 \times 7}$. This simplifies to $12\sqrt{14} + 2\sqrt{14}$ which is $14\sqrt{14}$ and, using index notation, this can be written as $14^{3/2}$. Hence $k = \frac{3}{2}$.

17. **D** One way to count the possible codes is in descending numerical order of the three-digit codes. The list begins: 789; 689, 679, 678; 589, 579, 578, 569, 568, 567; ... . Each initial digit n produces part of the list with the $(8 - n)$th triangular number of possible codes, where $n \leqslant 7$. The total number of possible codes is then the sum of these triangular numbers $1 + 3 + 6 + 10 + 15 + 21 + 28$ including 1 code starting with the digit 7, all the way to 28 codes starting with the digit 1. The total number of codes that Aaron can choose is 84.

18. **E** The four arcs are of equal length and their end-points lie on a circle, so the four end-points can be joined to make a square. As two of the arcs are 'turned over', the two unshaded regions inside the square have areas equal to the two shaded regions outside the square.
The total shaded area is therefore equal to the area of the square. The radius of the circle is given as 1 so, by Pythagoras' Theorem, the side-length of the square is $\sqrt{1^2 + 1^2} = \sqrt{2}$. So the area of the shaded region is $\sqrt{2} \times \sqrt{2} = 2$.

19. **D** Let S consist of h, j, k, l, m in ascending order of size. We want m to be as small as possible. Given three side-lengths, there is a quadrilateral with non-zero area with a specified fourth side-length if and only if the fourth side-length is less than the sum of the other three side-lengths. To ensure that j, k, l, m are not the side-lengths of such a quadrilateral, we must have $m \geqslant j + k + l$. Likewise, considering h, j, k, l, we must have $l \geqslant h + j + k$. Since the smallest possible values of h, j and k are 1, 2 and 3 respectively then $l \geqslant 1 + 2 + 3$ so 6 is the smallest value of l. Also $m \geqslant 2 + 3 + 6$ so 11 is the smallest value of m.

20. **E** Let the point Z' be directly below X, so that $XYZZ'$ is a rectangle. As the length of XY is 2 cm, the distance from Y to the nearest corner of the square is 3 cm. The area of $XYZZ'$ is $2 \text{ cm} \times 3 \text{ cm}$ which is 6 cm^2. The diagonals XZ and YZ' split $XYZZ'$ into quarters and each has area $1\frac{1}{2} \text{ cm}^2$. The central grey octagon is formed from a square with side $Z'Z$ of length 2 cm together with four triangles, each of area $1\frac{1}{2} \text{ cm}^2$. The total area of the shaded octagon is $2 \times 2 + 4 \times 1\frac{1}{2}$ which is 10 cm^2.

21. **C** As there are 10 discs, the adjacent lines drawn from the centre of the inner circle to the centre of each disc are separated by an angle of 36°. The line OB is a tangent to both the disc with centre A and the disc with centre C. So the points A, B and C lie on a straight line as angles OBA and OBC are both 90°.

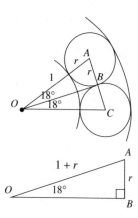

In the second diagram, from triangle OAB we have $\sin 18° = \dfrac{r}{1 + r}$ which rearranges to

$$\dfrac{\sin 18°}{1 - \sin 18°} = r.$$

The radius of the outer circle is

$$1 + 2r = 1 + \dfrac{2\sin 18°}{1 - \sin 18°} = \dfrac{1 + \sin 18°}{1 - \sin 18°}.$$

22. **C** Suppose first that Cam is telling the truth, so Ben and Dan are both lying. Then Ben's statement is actually correct, as is Dan's. There is a clear contradiction. So we know that Cam is in fact lying. Therefore at least one of Ben and Dan is telling the truth. If Ben is telling the truth, then we learn that Dan is telling the truth. If Dan is telling the truth then we learn that Ben is telling the truth. So both Ben and Dan are telling the truth. This means that only Cam is lying.

23. **E** For the cuboid to be contained within a sphere of smallest possible radius, all eight vertices of the cuboid must lie on the sphere. The radius r of the smallest sphere is then half of the length of the body diagonal of the cuboid, so $r = \sqrt{1^2 + 5^2 + 11^2} = \sqrt{147}$. If the largest cube which will fit inside this sphere has side-length $2x$, then $r = \sqrt{x^2 + x^2 + x^2}$. Thus $3x^2 = 147$, so $x^2 = 49$ and so $x = 7$. The side-length of the largest cube is 14.

24. **B** Let the square have side-length 2, $RT = h$ and let A be the point of contact between TU and the circle. Two tangents to a circle which meet at a point are of equal length. So as $QU = 1$ so does AU. Similarly $TA = TS = 2 - h$. Applying Pythagoras' Theorem to triangle URT gives $1^2 + h^2 = (1 + 2 - h)^2$ so $1 + h^2 = 9 - 6h + h^2$ and therefore $8 - 6h = 0$ which gives $h = \frac{4}{3}$. The required ratio is then $4 : 3$.

25. **D** For n to be the smallest integer for which $7n$ has 2016 digits, $7n$ must start with 1, be followed by 2014 zeros and end with a digit a. When this number is divided by 7, the answer is formed from the repeating sequence of 6 digits 142857. The remainders also form a repeating sequence 3, 2, 6, 4, 5, 1. These sequences are repeated 335 times as 6×335 is 2010. The last 4 zeros (to make 2014 zeros in total) and the final a create the last section of the division as shown:

$$\dfrac{\ldots\ldots 1\,4\,2\,8}{\ldots\ {}^1 0^3 0^2 0^6 0^4 a}.$$

Finally, $40 + a$ must be divisible by 7 and be as small as possible. So $a = 2$ and as $42 \div 7 = 6$ the units digit of n is 6.

The answers

The table below shows the proportion of pupils' choices. The correct answer is shown in bold. [The percentages are rounded to the nearest whole number.]

Qn	A	B	C	D	E	Blank
1	4	**91**	1	0	1	2
2	1	1	4	**86**	6	2
3	6	**62**	2	13	6	11
4	8	36	**40**	5	1	10
5	**57**	4	6	10	4	19
6	6	4	20	**39**	7	23
7	**66**	21	7	1	2	4
8	10	**57**	6	3	2	22
9	8	24	**48**	11	2	7
10	2	**64**	4	7	4	19
11	9	4	6	6	**40**	34
12	4	6	**37**	15	16	22
13	**54**	5	5	5	8	22
14	5	7	4	**71**	4	9
15	3	**55**	4	2	2	33
16	2	3	7	**31**	7	50
17	4	12	11	**38**	1	35
18	2	4	11	4	**17**	62
19	2	5	9	**4**	2	76
20	3	3	9	3	**22**	60
21	3	5	**5**	2	3	83
22	1	2	**43**	4	7	42
23	5	7	4	3	**7**	74
24	5	**8**	4	3	1	79
25	3	3	5	**6**	8	75

SMC 2016: Some comments on the pupils' choice of answers as sent to schools in the letter with the results

It is pleasing to see that this year the average mark is 61, significantly higher than last year.

We hope you will find the time to look at the table included with your results which tells you how the responses of your students compare with the national distribution. You are encouraged to discuss the questions with your pupils and, especially, those questions where they were not as successful as you might have hoped.

Both of the earlier questions where there were fewer correct answers than we expected covered geometry. In question 4 the difficulty may have been that *scalene* is not as widely understood as it should be. Although geometry problems often involve isosceles triangles, almost all triangles are scalene (you may wish to discuss with your pupils the sense in which this is true) and so this terminology should be known.

To answer Question 6, you need to know about similar triangles and how to work out the area of a trapezium. Nearly a quarter of the pupils chose not to answer this question. This suggests a lack of confidence about these topics. We hope that the *Questions for Investigation* which form part of the Extended Solutions (these may be downloaded from our website, www.ukmt.org.uk) will be used to help pupils with their understanding.

It is more encouraging to note that pupils did well on the questions which test logical thinking. The idea of a counterexample plays an important role in mathematics, and it is therefore good to see that over three-quarters of the entrants answered Question 14 correctly. The success of pupils on Question 22 also stands out. Unusually for a question so late on the paper, over half the pupils attempted the question, and three quarters of these selected the correct option.

As ever, it is good to see how many students achieved very high marks. Please make sure that the achievement of your high-scoring students is widely recognized in your school or college.

The SMC marks

The profile of marks obtained is shown below.

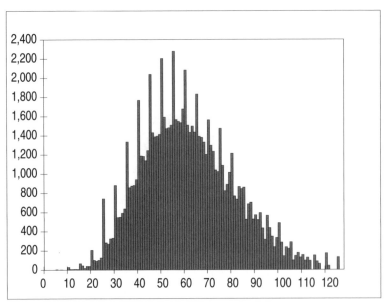

Bar chart showing the actual frequencies in the 2016 SMC

Since 2012, the UKMT has awarded certificates to the top 60% of SMC students. On this basis the cut-off marks were set at

GOLD – 88 or over   SILVER – 71 to 87   BRONZE – 55 to 70

Candidates who scored 106 or more were invited to take part in BMO 1 and those who scored from 90 to 105 were invited to take part in the Senior Kangaroo.

A sample of one of the certificates is shown below.

UK Senior Mathematical Challenge
2016

of

received a

GOLD CERTIFICATE

Institute
and Faculty
of Actuaries

Professor Chris Budd, OBE
Chairman, United Kingdom Mathematics Trust

The United Kingdom Senior Mathematical Challenge

The Senior Mathematical Challenge (SMC) is run by the UK Mathematics Trust. The SMC encourages mathematical reasoning, precision of thought, and fluency in using basic mathematical techniques to solve interesting problems. It is aimed at those in full-time education and with sufficient mathematical competence to undertake a post-16 course.

The problems on the SMC are designed to make students think. Most are accessible, yet still challenge those with more experience; they are also meant to be memorable and enjoyable.

Mathematics controls more aspects of the modern world than most people realise—from iPods, cash machines, telecommunications and airline booking systems to production processes in engineering, efficient distribution and stock-holding, investment strategies and 'whispering' jet engines. The scientific and industrial revolutions flowed from the realisation that mathematics was both the language of nature, and also a way of analysing—and hence controlling—our environment. In the last fifty years old and new applications of mathematical ideas have transformed the way we live.

All these developments depend on mathematical thinking—a mode of thought whose essential style is far more permanent than the wave of technological change which it has made possible. The problems on the SMC reflect this style, which pervades all mathematics, by encouraging students to think clearly about challenging problems.

The SMC was established as the National Mathematics Contest in 1961. In recent years there have been over 100,000 entries from around 2000 schools and colleges. Certificates are awarded to the highest scoring 60% of candidates (Gold : Silver : Bronze 1 : 2 : 3).

The UKMT is a registered charity. Please see our website www.ukmt.org.uk for more information.
Donations to support our work would be gratefully received; a link for on-line donations is below.

www.donate.ukmt.org.uk

The Next Stages

Subject to certain conditions, candidates who obtained a score of 106 or over in the 2016 Senior Mathematical Challenge were invited to take the British Mathematical Olympiad Round One and UK candidates who scored from 90 to 105 were invited to take part in the Senior Kangaroo. The latter makes use of Kangaroo questions as well as a few others and is not a multiple-choice paper but can be marked by character recognition as all the answers are three-digit numbers.

SENIOR 'KANGAROO' MATHEMATICAL CHALLENGE

Friday 2nd December 2016

Organised by the United Kingdom Mathematics Trust

The Senior Kangaroo paper allows students in the UK to test themselves on questions set for the best school-aged mathematicians from across Europe and beyond.

RULES AND GUIDELINES (to be read before starting):

1. Do not open the paper until the Invigilator tells you to do so.

2. Time allowed: **1 hour**.

3. The use of rough paper is allowed; **calculators** and measuring instruments are **forbidden**.

4. **Use B or HB pencil only** to complete your personal details and record your answers on the machine-readable Answer Sheet provided. **All answers are written using three digits, from 000 to 999.** For example, if you think the answer to a question is 42, write 042 at the top of the answer grid and then code your answer by putting solid black pencil lines through the 0, the 4 and the 2 beneath.

   Please note that the machine that reads your Answer Sheet will only see the solid black lines through the numbers beneath, not the written digits above. You must ensure that you code your answers or you will not receive any marks. There are further instructions and examples on the Answer Sheet.

5. The paper contains 20 questions. Five marks will be awarded for each correct answer. There is no penalty for giving an incorrect answer.

6. The questions on this paper challenge you **to think**, not to guess. Though you will not lose marks for getting answers wrong, you will undoubtedly get more marks, and more satisfaction, by doing a few questions carefully than by guessing lots of answers.

Enquiries about the Senior Kangaroo should be sent to:
Maths Challenges Office, School of Maths Satellite,
University of Leeds, Leeds, LS2 9JT
Tel. 0113 343 2339
www.ukmt.org.uk

1. Using this picture we can observe that
    $1 + 3 + 5 + 7 = 4 \times 4$.
    What is the value of
    $1 + 3 + 5 + 7 + 9 + 11 + 13 + 15 + 17 + 19 + 21$?

2. Both rows of the following grid have the same sum. What is the value of * ?

1	2	3	4	5	6	7	8	9	10	1050
11	12	13	14	15	16	17	18	19	20	*

3. Andrew has two containers for carrying water. The containers are cubes without tops and have base areas of 4 dm² and 36 dm² respectively. Andrew has to completely fill the larger cube with pond water, which must be carried from the pond using the smaller cube. What is the smallest number of visits Andrew has to make to the pond with the smaller cube?

4. How many four-digit numbers formed only of odd digits are divisible by five?

5. The notation $|x|$ is used to denote the absolute value of a number, regardless of sign. For example, $|7| = |-7| = 7$.
    The graphs $y = |2x| - 3$ and $y = |x|$ are drawn on the same set of axes. What is the area enclosed by them?

6.

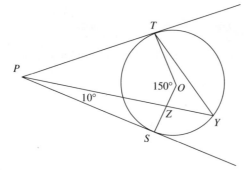

    In the diagram, PT and PS are tangents to a circle with centre O. The point Y lies on the circumference of the circle; and the point Z is where the line PY meets the radius OS.

    Also, $\angle SPZ = 10°$ and $\angle TOS = 150°$.

    How many degrees are there in the sum of $\angle PTY$ and $\angle PYT$?

7. Bav is counting the edges on a particular prism. The prism has more than 310 edges, it has fewer than 320 edges and its number of edges is odd. How many edges does the prism have?

8. The real numbers x, y and z are a solution (x, y, z) of the equation
    $(x^2 - 9)^2 + (y^2 - 4)^2 + (z^2 - 1)^2 = 0$. How many different possible values are there for
    $x + y + z$?

9. The diagram shows two concentric circles. Chord AB of the larger
    circle is tangential to the smaller circle.

    The length of AB is 32 cm and the area of the shaded region is
    $k\pi$ cm^2.

    What is the value of k?

10. Consider the expression $1 * 2 * 3 * 4 * 5 * 6$.

    Each star in the expression is to be replaced with either '+' or '×'.

    N is the largest possible value of the expression. What is the largest prime factor of N?

11. Stephanie enjoys swimming. She goes for a swim on a particular date if, and only if, the day,
    month (where January is replaced by '01' through to December by '12') and year are all of the
    same parity (that is they are all odd, or all are even). On how many days will she go for a
    swim in the two-year period between January 1st of one year and December 31st of the
    following year inclusive?

12. Delia is joining three vertices of a square to make four right-angled triangles.

    She can create four triangles doing this, as shown.

    How many right-angled triangles can Delia make by joining three vertices of a regular
    polygon with 18 sides?

13. This year, 2016, can be written as the sum of two positive integers p and q where $2p = 5q$ (as
    $2016 = 1440 + 576$). How many years between 2000 and 3000 inclusive have this property?

14. The lengths of the sides of a triangle are the integers $13, x, y$. It is given that $xy = 105$. What
    is the length of the perimeter of the triangle?

15. The large equilateral triangle shown consists of 36 smaller equilateral triangles. Each of the smaller equilateral triangles has area 10 cm². The area of the shaded triangle is K cm². Find K.

16. A function $f(x)$ has the property that, for all positive x, $3f(x) + 7f\left(\dfrac{2016}{x}\right) = 2x$. What is the value of $f(8)$?

17. Students in a class take turns to practise their arithmetic skills. Initially a board contains the integers from 1 to 10 inclusive, each written ten times. On each turn a student first deletes two of the integers and then writes on the board the number that is one more than the sum of those two deleted integers. Turns are taken until there is only one number remaining on the board. Assuming no student makes a mistake, what is the remaining number?

18. The sum of the squares of four consecutive positive integers is equal to the sum of the squares of the next three consecutive integers. What is the square of the smallest of these integers?

19. Erin lists all three-digit primes that are 21 less than a square. What is the mean of the numbers in Erin's list?

20. A barcode of the type shown in the two examples is composed of alternate strips of black and white, where the leftmost and rightmost strips are always black. Each strip (of either colour) has a width of 1 or 2. The total width of the barcode is 12. The barcodes are always read from left to right. How many distinct barcodes are possible?

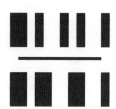

Further remarks

A solutions leaflet was provided.

SENIOR 'KANGAROO' MATHEMATICAL CHALLENGE

Friday 2nd December 2016

Organised by the United Kingdom Mathematics Trust

SOLUTIONS

1. **121** The sum $1 + 3 + 5 + 7 + 9 + 11 + 13 + 15 + 17 + 19 + 21$ has eleven terms. Therefore the value of the required sum is $11 \times 11 = 121$.

2. **950**

1	2	3	4	5	6	7	8	9	10	1050
11	12	13	14	15	16	17	18	19	20	*

We observe that in all but the rightmost column the value in the second row is ten larger than the value in the first row. There are 10 such columns. Therefore the sum of the leftmost ten elements of the second row is 100 more than the corresponding sum in the first row. To achieve the same total in each row, * will need to be 100 less than the value above it. Therefore * = 950.

3. **27** We first observe that any pair of cubes are mathematically similar. These cubes' surface areas are in the ratio 1:9, so that their lengths are in ratio 1:3 and that their volumes are in ratio 1:27.

Therefore Andrew may fill the larger cube in 27 visits, provided the smaller cube is completely filled on each occasion.

4. **125** The number will be of the form '*abcd*' where a, b and c are any odd digits and $d = 5$. Hence there are 5, 5, 5 and 1 possibilities for a, b, c and d respectively. Therefore there are $5 \times 5 \times 5 \times 1 = 125$ such numbers.

5. **9** The enclosed area is a concave quadrilateral with vertices at $(-3, \ 3), (0, \ 0), (3, \ 3)$ and $(0, -3)$. Considering this as two conjoined congruent triangles we find the area as $2 \times \frac{1}{2} \times 3 \times 3 = 9$.

6. **160** The tangent-radius property gives $\angle PSO = \angle PTO = 90°$. From the angle sum of quadrilateral $PTOS$ we may conclude that $\angle TPS = 30°$ and therefore that $\angle TPY = 20°$. By considering the angle sum of triangle PTY we conclude that the required total is $160°$.

7. **315** Suppose that the cross-section of the prism is an N-gon with N edges. The prism will have N edges in each of its 'end' faces and a further N edges connecting corresponding vertices of the end faces. Therefore the number of edges is $3N$ and hence is a multiple of 3. The only multiples of 3 in the given range are 312, 315 and 318. Since we know the total is odd, the prism has 315 edges.

8. **7** Since squares of real numbers are non-negative, the sum can only be 0 if each expression in brackets is zero. Therefore the solutions of the equation are $x = \pm 3$, $y = \pm 2$ and $z = \pm 1$. We observe that the maximum and minimum values for $x + y + z$ are 6 and -6, and that since $x + y + z$ is the sum of one even and two odd numbers, that $x + y + z$ itself will be even.

It suffices to show that each even total between $+6$ and -6 can be attained.

$$(+3) + (+2) + (+1) = +6 \qquad (+3) + (+2) + (-1) = +4$$
$$(+3) + (-2) + (+1) = +2 \qquad (+3) + (-2) + (-1) = 0$$
$$(-3) + (+2) + (-1) = -2 \qquad (-3) + (-2) + (+1) = -4$$
$$(-3) + (-2) + (-1) = -6$$

Hence there are seven possible values for $x + y + z$.

9. **256** Let the radii of the larger and smaller circles be R and r respectively. Draw radius OA of the larger circle and drop the perpendicular from O to AB. By the tangent-radius property this perpendicular will be a radius of the smaller circle.

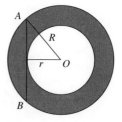

Now the area of the shaded region = area of larger circle − area of smaller circle.

The area of the shaded region $= \pi R^2 - \pi r^2 = \pi(R^2 - r^2)$.
But $R^2 - r^2 = 16^2 = 256$ (by Pythagoras' theorem), hence the area of the shaded region $= 256\pi$ and therefore $k = 256$.

10. **103** Note that $6! = 1 \times 2 \times 3 \times 4 \times 5 \times 6 = 720$. We observe that if any multiplication sign, other than the first, is replaced by an addition sign then each remaining product is at most 360. Therefore we retain each multiplication sign except the first which may be replaced by an addition sign to obtain a maximal value of 721.

The prime factors of 721 are 7 and 103, of which 103 is the largest.

11. **183** We first observe that exactly one odd year and exactly one even year are under consideration.

In an odd year we need only consider odd months. January, March, May and July each has 16 odd days while September and November has 15. Therefore the number of days Stephanie will swim in the odd year is $4 \times 16 + 2 \times 15 = 94$.

In an even year we need only consider even months. April, June, August, October and December has 15 even days and February has 14 (regardless of whether or not it is a leap year). Therefore the number of days Stephanie will swim in the even year is $5 \times 15 + 14 = 89$. Hence she will swim for $94 + 89 = 183$ days over the two years.

12. 144 The regular 18-gon has a circumcircle, that is, a circle passing through all of its vertices. This is also the circumcircle of each right-angled triangle formed. In order for one of these triangle's angles to be a right angle, the opposite side needs to be a diameter, There are 9 possible choices of diameter. For each choice of diameter, there are 8 vertices on each side for the right angle, making 16 choices overall. For each choice of diameter there are 16 choices for the third vertex of the right-angled triangle.

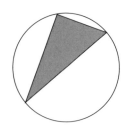

13. 143 For a year Y to be expressible as as the sum of two positive integers p and q where $2p = 5q$ we require $p + q = Y$ and $2p = 5q$. From the first of these, it follows that $2p + 2q = 2Y$ and hence $5q + 2q = 2Y$.

Therefore $7q = 2Y$ from which it follows that Y is also divisible by 7 (since 2 and 7 are coprime).

We observe that $q = \frac{2Y}{7}$ will be an integer less than Y for all Y that are multiples of 7.

Then $p = Y - q$ will also be an integer.

We now must count all the multiples of 7 between 2000 and 3000 inclusive.

Since $1995 = 285 \times 7$ and $2996 = 428 \times 7$ there are $428 - 285 = 143$ multiples of 7 between 2000 and 3000 and hence there are 143 such years.

14. 35 Assume, without loss of generality, that $x \leqslant y$. Since x, y are positive integers and $xy = 105$, the possible values of (x, y) are $(1, 105)$, $(3, 35)$, $(5, 21)$, $(7, 15)$.

Since we require $13 + x > y$ for the triangle to exist, we may eliminate the first three of these possibilities, leaving only $(7, 15)$ and conclude that the perimeter is $13 + 7 + 15 = 35$.

15. 110 For each small equilateral triangle, let the length of each side be x and the perpendicular height be h.

We may trap the shaded triangle in a rectangle as shown, where one vertex is coincident with one of the vertices of the rectangle and the other two vertices lie on sides of the rectangle.

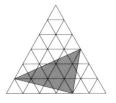

The rectangle has width $4x$ and height $3h$. Therefore the rectangle's area is $12xh$.

The three additional (unshaded) right-angled triangles in the rectangle have areas $\frac{1}{2} \times 4x \times 2h = 4xh$, $\frac{1}{2} \times \frac{1}{2}x \times 3h = \frac{3}{4}xh$ and $\frac{1}{2} \times \frac{7}{2}x \times h = \frac{7}{4}xh$.

Therefore their total area is $4xh + \frac{3}{4}xh + \frac{7}{4}xh = \frac{13}{2}xh$.

Therefore $K = 12xh - \frac{13}{2}xh = \frac{11}{2}xh$.

Each of the 36 smaller equilateral triangles has area $\frac{1}{2}xh$ so we know that $\frac{1}{2}xh = 10$ and therefore that $xh = 20$.

Therefore $K = \frac{11}{2} \times 20 = 110$.

16. 87 The function $f(x)$ has the property that $3f(x) + 7f\left(\dfrac{2016}{x}\right) = 2x$. First observe that $\dfrac{2016}{8} = 252$. Therefore $3f(8) + 7f(252) = 16$ and $3f(252) + 7f(8) = 2 \times 252$. Let $f(8) = V$ and $f(252) = W$. Therefore $3V + 7W = 16$ and $3W + 7V = 504$. When these equations are solved simultaneously, we obtain $V = 87$ and $W = -35$ so that $f(8) = 87$.

17. 649 We observe that the total of all integers on the board at the start of the process is $10(1 + 2 + 3 + 4 + 5 + 6 + 7 + 8 + 9 + 10) = 550$.

On each turn this total is increased by 1. Since we start with one hundred integers on the board and at each turn this number of integers is decreased by one, then 99 turns will be required to complete the process. Therefore the total of all integers on the board will increase by 99 over the course of the process. Hence the remaining number will be $550 + 99 = 649$.

18. 441 Let the smallest number be x. Therefore
$x^2 + (x + 1)^2 + (x + 2)^2 + (x + 3)^2 = (x + 4)^2 + (x + 5)^2 + (x + 6)^2$ and hence
$x^2 + x^2 + 2x + 1 + x^2 + 4x + 4 + x^2 + 6x + 9 = x^2 + 8x + 16 + x^2 + 10x + 25 + x^2 + 12x + 36$.
This can be rewritten as $4x^2 + 12x + 14 = 3x^2 + 30x + 77$ or $x^2 - 18x - 63 = 0$.
Hence $(x - 21)(x + 3) = 0$, which has solutions $x = 21$ and $x = -3$. The question tells us that x is positive and therefore $x = 21$.

The square of the smallest of these integers is therefore $21^2 = 441$.

19. 421 When an odd number is subtracted from an odd square, an even (and hence composite) number is obtained. Similarly, when a multiple of 3 (or 7) is subtracted from a square of a multiple of 3 (or 7), a multiple of 3 (or 7) is obtained which is also composite. Therefore we need only consider three-digit squares that are neither odd nor a multiple of 3 (or 7). Hence the only squares we need to consider are $16^2 = 256, 20^2 = 400$, $22^2 = 484$ and $26^2 = 676$ which yield differences of 235, 379, 463 and 655 respectively. It is easy to see that 235 and 655 are multiples of 5 and hence composite. Therefore only 379 and 463 remain as possible primes satisfying the given condition. After checking divisibilty by 11, 13, 17 and 19 for both, both are indeed seen to be prime and their mean is 421.

20. 116 Any code will start with a black strip and a white strip followed by a shorter barcode. Let $C(m)$ be the number of distinct barcodes of width m.

Those codes which start with BW will be followed by a code of width $m - 2$; so there will be $C(m - 2)$ of these. Likewise, there will be $C(m - 3)$ codes starting BBW, the same number starting BWW, and $C(m - 4)$ starting BBWW; and that exhausts the possibilites. So it follows that $C(m) = C(m - 2) + 2C(m - 3) + C(m - 4)$.

When $m \leqslant 4$, it is simple to list all possible barcodes; namely B, BB, BWB and BBWB, BWBB, BWWB. Therefore $C(1) = C(2) = C(3) = 1$ and $C(4) = 3$. We can now calculate $C(m)$ for $m > 4$.

Thus $C(5) = C(3) + 2C(2) + C(1) = 1 + 2 + 1 = 4$, and continuing like this, we get $C(6) = 6$, $C(7) = 11$, $C(8) = 17$, $C(9) = 27$, $C(10) = 45$, $C(11) = 72$, $C(12) = 116$.

Certificates

These were awarded at two levels, Merit and Qualification.

2016 Senior Kangaroo

....

of

....

received a

CERTIFICATE of MERIT

Professor Chris Budd, OBE
Chairman, United Kingdom Mathematics Trust

THE UKMT SENIOR KANGAROO

The Senior Kangaroo is one of the follow-on rounds for the Senior Mathematical Challenge (SMC) and is organised by the UK Mathematics Trust (UKMT). Around 3,500 high-scoring students in the SMC are invited to participate in the Senior Kangaroo and to test themselves on questions set for the best school-aged mathematicians from across Europe and beyond.

The Senior Kangaroo is a one-hour examination comprising 20 questions; all answers are written using 3 digits, from 000 to 999. The problems involve amusing and thought-provoking situations which require the use of logic as well as mathematical understanding.

The UKMT is a registered charity.
For more information please see our website www.ukmt.org.uk
Donations to support our work would be gratefully
received and can be made by visiting
www.donate.ukmt.org.uk

Mathematical Olympiad for Girls

The UK Mathematical Olympiad for Girls (UK MOG) is held annually to identify students to engage in training for European Girls' Mathematical Olympiad (EGMO). Students who are not involved in training are still eligible for selection for the team.

The 2016 MOG paper was held on 11th October. The time allowed was $2\frac{1}{2}$ hours. The question paper and solutions follow with a prize-winner list.

United Kingdom Mathematics Trust
UK Mathematical Olympiad for Girls
Tuesday 11th October 2016

Instructions

1. Do not turn over until told to do so.

2. Time allowed: $2\frac{1}{2}$ hours.

3. Each question carries 10 marks. Full marks will be awarded for written solutions – not just answers – with complete proofs of any assertions you may make.

   Marks awarded will depend on the clarity of your mathematical presentation. Work in rough first, and then write up your best attempt.

4. Partial marks may be awarded for good ideas, so try to hand in everything that documents your thinking on the problem – the more clearly written the better.

   However, one complete solution will gain more credit than several unfinished attempts.

5. Earlier questions tend to be easier. Some questions have two parts. Part (a) introduces results or ideas useful in solving part (b).

6. The use of rulers and compasses is allowed, but calculators and protractors are forbidden.

7. Start each question on a fresh sheet of paper. Write on one side of the paper only.

   On each sheet of working write the number of the question in the top left-hand corner and your name, initials and school in the top right-hand corner.

8. Complete the cover sheet provided and attach it to the front of your script, followed by your solutions in question number order.

9. Staple all the pages neatly together in the top left-hand corner.

10. To accommodate candidates sitting in other time zones, please do not discuss the paper on the internet until 08:00 BST on Wednesday 12th October.

Enquiries about the Mathematical Olympiad for Girls should be sent to:
UKMT, School of Mathematics Satellite, University of Leeds, Leeds LS2 9JT
0113 343 2339 : enquiry@ukmt.org.uk : www.ukmt.org.uk

138

1. The diagram shows a figure consisting of six line segments and a circle, each containing three points.

Each point is labelled with a real number. The sum of the three numbers on each line segment or circle is T.

Prove that each number is equal to $\frac{1}{3}T$.

2. The diagram shows two circles C_1 and C_2 with diameters PA and AQ. The circles meet at the points A and B, and the line PA is a tangent to C_2 at A.

Prove that

$$\frac{PB}{BQ} = \frac{\text{area } C_1}{\text{area } C_2}.$$

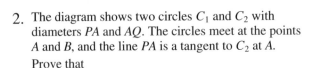

3. Punam puts counters onto some of the cells of a 5×5 board. She can put more than one counter on each cell, and she can leave some cells empty. She tells Quinn how many counters there are in each row and column. These ten numbers are all different.

Can Quinn always work out which cells, if any, are empty?

4. (a) In the trapezium $ABCD$, the edges AB and DC are parallel. The point M is the midpoint of BC, and N is the midpoint of DA.
   Prove that $2MN = AB + CD$.

   (b) The diagram shows part of a tiling of the plane by squares and equilateral triangles.
   Each tile has edges of length 2.
   The points X and Y are at the centres of square tiles.
   What is the distance XY?

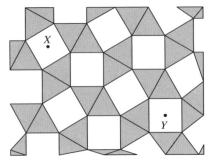

5. Alia, Bella and Catherine are multiplying fractions, aiming to obtain integers. Each of them can multiply as many fractions as she likes (including just one), and can use the same fraction more than once.

Alia's fractions are of the form $\dfrac{n + 1}{n}$, where n is a positive integer.

Bella's fractions are of the form $\dfrac{6p - 5}{3p + 6}$, where p is a positive integer.

Catherine's fractions are of the form $\dfrac{4q - 1}{2q + 1}$, where q is a positive integer.

Which integers can each of them obtain?

Time allowed: $2\frac{1}{2}$ hours

Mathematical Olympiad for Girls: Solutions

These are polished solutions and do not illustrate the process of failed ideas and rough work by which candidates may arrive at their own solutions. Some of the solutions include comments, which are intended to clarify the reasoning behind the selection of a particular method.

The mark allocation on Mathematical Olympiad papers is different from what you are used to at school. To get any marks, you need to make significant progress towards the solution. This is why the rubric encourages candidates to try to finish whole questions rather than attempting lots of disconnected parts.

Each question is marked out of 10.

3 or 4 marks   roughly means that you had most of the relevant ideas, but were not able to link them into a coherent proof.

8 or 9 marks   means that you have solved the problem, but have made a minor calculation error or have not explained your reasoning clearly enough. One question we often ask is: if we were to have the benefit of a two-minute interview with this candidate, could they correct the error or fill the gap?

These solutions may be used freely within your school or college. You may, without further permission, post these solutions on a website that is accessible only to staff and students of the school or college, print out and distribute copies within the school or college, and use them in the classroom. If you wish to use them in any other way, please consult us.

---

1. The diagram shows a figure consisting of six line segments and a circle,   each containing three points.

   Each point is labelled with a real number. The sum of the three numbers on each line segment or circle is T.

   Prove that each number is equal to $\frac{1}{3}T$.

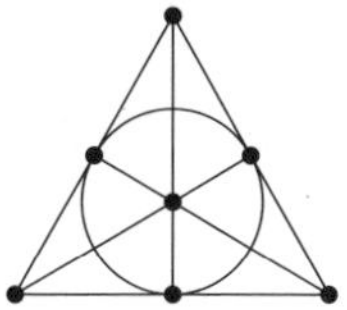

Commentary

This question is about sums of numbers, so a sensible first step seems to be to give each number a name so we can write some equations.

Label the numbers as shown in the diagram below. There are seven unknowns and we can write seven equations. You may know several different methods for solving such systems of equations, for example elimination and substitution. In this case, substituting from one equation into another is likely to produce long expressions.

A better method is to look for equations which share one or more unknowns and eliminate those unknowns. For example, $a + b + c = T$ and $a + d + e = T$. You can subtract the two equations to obtain $b + c - d - e = 0$ and so $b + c = d + e$.

You can then look for another two equations that contain those four unknowns, for example $g + d + b = T$ and $g + e + c = T$. Subtracting those two gives $d + b = e + c$. Adding this to the equation we found above gives $2b + c + d = 2e + c + d$ and so $b = e$.

You can use the symmetry of the situation to see that we can produce an analogous proof showing that $b = f$. Having found that several of the unknowns are equal to each other, it may be a good idea to relabel the diagram to show this. We can then complete the proof, as we have done below

Solution

Let the numbers labelling the points be as shown in the diagram.

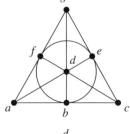

Since $T = a + b + c = a + d + e$, we have $b + c = d + e$. Also, $T = b + d + g = c + e + g$ and so $b + d = c + e$. Therefore $2b + c + d = 2e + c + d$ and so $b = e$.

Substituting this back into $b + d = c + e$ we obtain $d = c$.

Analogously, we can prove that $b = f$, and that $d = a$ and $d = g$.

We can therefore relabel the diagram as shown on the right.

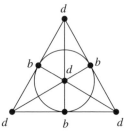

Considering the three points on the circle, we have $3b = T$ and so $b = \frac{1}{3}T$. Considering the base of the triangle, $2d + b = T$ and so $d = \frac{1}{3}T$ as well.

Thus each number is equal to $\frac{1}{3}T$, as required.

Note

The configuration in the question is known as the Fano plane (after Gino Fano, 1871–1952).

The Fano plane is an example of a "finite projective plane". It has only seven points and seven lines (represented as the six line segments and the circle in our diagram). Notice that every pair of lines have one common point; hence, in this plane, every two lines intersect and there are no parallel lines.

2. The diagram shows two circles C_1 and C_2 with diameters PA and AQ. The circles meet at the points A and B, and the line PA is a tangent to C_2 at A.

Prove that

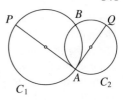

$$\frac{PB}{BQ} = \frac{\text{area } C_1}{\text{area } C_2}.$$

Commentary

In geometry questions, there are often lots of different extra lines we could draw, and different lengths and angles we could calculate, so it can be difficult to decide where to start. A useful strategy is to think about what we are trying to prove, and focus on lines, angles or triangles which we think might be useful. This is essentially "working backwards" from the answer; in writing up the solution, you need to be careful to start with the given facts and end with the required conclusion.

Results about ratios of lengths can often be proved using similar triangles. In this question we are also interested in the ratio of areas of the two circles. But the area of the circle is proportional to the square of its diameter, so the required result is equivalent to $\dfrac{PB}{BQ} = \dfrac{AP^2}{AQ^2}$.

The four lengths from the above equation appear in triangles ABP and ABQ. If you can show that those two triangles are similar, you may be able to use the ratios of their sides to get the required result.

To prove that two triangles are similar you need to find two pairs of equal angles. At the first glance it looks like there are no angles given in this question. However, diameters and tangents in circles create right angles, so this is a good place to start.

We present three possible solutions. The first two use similar triangles. The third uses the tangent-secant theorem, which says that in the diagram on the right, if XT is a tangent to the circle, then $XM \times XN = XT^2$.

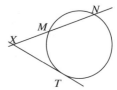

The third solution also uses the result that the angle between a diameter and the tangent at an endpoint of the diameter is a right angle. In fact it uses this result twice. First we use the fact that PA is tangent to C_2 to conclude that PAQ is a right angle. Then we use the converse of the result: since PAQ is a right angle and AP is a diameter of C_1, AQ is also a tangent to C_1.

142

Solution

Method 1

The angle in a semicircle is a right angle. Since AP is a diameter of C_1, $\angle PBA = 90°$, and since AQ is a diameter of C_2, $\angle ABQ = 90°$.

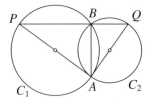

Also, the angle between the tangent and the diameter of a circle at the point of contact is a right angle. Since PA is a tangent to C_2, $\angle PAQ = 90°$. Hence $\angle APB = 90° - \angle PAB = \angle AQB$.

Each of triangles PBA and ABQ has a right angle at B, and $\angle APB = \angle AQB$. Hence they are similar (AA). Therefore, by considering the ratios of their sides, we obtain

$$\frac{PB}{AB} = \frac{PA}{AQ}$$

so that

$$PB = \frac{PA \times AB}{AQ}, \tag{1}$$

and again from the similar triangles

$$\frac{BA}{BQ} = \frac{PA}{AQ}.$$

so that

$$BQ = \frac{BA \times AQ}{PA}. \tag{2}$$

Dividing equation (1) by equation (2), we get

$$\frac{PB}{BQ} = \frac{PA^2}{AQ^2}.$$

But area $C_1 = \frac{1}{4}\pi AP^2$ and area $C_2 = \frac{1}{4}\pi AQ^2$. Therefore $\dfrac{PB}{BQ} = \dfrac{\text{area } C_1}{\text{area } C_2}$, as required.

Method 2

As in Method 1, $\angle PBA = 90°$ and $\angle ABQ = 90°$. Therefore

$$\angle PBQ = \angle PBA + \angle ABQ = 180°,$$

and so PBQ is a straight line segment.

Triangles PAQ and PBA share an angle at P and have right angles at A and B respectively, so they are similar (AA).

Triangles PAQ and ABQ also share an angle, the one at Q, and also have right angles at A and B respectively. Therefore they too are similar (AA).

From the similarity $PBA \sim PAQ$ we have $\dfrac{PB}{PA} = \dfrac{PA}{PQ}$, and from the similarity

$ABQ \sim PAQ$ we have $\dfrac{BQ}{AQ} = \dfrac{AQ}{PQ}$. Therefore

$$PB = \frac{PA^2}{PQ} \quad \text{and} \quad BQ = \frac{AQ^2}{PQ},$$

so that

$$\frac{PB}{BQ} = \frac{PA^2}{AQ^2},$$

which is equivalent to the required result.

Method 3

First, prove that PBQ is a straight line segment as in the previous solution.

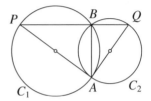

Since PA is tangent to the circle C_2 at A, $\angle PAQ = 90°$. But AP is the diameter of C_1, so AQ is a tangent to C_1 at A.

Using the tangent-secant theorem for circle C_2 and point P, we obtain

$$PB \times PQ = PA^2.$$

Using the same theorem for circle C_1 and point Q, we get

$$QB \times QP = QA^2.$$

Dividing the first equation by the second gives

$$\frac{PB}{QB} = \frac{PA^2}{QA^2},$$

and the required result follows.

---

3. Punam puts counters onto some of the cells of a 5×5 board. She can put more than one counter on each cell, and she can leave some cells empty. She tells Quinn how many counters there are in each row and column. These ten numbers are all different.

   Can Quinn always work out which cells, if any, are empty?

> *Commentary*
>
> It is usually a good idea to start by trying to produce some examples of arrangements of counters that satisfy the given condition.
>
> You then need to decide what you are trying to prove, drawing on your experience from experimenting with some examples of ways of arranging the counters.
>
> If you think that Quinn can always work out which cells are empty then you need

to show that this is the case for all possible arrangements for which the ten row and column totals are all different.

If you think that Quinn cannot identify the empty cells, then you need to find an example of two different arrangements which have the same row and column totals, but the empty cells in different places.

Solution

No, it is not always possible for Quinn to identify the empty cells. Consider two arrangements X, Y of Punam's counters that are the same except in the top left

2×2 square, where, say, X has
$\begin{array}{|c|c|} \hline 0 & 1 \\ \hline 1 & 0 \\ \hline \end{array}$
while Y has
$\begin{array}{|c|c|} \hline 1 & 0 \\ \hline 0 & 1 \\ \hline \end{array}$.

For example, X and Y could be as shown in the figures below.

0	1	0	0	0
1	0	1	0	0
0	0	0	0	3
0	3	1	0	0
9	8	7	0	5

X

1	0	0	0	0
0	1	1	0	0
0	0	0	0	3
0	3	1	0	0
9	8	7	6	5

Y

The row totals in these examples are 1, 2, 3, 4, 35 and the column totals are 10, 12, 9, 6, 8, all different.

Since Quinn knows only the total numbers of counters in each row and column, she could not distinguish X from Y, and therefore she cannot work out which cells are empty and which have one or more counters on them.

Note

If the problem is modified so that Punam can put at most one counter on each cell, then Quinn can use the row and column totals to work out which cells are empty. Can you prove this?

4. (a) In the trapezium *ABCD*, the edges *AB* and *DC* are parallel. The point *M* is the midpoint of *BC*, and *N* is the midpoint of *DA*.
   Prove that $2MN = AB + CD$.

   (b) The diagram shows part of a tiling of the plane by squares and equilateral triangles.
   Each tile has edges of length 2.
   The points *X* and *Y* are at the centres of square tiles.
   What is the distance *XY*?

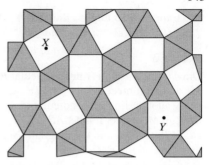

Solution

Part (a)

Commentary

There are several different ways to approach this part, and we present two possible proofs here.

In the first proof, since we are interested in the length AB + CD, we are going to extend the two bases of the trapezium, as shown in the diagram below. The two identical copies of the trapezium make up a parallelogram with base length *AB* + *CD*, so we just need to prove that *NMP* is a straight line parallel to the base.

You may have seen this construction when deriving the formula for the area of the trapezium. Our second proof explicitly uses the area of the trapezium: we create a rectangle with base length *NM* and the area equal to the area of the trapezium.

Method 1

Extend the side *AB* to point *E* and the side *DC* to point *F* such that *BE* = *DC* and *CF* = *AB*. Then *AEFD* is a parallelogram, since the opposite sides *AE* and *DF* are parallel and both have length *AB* + *CD*. It follows that *EF* and *AD* are parallel and equal in length.

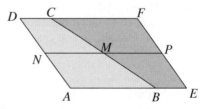

Let *P* be the midpoint of *EF*. Then *AN* and *EP* are parallel and have equal lengths, so *AEPN* is also a parallelogram, and hence *NP* = *AE* = *AB* + *CD*.

The trapezia *ABCD* and *FCBE* are congruent: we have already proved that the corresponding sides are equal, $\angle BAD = \angle CFE$ and $\angle ADC = \angle FEB$ from the parallelogram, and $\angle ABC = \angle FCB$ because the lines *AE* and *DF* are parallel.

M is the midpoint of BC, which is the shared side of the two trapezia. Therefore $\angle NMC = \angle BMP$. It follows that *NMP* is a straight line. The congruence of the two trapezia also implies that $NM = MP$.

Therefore $NP = 2MN$ and so $2MN = AB + CD$, as required.

Method 2

Draw a line through N perpendicular to AB, and let it meet AB at P and DC at S. Draw another line perpendicular to AB through M, and let it meet AB at Q and DC at R, as shown in the diagram. Note that some of the P, Q, R and S will be on the sides and some on the extensions of sides AB and DC; it can be checked that the proof works in all possible cases.

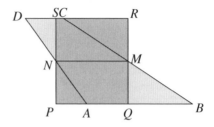

$PQRS$ has four right angles, so it is a rectangle. Its base is equal in length to MN and its height is equal to the height of the trapezium, h. Hence the area of the rectangle $PQRS$ is $MN \times h$.

Triangles PAN and SDN are congruent: they are both right-angled, have equal angles at N and $AN = DN$ (since N is the midpoint of AD). Similarly, triangles QBM and RDM are congruent. Hence the area of the rectangle $PQRS$ equals the area of the trapezium $ABCD$. Therefore we have:

$$MN \times h = \tfrac{1}{2}(AB + CD)h.$$

It follows that $2MN = AB + CD$, as required.

Part (b)

Commentary

The first thing you should ask is how you can use the result from part (a). X and Y are midpoints of the diagonals of the two squares, so it seems sensible to look for a trapezium with those two diagonals as sides. The parallel sides of this trapezium are made up of the sides and heights of the equilateral triangle, so you can calculate their lengths.

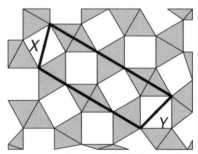

There are two things you need to prove before you can do the calculations. First, you need to show that the sides labeled DC and AB in the diagram below are in fact parallel. Second, you need to show that those lines pass through the points S, R, P and Q.

We claim that $XY = 3 + 3\sqrt{3}$. Here is a proof.

Extract four squares from the shaded part of the pattern, as shown in the diagram below. Let A, B, C, D be the vertices of the squares containing the points X, Y, as shown. Also, going from left to right on the "lower" zig-zag boundary of the figure, label the "bottom" vertices of the two inner squares P, Q, and going from right to left on its "upper" boundary, label the two "top" vertices of those squares R, S.

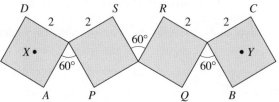

The bisector of the middle 60° angle is a line of symmetry of the figure. Reflection in that line interchanges A and B and interchanges C and D. Consequently both AB and CD are perpendicular to that line, and so AB is parallel to CD, that is, $ABCD$ is a trapezium. Therefore, using the result of part (a), $2XY = AB + CD$.

The isosceles triangle with base AP has angle 60° at its apex, so its other two angles are 60° also, and therefore it is equilateral. The isosceles triangle that has PQ as its base has angle 120° at its apex, hence angles 30° at P and Q.

Consequently $\angle APQ = 60° + 90° + 30° = 180°$, that is, APQ is a straight line. Similarly (or by symmetry) PQB is a straight line. Thus the line segment AB passes through P and Q. A very similar argument shows that the line segment CD passes through R and S.

Now $AP = QB = SR = 2$, since those are the sides of equilateral triangles.

The length PQ is equal to twice the height of the equilateral triangle, as can be seen from the diagram of the full tiling above (in the commentary). Using Pythagoras' Theorem, the height of the equilateral triangle of side 2 is 3. Hence $PQ = DS = RC = 2\sqrt{3}$.

Therefore $AB = 2 + x + 2 = 4 + 2\sqrt{3}$ and $DC = x + 2 + x = 2 + 4\sqrt{3}$. By part (a), $2XY = (AB + CD) = 6 + 6\sqrt{3}$, so $XY = 3 + 3\sqrt{3}$ as claimed.

---

5. Alia, Bella and Catherine are multiplying fractions, aiming to obtain integers. Each of them can multiply as many fractions as she likes (including just one), and can use the same fraction more than once.

   Alia's fractions are of the form $\dfrac{n + 1}{n}$, where n is a positive integer.

   Bella's fractions are of the form $\dfrac{6p - 5}{3p + 6}$, where p is a positive integer.

   Catherine's fractions are of the form $\dfrac{4q - 1}{2q + 1}$, where q is a positive integer.

   Which integers can each of them obtain?

Solution

Commentary

The first thing to do is to try multiplying some fractions and see what integers you can get. Hopefully you can find how to obtain any integer greater than 1 using Alia's fractions, and decide that Bella cannot obtain any integers.

Catherine's task is more challenging. You may want to start by listing several of her fractions — $\dfrac{3}{3}, \dfrac{7}{5}, \dfrac{11}{7}, \dfrac{15}{9}, \ldots$ — and seeing what integers can be obtained from them. After some experimenting, you may start to suspect that you can obtain larger odd integers by using some of the smaller ones. For example, if you can obtain 7 then you can use it to obtain 11 by doing $\dfrac{11}{7} \times 7$.

Integers that do not appear as numerators of Catherine's fractions are a bit more difficult. For example, to obtain 13 you need to realise that 39 appears as a numerator in $\dfrac{39}{21}$, and so you can obtain 13 as $\dfrac{39}{21} \times 7$.

This suggests that you should look for a slightly different calculation depending on whether the required odd integer is of the form $4m - 1$ or $4m + 1$. Integers of the form $4m - 1$ appear as numerators of Catherine's fractions, so if you can obtain $2m + 1$ then you can also obtain $4m - 1 = (2m + 1) \times \dfrac{4m - 1}{2m + 1}$. To obtain an integer of the form $4m + 1$ you need to look at $3(4m + 1) = 12m + 3$, because this does appear as the numerator of the fraction $\dfrac{12m + 3}{6m + 3}$.

Taking $n = 1$, Alia gets the integer 2. Now if $n > 2$, then Alia can obtain n as $\dfrac{2}{1} \times \dfrac{3}{2} \times \ldots \times \dfrac{N}{N - 1}$. Thus Alia can obtain any positive integer except 1. (She cannot obtain 1 because all her fractions are greater than 1.)

Bella, however, cannot obtain any positive integers. Her store consists of fractions of the form $\dfrac{N}{3D}$, where the positive integer N is not a multiple of 3.

If she multiplies m of these fractions together she will obtain a fraction of the form $\dfrac{X}{3^m Y}$, where the positive integer X is not multiple of 3. Since the term 3^m cannot cancel, this will never be a positive integer (we must have $M \geqslant 1$).

Since the fractions available to Catherine have odd numerator and odd denominator, the same will be true of any fraction she can create by multiplying them. Therefore she certainly cannot reach any even positive integers. She can, however, reach every odd positive integer.

This may be seen as follows. Let $f(q)$ be the fraction $\dfrac{4q - 1}{2q + 1}$.

Then $f(1) = 1$, $f(4) \times f(7) = \dfrac{15}{9} \times \dfrac{27}{15} = 3$, and $3 \times f(4) = 3 \times \dfrac{15}{9} = 5$.

Thus Catherine can obtain 1, 3 and 5.

Suppose now that $m \geqslant 2$ and Catherine has managed to obtain all odd numbers up to and including $4m = 3$. We know that she can do this for $m = 2$. Since $2m + 1 \leqslant 4m - 3$, she can obtain $2m + 1$, and so she can use the calculations

$$4m - 1 = (2m + 1) \times \frac{4m - 1}{2m + 1} = (2m + 1) \times f(m) \qquad \text{and}$$

$$4m + 1 = (2m + 1) \times \frac{12m + 3}{6m + 3} = (2m + 1) \times f(3m + 1)$$

to add $4m - 1$ and $4m + 1$ to her list, so as to extend it to all odd numbers up to and including $4m + 1 = 4(m + 1) - 3$.

This means that, having obtained 5, she can obtain 7 and 9, then 11 and 13, and so on. Hence Catherine can obtain any odd positive integer.

Note

The method we used for Catherine, where we prove a result about a certain positive integer by using the same result for a smaller integer, is called *proof by induction*. You may learn about it in your future studies; it is a very useful method for proving results about positive integers.

The Mathematical Olympiad for Girls Prize Winners

The following contestants were awarded prizes:

Aalia Adam	Henrietta Barnett School
Molly Barker	Highworth Grammar School
Naomi Bazlov	KEHS
Emma Brown	St Helen's School, Northwood
Kristina Buck	St Ninian's High School
Louisa Cullen	Pocklington School
Coral Dalitz	Cheney School
Hannah Erlebach	Leicester High School for Girls
Wendi Fan	North London Collegiate
Emilia Feldman	The Perse School
Katherine Horton	King College London Mathematics School
Shuqi Huang	St Swithun's School, Winchester
Phoebe Jackson	Moreton Hall
Yilan (Ellen) Jiang	The Stephen Perse Foundation
Georgina Lang	Moreton Hall
Zijia (Emily) Li	Rydal Penrhos School
Weida Liao	Churston Ferrers Grammar School
Niamh Lister	Truro College
Florence Miller	County Upper School
Melissa Quail	Longsands Academy
Amelia Rout	Chislehurst and Sidcup Grammar School
Megumi Sano	Southbank International School
Andrea Sendula	Kenilworth School
Alevtina Studenikina	Cheltenham Ladies' College
Roan Talbut	The Perse School
Chloe Thickett	The Sixth Form College Farnborough
Alice Vaughan-Williams	Nailsea School
Naomi Wei	City of London School for Girls
Fiona Wilson	Wallington High School for Girls
Guo Yu	Marymount International School London
Ruihua Zhang	Sevenoaks School
Siana Zhekova	King College London Mathematics School

British Mathematical Olympiads

Within the UKMT, the British Mathematical Olympiad Subtrust has control of the papers and everything pertaining to them. The BMOS produces an annual account of its events which, for 2016-2017, was edited by James Aaronson (University of Oxford). Much of this report is included in the following pages.

United Kingdom Mathematics Trust

British Mathematical Olympiad

Round 1 : Friday, 2 December 2016

Time allowed *Three and a half hours.*

Instructions • *Full written solutions − not just answers − are required, with complete proofs of any assertions you may make. Marks awarded will depend on the clarity of your mathematical presentation. Work in rough first, and then write up your best attempt.*

Do not hand in rough work.

• *One **complete** solution will gain more credit than several unfinished attempts. It is more important to complete a small number of questions than to try all the problems.*

• *Each question carries 10 marks. However, earlier questions tend to be easier. In general you are advised to concentrate on these problems first.*

• *The use of rulers, set squares and compasses is allowed, but calculators and protractors are forbidden.*

• *Start each question on a fresh sheet of paper. Write on one side of the paper only. On each sheet of working write the number of the question in the top **left**-hand corner and your name, initials and school in the top **right**-hand corner.*

• *Complete the cover sheet provided and attach it to the front of your script, followed by your solutions in question number order.*

• *Staple all the pages neatly together in the top **left**-hand corner.*

• *To accommodate candidates sitting in other time zones, please do not discuss the paper on the internet until 8 am GMT on Saturday 3 December when the solutions video will be released at https://bmos.ukmt.org.uk*

Do not turn over until **told to do so.**

United Kingdom Mathematics Trust

2016/17 British Mathematical Olympiad
Round 1: Friday, 2 December 2016

1. The integers 1, 2, 3, . . . , 2016 are written down in base 10, each appearing exactly once. Each of the digits from 0 to 9 appears many times in the list. How many of the digits in the list are odd? *For example, 8 odd digits appear in the list* 1, 2, 3, ... , 11.

2. For each positive real number x, we define $\{x\}$ to be the greater of x and $1/x$, with $\{1\} = 1$. Find, with proof, all positive real numbers y such that

$$5y\{8y\}\{25y\} = 1.$$

3. Determine all pairs (m, n) of positive integers which satisfy the equation $n^2 - 6n = m^2 + m - 10$.

4. Naomi and Tom play a game, with Naomi going first. They take it in turns to pick an integer from 1 to 100, each time selecting an integer which no-one has chosen before. A player loses the game if, after their turn, the sum of all the integers chosen since the start of the game (by both of them) cannot be written as the difference of two square numbers. Determine if one of the players has a winning strategy, and if so, which.

5. Let ABC be a triangle with $\angle A < \angle B < 90°$ and let Γ be the circle through A, B and C. The tangents to Γ at A and C meet at P. The line segments AB and PC produced meet at Q. It is given that

$$[ACP] = [ABC] = [BQC].$$

Prove that $\angle BCA = 90°$.
Here $[XYZ]$ denotes the area of triangle XYZ.

6. Consecutive positive integers m, $m + 1$, $m + 2$ and $m + 3$ are divisible by consecutive odd positive integers n, $n + 2$, $n + 4$ and $n + 6$ respectively.
Determine the smallest possible m in terms of n.

The British Mathematical Olympiad 2016-2017

The Round 1 paper was marked by volunteers in December. Below is a list of the prize winners.

Round 1 Prize Winners

The following contestants were awarded prizes:

Gold Medals

Joe Benton	St Paul's School, Barnes, London
Alex Chen	Westminster School, London
Neel Nanda	Latymer School, London
Michael Ng	Aylesbury Grammar School
Thomas Read	The Perse School, Cambridge
Harvey Yau	Ysgol Dyffryn Taf, Carmarthenshire
Dougie Dolleymore	King Edward's School, Birmingham
Eric Chen	Concord College, Shrewsbury
Hugo Aaronson	St Paul's School, Barnes, London
Agnijo Banerjee	Grove Academy, Dundee
Kyung Chan Lee	Garden International School, Malaysia
Thomas Pycroft	Whitchurch High School, Cardiff
Zherui Xu	Ruthin School, Denbighshire
Pino Cholsaipant	Shrewsbury International School, Thailand
Amelia Rout	Chislehurst & Sidcup Grammar School, Kent
Zhuangfei Shang	RDFZ, Beijing
Rosie Cates	Hills Road VI Form College, Cambridge
Ryan Lee	Magdalen College School, Oxford
Protik Moulik	Westminster School, London

Silver medals:

John Bamford	Bilborough VI Form College, Nottingham
Sam Bealing	Bridgewater High School, Warrington
Nathan Creighton	Mossbourne Community Academy, Hackney
Weida Liao	Churston Ferrers Grammar School, Devon
Alex Song	Westminster School, London
Roan Talbut	The Perse School, Cambridge
Yicen Tian	Stamford High School, Lincs
Shilin Wu	Concord College, Shrewsbury
Cindy Anggrenia	INTO University of East Anglia, Norwich
Patrick Bevan	The Perse School, Cambridge

Alexander Fruh	St Aloysius' College, Glasgow
Oscar Heath	Harris Westminster Sixth Form
Isuru S. Jayasekera	Wilson's School, Surrey
Shikhar Kumar	Birkenhead School
Pratap Singh	The Perse School, Cambridge
Ziyue Su	Glenalmond College, Perth and Kinross
Euan Tebbutt	Twycross House School, Warks
Naomi Wei	City of London Girls' School
Lennie Wells	St Paul's School, Barnes, London
Daniel Yue	King Edward's School, Birmingham
Jacob Coxon	Magdalen College School, Oxford
Isaac Kaufmann	City of London School
Sebastian Monnet	King's College London Mathematics School
Melissa Quail	Longsands Academy, St Neots, Cambs
Mervyn Tong	Sevenoaks School, Kent
Zhengda Che	Abbey College, Cambridge
Shuqi Huang	St Swithun's School, Winchester
Yuriy Tumarkin	Durham Johnston School
Jingying Zhang	Ruthin School, Denbighshire
Leran Dai	Shrewsbury School
Shiya Sun	Ruthin School, Denbighshire
Tommy Walker Mackay	Stretford Grammar School, Manchester
George Clements	Norwich School
Edwin Winata Hartanto	Anglo-Chinese School (Independent), Singapore
Peihang Luo	Ruthin School, Denbighshire
Otto Pyper	Eton College, Windsor
Yuta Tsuchiya	Queen Elizabeth's School, Barnet
Liam Zhou	Westminster School, London

Bronze medals:

Lan (Cornelia) Chen	Concord College, Shrewsbury
Zijing Tan	Headington School, Oxford
Chengran Yang	Loughborough Grammar School
Robert Hall	Dr Challoner's Grammar School, Amersham
Matthew Hutton	Royal Grammar School, Newcastle
Jie Jiao	Ivy Experimental School, Jiangsu, China
Moses Mayer	The British International School Jakarta, Indonesia
Richard (Zhuowen) Su	Charterhouse, Godalming, Surrey
Haolin (Linda) Wang	Rydal Penrhos School, Colwyn Bay, Conwy
Jacob Chevalier Drori	Highgate School, London

Gabriele Corso   Colchester Royal Grammar School
George Cull   Reigate Grammar School, Surrey
Raymond Douglas   Magdalen College School, Oxford
Zhongyi Hu   Ruthin School, Denbighshire
Ryan Kang   Westminster School, London
Charlie Liao   Bedstone College, Shropshire
Mengzhen Liu   Beijing National Day School, China
James Sun   Reading School
Patrick Winter   Barton Peveril College, Eastleigh
Zonglin Wu   RDFZ, Beijing
Kerun Xu   Ningbo Xiaoshi High School, China
Lu Yubing   Mount Kelly College, Devon
Minghao Zhang   Dulwich College
Connie (Guanlan) Zhao   Ruthin School, Denbighshire
Emily Beatty   King Edward VII School, Sheffield
David Bick   London Oratory School
Toby Chamberlain   Malmesbury School, Wiltshire
Yan Yau Cheng   Discovery College, Hong Kong
Alex Darby   Sutton Grammar School for Boys, Surrey
Sungyoung Kim   Dubai College
Callum McDougall   Westminster School, London
Matthew Penn   Redland Green School, Bristol
Benedict Randall Shaw   Westminster School, London
Mukul Rathi   Nottingham High School
Matthew Richmond   Hills Road VI Form College, Cambridge
Arthur Ushenin   Eton College, Windsor
Zeli Wang   Harrow International School, Hong Kong
Lan An   RDFZ, Beijing
Boon Han Nathaniel Ang Anglo-Chinese School (Independent), Singapore
Charlie Hu   City of London School
Dingyun Huang   Lime House School, Carlisle
Robbie King   King's College School, Wimbledon
Olivia Pricilia   Bellerbys College, Brighton
Huanqiao Tong   Ruthin School, Denbighshire
Thiem Udomsrirungruang Shrewsbury International School, Thailand
David Veres   King Edward VI School, Southampton
Yannis Wells   Exeter Mathematics School
Isaac Wood   Redland Green School, Bristol
Elliot Young   Norwich School
Ping'an Yu   Wuxi Number 1 High School, China

United Kingdom Mathematics Trust

British Mathematical Olympiad
Round 2: Thursday, 26 January 2017

Time allowed *Three and a half hours.*

Each question is worth 10 marks.

Instructions • *Full written solutions – not just answers – are required, with complete proofs of any assertions you may make. Marks awarded will depend on the clarity of your mathematical presentation. Work in rough first, and then draft your final version carefully before writing up your best attempt.*

Rough work **should** *be handed in, but should be clearly marked.*

• *One or two* **complete** *solutions will gain far more credit than partial attempts at all four problems.*

• *The use of rulers and compasses is allowed, but calculators and protractors are forbidden.*

• *Staple all the pages neatly together in the top* **left-***hand corner, with questions 1, 2, 3, 4 in order, and the cover sheet at the front.*

• To accommodate candidates sitting in other time zones, please do not discuss any aspect of the paper on the internet until 8 am GMT on Friday 27 January.

In early March, twenty students eligible to represent the UK at the International Mathematical Olympiad will be invited to attend the training session to be held at Trinity College, Cambridge (30 March – 3 April 2017). At the training session, students sit a pair of IMO-style papers and eight students will be selected for further training and selection examinations. The UK Team of six for this year's IMO (to be held in Rio de Janeiro, Brazil 12–23 July 2017) will then be chosen.

Do not turn over until told to do so.

United Kingdom Mathematics Trust

2016/17 British Mathematical Olympiad
Round 2

1. This problem concerns triangles which have vertices with integer coordinates in the usual x, y-coordinate plane. For how many positive integers $n < 2017$ is it possible to draw a right-angled isosceles triangle such that exactly n points on its perimeter, including all three of its vertices, have integer coordinates?

2. Let $\lfloor x \rfloor$ denote the greatest integer less than or equal to the real number x. Consider the sequence a_1, a_2, ... defined by

$$a_n = \frac{1}{n}\left(\left\lfloor\frac{n}{1}\right\rfloor + \left\lfloor\frac{n}{2}\right\rfloor + \; ... \; + \left\lfloor\frac{n}{n}\right\rfloor\right)$$

for integers $n \geqslant 1$. Prove that $a_{n+1} > a_n$ for infinitely many n, and determine whether $a_{n+1} < a_n$ for infinitely many n.
   [*Here are some examples of the use of* $\lfloor x \rfloor$: $\lfloor \pi \rfloor = 3, \lfloor 1729 \rfloor = 1729$ *and* $\lfloor \frac{2017}{1000} \rfloor = 2.$]

3. Consider a cyclic quadrilateral $ABCD$. The diagonals AC and BD meet at P, and the rays AD and BC meet at Q. The internal angle bisector of angle BQA meets AC at R and the internal angle bisector of angle APD meets AD at S. Prove that RS is parallel to CD.

4. Bobby's booby-trapped safe requires a 3-digit code to unlock it. Alex has a probe which can test combinations without typing them on the safe. The probe responds *Fail* if no individual digit is correct. Otherwise it responds *Close*, including when all digits are correct. For example, if the correct code is 014, then the responses to 099 and 014 are both Close, but the response to 140 is Fail. If Alex is following an optimal strategy, what is the smallest number of attempts needed to guarantee that he knows the correct code, whatever it is?

The British Mathematical Olympiad 2016-2017
Round 2

The second round of the British Mathematical Olympiad was held on Thursday 26th January 2017. Some of the top scorers from this round were invited to a residential course at Trinity College, Cambridge.

Leading Scorers

40	Joe Benton	St Paul's School, Barnes, London
	Neel Nanda	Latymer School, London
	Thomas Read	The Perse School, Cambridge
	Harvey Yau	Ysgol Dyffryn Taf, Carmarthenshire
39	Kyung Chan Lee	Garden International School, Malaysia
32	Yuta Tsuchiya	Queen Elizabeth's School, Barnet
	Zherui Xu	Ruthin School, Denbighshire
30	Hugo Aaronson	St Paul's School, Barnes, London
	Rosie Cates	Hills Road VI Form College, Cambridge
	Nathan Creighton	Mossbourne Community Academy, Hackney
	Michael Ng	Aylesbury Grammar School
	Thomas Pycroft	Whitchurch High School, Cardiff
	Naomi Wei	City of London Girls' School
29	Artem Baryshnikov	Dulwich College
	Jacob Coxon	Magdalen College School, Oxford
28	Sam Bealing	Bridgewater High School, Warrington
27	Isuru Shavinda Jayasekera	Wilson's School, Surrey
	Chengran Yang	Loughborough Grammar School
26	Jacob Mair	Burnham Grammar School, Slough
	Alex Song	Westminster School, London
25	Alex Chen	Westminster School, London
	Zhuangfei Shang	RDFZ, Beijing
	Alevtina Studenikina	Cheltenham Ladies' College
24	Benedict R. Shaw	Westminster School, London
23	Emily Beatty	King Edward VII School, Sheffield
	Melissa Quail	Longsands Academy, St Neots, Cambs
	Matthew Richmond	Hills Road VI Form College, Cambridge
	Lennie Wells	St Paul's School, Barnes, London

Introduction to the BMO problems and full solutions

The 'official' solutions are the result of many hours' work by a large number of people, and have been subjected to many drafts and revisions. The contestants' solutions included here will also have been redrafted several times by the contestants themselves, and also shortened and cleaned up somewhat by the editors. As such, they do not resemble the first jottings, failed ideas and discarded pages of rough work with which any solution is started.

Before looking at the solutions, pupils (and teachers) are encouraged to make a concerted effort to attack the problems themselves. Only by doing so is it possible to develop a feel for the question, to understand where the difficulties lie and why one method of attack is successful while others may fail. Problem solving is a skill that can only be learnt by practice; going straight to the solutions is unlikely to be of any benefit.

It is also important to bear in mind that solutions to Olympiad problems are not marked for elegance. A solution that is completely valid will receive a full score, no matter how long and tortuous it may be. However, elegance has been an important factor influencing our selection of contestants' answers.

The 'Christopher Bradley Elegance Prize' was awarded to Harvey Yau, for a particularly beautiful solution to BMO2 Problem 1.

BMO Round 1

Problem 1 (Proposed by David Monk)

The integers 1, 2, 3, . . . , 2016 are written down in base 10, each appearing exactly once. Each of the digits from 0 to 9 appears many times in the list. How many of the digits in the list are odd? *For example, 8 odd digits appear in the list* 1, 2, 3, … , 11.

The main part of this problem is proving that half of the digits are odd. We might get the idea to pair off numbers that add up to 1999 because there are no carries in the addition.

Solution by the Editor: Observe that we may add leading zeroes without changing the number of odd digits. Among numbers from 0000 to 1999, exactly half of the digits are odd. We can see this by pairing up x with $1999 - x$. This contributes 4000 odd digits to the total.

We can manually count the number of odd digits from 2000 to 2016. The total is 15, and thus the answer is 4015.

Problem 2 (Proposed by Dan Griller)

For each positive real number x, we define $\{x\}$ to be the greater of x and $1/x$, with $\{1\} = 1$. Find, with proof, all positive real numbers y such that

$$5y\{8y\}\{25y\} = 1.$$

The equation has different definitions on various ranges, so it is natural to split the problem up into those ranges.

Solution by the Editor:

- If $y \leqslant \dfrac{1}{25}$, then the equation becomes $5y = 200y^2$, and thus $y = \dfrac{1}{40}$, which works.

- If $\dfrac{1}{25} < y \leqslant \dfrac{1}{8}$, then the equation becomes $125y^2 = 8y$, and thus $y = \dfrac{8}{125}$, which works.

- If $\dfrac{1}{8} < y$, then the equation becomes $1000y^3 = 1$, and thus $y = \dfrac{1}{10}$. This does not work, as $\dfrac{1}{10} < \dfrac{1}{8}$.

Thus, the two solutions for y are $\dfrac{1}{40}$ and $\dfrac{8}{125}$.

Problem 3 (Proposed by Tom Bowler)

Determine all pairs (m, n) of positive integers which satisfy the equation $n^2 - 6n = m^2 + m - 10$.

In order to make any progress with this problem, it will be important to find a factorisation somehow. Completing the square turns out to be helpful.

Solution 1 *by the Editor*: Completing the square gives

$$(n - 3)^2 - 9 = \left(m + \tfrac{1}{2}\right)^2 - \tfrac{1}{4} - 10,$$

which leads to

$$5 = (2m + 1)^2 - (2n - 6)^2$$

and thus

$$(2m + 2n - 5)(2m - 2n + 7) = 5.$$

There are four possible factorisations of 5, namely 1×5, 5×1, $(-1) \times (-5)$ and $(-5) \times (-1)$. These give $(m, n) = (1, 2), (1, 4), (-2, 4)$ and $(-2, 2)$ respectively, of which only the first two are valid.

Solution 2 *by the Editor*: Completing the square on the left-hand side gives

$$(n - 3)^2 = m^2 + m - 1.$$

For $m > 1$ we have

$$m^2 < m^2 + m - 1 < (m + 1)^2,$$

and so $m^2 + m - 1$ cannot be a square. So the only possibility is $m = 1$, giving $n = 2$ or $n = 4$.

Problem 4 (Proposed by Tom Bowler)

Naomi and Tom play a game, with Naomi going first. They take it in turns to pick an integer from 1 to 100, each time selecting an integer which no-one has chosen before. A player loses the game if, after their turn, the sum of all the integers chosen since the start of the game (by both of them) cannot be written as the difference of two square numbers. Determine if one of the players has a winning strategy, and if so, which.

This problem naturally falls into two parts; deciding which integers are the difference of two squares, and then figuring out the winning strategy.

Solution by the Editor:

First, observe that a positive integer n cannot be written as the difference of two square numbers if and only if $n \equiv 2 \bmod 4$. This is because, if

$$n = x^2 - y^2 = (x - y)(x + y),$$

then

$$(x - y) \equiv (x + y) \bmod 2,$$

and thus if n is even, then both $(x - y)$ and $(x + y)$ must be even and so $4 \mid n$.

Conversely, if n is odd, choose $x = \frac{1}{2}(n + 1)$ and $y = \frac{1}{2}(n - 1)$. If $n = 4k$, choose $x = k + 1, y = k - 1$.

Naomi has a winning strategy. She will start by choosing 100. On subsequent turns, if Tom has chosen T on the previous turn, Naomi will choose $100 - T$. Naomi will not lose as the total is divisible by 4 at the end of each of her turns. She will always be able to play because if Tom chooses 50, he will lose. Thus, Tom will eventually be the first player to choose a number of the form 2 mod 4, and thus he will lose.

164

Problem 5 (Proposed by Jack Smith)

Let ABC be a triangle with $\angle A < \angle B < 90°$ and let Γ be the circle through A, B and C. The tangents to Γ at A and C meet at P. The line segments AB and PC produced meet at Q. It is given that

$$[ACP] = [ABC] = [BQC].$$

Prove that $\angle BCA = 90°$.

Here $[XYZ]$ denotes the area of triangle XYZ.

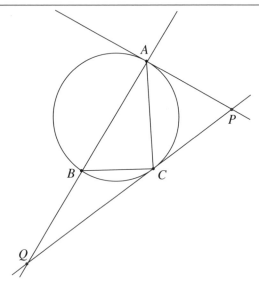

Solution by the Editor:

In order to show that $\angle BCA = 90°$, it will be enough to show that $\angle CAB + \angle CBA = 90°$. But, by the alternate segment theorem $\angle CBA = \angle CAP$, so it is enough to show that $\angle PAB = 90°$, in other words, that AB is a diameter. Or by Thales' theorem, since AB is a diameter $\angle BCA = 90°$.

By equal heights, $BQ = AB = c$.

By tangent-secant, $QC = \sqrt{QB \times QA} = c\sqrt{2}$.

By equal tangents and equal heights,

$$PA = PC = \frac{QC}{2} = \frac{c}{\sqrt{2}}.$$

Hence $PA^2 + AQ^2 = \frac{c^2}{2} + (2c)^2 = \left(\frac{3c}{\sqrt{2}}\right)^2 = PQ^2$, as required.

Problem 6 (Proposed by Andras Hrasko)

Consecutive positive integers m, $m + 1$, $m + 2$ and $m + 3$ are divisible by consecutive odd positive integers n, $n + 2$, $n + 4$ and $n + 6$ respectively.

Determine the smallest possible m in terms of n.

Solution by the Editor:

$2m$, $2m + 2$, $2m + 4$ and $2m + 6$ are divisible by n, $n + 2$, $n + 4$ and $n + 6$ respectively, and thus $2m - n$ is divisible by all four of n, $n + 2$, $n + 4$ and $n + 6$.

If n is not divisible by 3, then n, $n + 2$, $n + 4$ and $n + 6$ are coprime. So $2m - n$ is an odd multiple of $n(n + 2)(n + 4)(n + 6)$, and thus the smallest solution is

$$m = \frac{n(n + 2)(n + 4)(n + 6) + n}{2}.$$

If n is divisible by 3, then the least common multiple of n, $n + 2$, $n + 4$ and $n + 6$ is $\dfrac{n(n + 2)(n + 4)(n + 6)}{3}$. So $2m - n$ is an odd multiple of $\dfrac{n(n + 2)(n + 4)(n + 6)}{3}$, and thus the smallest solution is

$$m = \frac{\dfrac{n(n + 2)(n + 4)(n + 6)}{3} + n}{2}.$$

BMO Round 2

Problem 1 (Proposed by Tom Bowler)

This problem concerns triangles which have vertices with integer coordinates in the usual x, y-coordinate plane. For how many positive integers $n < 2017$ is it possible to draw a right-angled isosceles triangle such that exactly n points on its perimeter, including all three of its vertices, have integer coordinates?

This problem boils down to showing that it is possible to draw such a triangle if and only if n is divisible by 3 or 4.

Solution 1 by Michael Ng, Aylesbury Grammar School:

First, observe that, if n is divisible by 3 or 4, it is possible. If $n = 3k$, set the triangle to have vertices $(0, 0)$, $(k, 0)$, $(0, k)$. If $n = 4k$, set the triangle to have vertices $(0, 0)$, (k, k), $(k, -k)$.

We must now prove that it is possible only if n is divisible by 3 or 4. Translate the triangle such that the vertex with the right angle is at the origin. The coordinates of the other two vertices can then be taken as (a, b) and $(b - a)$.

Now, observe that the number of integer points on an edge joining (a, b) to (c, d), ignoring the endpoints, is $\gcd(a - c, b - d) - 1$. Thus, the total number of integer points will be $2 \gcd(a, b) + \gcd(a - b, a + b)$.

Now, $\gcd(a, b)$ clearly divides $\gcd(a - b, a + b)$. But $\gcd(a - b, a + b)$ divides $(a - b) + (a + b) = 2a$, and similarly it also divides $2b$. Hence, $\gcd(a - b, a + b) \mid 2\gcd(a, b)$, and thus $\gcd(a - b, a + b) = \gcd(a, b)$ or $2 \gcd(a, b)$.

Thus, the number of integer points will either be $3 \gcd(a, b)$ or $4 \gcd(a, b)$.

Finally, observe that in a block of 12 consecutive numbers, exactly six of them will be divisible by 3 or 4. Thus, there are 1008 valid numbers less than or equal to 2016. Since 3 and 4 do not divide 2017, the overall count is 2016.

Solution 2 *by Harvey Yau, Ysgol Dryffyn Taf:*

We provide an alternative argument to show that n must be divisible by 3 or 4.

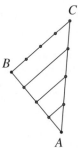

Suppose that the triangle has vertices A, B and C, with a right angle at B. Let $P_0 = A$, P_1, P_2, ... , $P_a = B$ be the (equally spaced) integer points on AB, and $P_a = B$, P_{a+1}, ... , $P_{2a} = C$ be the integer points on BC. We have integer points $Q_0 = A$, Q_1, ... , $Q_a = C$ on side AC by projecting P_0, ... , P_a parallel to BC.

We have now found all of the integer points on AB and BC, as well as some of the integer points on AC. It is possible that this is all of them, in which case the total number of lattice points is $3a$. Otherwise there are some other integer points on AC.

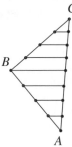

However, by projecting any other points perpendicularly to AC, we see that any other integer points on AC must lie at the midpoint of Q_iQ_{i+1}, and if there are any such integer points then all the midpoints must be integer points.

Thus, in this situation, the total number of integer points is $4a$, as required.

168

Problem 2 (Proposed by Andras Hrasko)

Let $\lfloor x \rfloor$ denote the greatest integer less than or equal to the real number x. Consider the sequence a_1, a_2, ... defined by

$$a_n = \frac{1}{n}\left(\left\lfloor \frac{n}{1} \right\rfloor + \left\lfloor \frac{n}{2} \right\rfloor + \ldots + \left\lfloor \frac{n}{n} \right\rfloor\right)$$

for integers $n \geqslant 1$. Prove that $a_{n+1} > a_n$ for infinitely many n, and determine whether $a_{n+1} < a_n$ for infinitely many n.

[*Here are some examples of the use of* $\lfloor x \rfloor$: $\lfloor \pi \rfloor = 3$, $\lfloor 1729 \rfloor = 1729$ *and* $\lfloor \frac{2017}{1000} \rfloor = 2$.]

Solution by Rosie Cates, Hills Road VI Form College:

First, we will record some properties of the $\lfloor \cdot \rfloor$ function and a_n.

1. If $x \mid (n+1)$, then $\left\lfloor \frac{n+1}{x} \right\rfloor = \left\lfloor \frac{n}{x} \right\rfloor + 1$. Otherwise, $\left\lfloor \frac{n+1}{x} \right\rfloor = \left\lfloor \frac{n}{x} \right\rfloor$.

2. $1 + \frac{1}{2} + \frac{1}{3} + \ldots + \frac{1}{2^x - 1} < x$. This is because the left-hand side is less than or equal to $1 + 2 \times \frac{1}{2} + \ldots + 2^{x-1} \times \frac{1}{2^{x-1}} = x$.

3. $(n+1)a_{n+1} - na_n$ is the number of factors of $n+1$. This is because the left-hand side can be written as the sum of terms of the form $\left\lfloor \frac{n+1}{x} \right\rfloor - \left\lfloor \frac{n}{x} \right\rfloor$, which is 1 for each factor x of $n+1$, and 0 otherwise, by point 1.

4. If $n > 7$, then $a_n > 2$. This is because

$$na_n > n + \left\lfloor \frac{n}{2} \right\rfloor + (n-2)$$

$$> n + 3 + n - 2$$

$$= 2n + 1.$$

Now, we claim that, if $n = 2^m - 1$, then $a_n < a_n + 1$. To prove this, observe that by point 3, $(2^m - 1)a_{2^m - 1} + m + 1 = 2^m a_{2^m}$.

Point 2 tells us that $a_{2^m - 1} < m + 1$, and so $2^m a_{2^m - 1} < 2^m a_{2^m}$, as required.

Now, we claim that, if $n + 1$ is a prime greater than 7, then $a_{n+1} < a_n$. To prove this, observe that point 4 tells us that $a_n > 2$. But by point 3, $na_n + 2 = (n+1)a_{n+1}$, and so $(n+1)a_n > (n+1)a_{n+1}$, as required.

Problem 3 (Proposed by David Monk)

Consider a cyclic quadrilateral *ABCD*. The diagonals *AC* and *BD* meet at *P*, and the rays *AD* and *BC* meet at *Q*. The internal angle bisector of angle *BQA* meets *AC* at *R* and the internal angle bisector of angle *APD* meets *AD* at *S*. Prove that *RS* is parallel to *CD*.

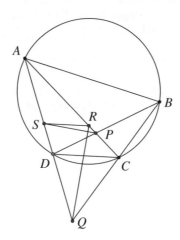

Solution by Thomas Read, The Perse School:

Let $\angle ADB = \angle ACB = \phi$ and $\angle CBD = \angle CAD = \theta$, by angles in the same segment. Then

$$\frac{AS}{SD} = \frac{AP}{PD} \quad \text{(angle bisector theorem)}$$

$$= \frac{\sin \phi}{\sin \theta} \quad \text{(sine rule in } DAP)$$

$$= \frac{\sin (\pi - \phi)}{\sin \theta}$$

$$= \frac{QA}{QC} \quad \text{(sine rule in } QAC)$$

$$= \frac{AR}{RC} \quad \text{(angle bisector theorem)}.$$

Therefore, triangles *ARS* and *ACD* are similar, and so *RS* and *CD* are parallel.

Problem 4 (Proposed by Paul Jefferys)

Bobby's booby-trapped safe requires a 3-digit code to unlock it. Alex has a probe which can test combinations without typing them on the safe. The probe responds *Fail* if no individual digit is correct. Otherwise it responds *Close*, including when all digits are correct. For example, if the correct code is 014, then the responses to 099 and 014 are both Close, but the response to 140 is Fail. If Alex is following an optimal strategy, what is the smallest number of attempts needed to guarantee that he knows the correct code, whatever it is?

This problem falls naturally into two parts; first, showing that Alex needs more than 12 guesses, and second, that she can always succeed within 13 guesses.

Solution by Neel Nanda, Latymer School:

This is a solution to the first part, in which we prove that at least 13 guesses are required. Suppose that the first six attempts are Fail. Then, there must be at least 4 possibilities remaining for each of the digits, for a total of 64. We can check that, regardless of Alex's next question, there can be more than 32 possible codes:

- None of the digits are possible; in other words, they have all been ruled out by previous guesses. Then an answer of Fail would leave 64 possible codes.
- One of the digits in the guess is possible, and the other two have been ruled out by previous guesses. Then an answer of Fail would leave 48 possible codes.
- Two of the digits in the guess are possible, and the other one has been ruled out by previous guesses. Then an answer of Fail would leave 36 possible codes.
- Three of the digits in the guess are possible. Then an answer of Close would leave 37 possible codes.

With the five remaining guesses, there can be at most 32 possible outcomes in total, and thus not all of the possibilities can be distinguished. Thus, at least 13 guesses are required.

Solution 2 *by Hugo Aaronson, St Paul's School*:

This is a solution to the second part, in which we provide a strategy that can guess the code within 13 guesses.

Start by guessing the possibilities 000, 111, . . . , 999. There are 3 cases, depending on the number of outcomes which were Close.

If there was only one Close, then that must have been the combination.

If there were two Closes, suppose that they were *aaa* and *bbb*. Let x be neither a nor b. Guess *axx*, *xax* and *xxa*; this will tell us the value of each digit, and thus the entire code.

If there were three Closes, suppose that they were *aaa*, *bbb* and *ccc*. Let x be none of a, b or c. Start by guessing *axx* and *bxx*. This will tell us the value of the first digit. We can distinguish the remaining two possibilites with our final guess – for example, if the first digit is a, then guess *xbx*.

Thus, 13 guesses are needed.

Olympiad Training and Overseas Competitions

Each year UKMT hold several camps to select and prepare students for participation in the UK team at the International Mathematical Olympiad (IMO). Teams are also sent to other international events as part of the training process.

Oxford Training Camp August 2016

The first event of the UKMT year, Oxford Training Camp, was held again at Queen's College, Oxford and ran from Sunday 28th August to Saturday 3rd September 2016. As always, our thanks go to Peter Neumann who organised and directed this very successful camp again. Twenty two students were invited to the camp this year – 13 from Y11, 6 from Y10, 2 from Y9/S2 and 1 from Y8. Unfortunately, one Y10 girl was ill and had to withdraw, so only 21 students attended the camp.

The academic programme was structured and intense. This year there were three 'lecture/tutorial courses', two in the morning, one in the afternoon. In the afternoons there also were lectures/presentations on a wide variety of topics. There were courses on *Geometry* by Geoff Smith (5 sessions of 100 minutes), on *Number theory* by Vicky Neale (5 sessions of 100 minutes), and on *Problem-solving* by Paul Russell (4 sessions of 60 minutes). On Monday, Tuesday, Thursday and Friday there were two further afternoon sessions, each lasting 60 to 75 minutes: sessions on *Combinatorics* (2) by James Cranch; *Counting strategies* (3) by Dominic Yeo; *Sequences* (1) by Maria Holdcroft; *Functional equations* (1) by Olivia Aaronson; *Geometric inequalities* (1) by Oliver Feng.

Students attending the Oxford Training Camp this year were: Naomi Bazlov (King Edward VI Girls' High School, Birmingham), Sam Bealing (Bridgewater High School), Emily Beatty (King Edward VII School, Sheffield), Jonathan Bostock (Eltham College), Elena Cates (The Perse School, Cambridge), Nathan Creighton (Mossbourne Community Academy, London), Stanley Dodds (Weydon School, Farnham), Dougie Dolleymore (King Edward's School, Birmingham), Hannah Erlebach (Leicester High School for Girls), Freddie Hand (Judd School, Tonbridge), Shavindra Jayasekara (Wilson's School, Wallington), Georgina Lang (Moreton Hall, Bury St Edmund's), Zijia Li (Westbourne School), Sophie McInerny (Tonbridge Grammar School), Navoil Neogi (Tiffin School, Kingston upon Thames), Jimin Park (Sutton High School), Chen-Xin Qui (Douglas Academy), Amelia Rout (Chislehurst & Sidcup Grammar School), Thalia Seale (Highgate School, London), Andrea Sendula (Kenilworth School), Romy Williamson (St Anne's Catholic School, Southampton).

Hungary Camp 2016/17

Each year UKMT send a group of twenty students and a number of volunteers to Hungary over the New Year to train with the Hungarian IMO squad. As in previous years the group travelled out on 27th December and returned on 4th January. Thanks go to this year's volunteers, Dominic Yeo who led the team, Gabriel Gendler and Kasia Warburton.

The UKMT students attending the camp this year were: Agnijo Banerjee (Grove Academy), Naomi Bazlov (King Edward VI Girls' High School, Birmingham), Emily Beatty (King Edward VII School, Sheffield), Joe Benton (St Paul's School), Rosie Cates (Hills Road Sixth Form College), Alexander Chen (Westminster School), Nathan Creighton (Mossbourne Community Academy, London), Dougie Dolleymore (King Edward's School, Birmingham), Isaac Kaufmann (City of London School), Neel Nanda (Latymer School), Michael Ng (Aylesbury Grammar School), Melissa Quail (Longsands Academy), Benedict Randall Shaw (Westminster School), Thomas Read (The Perse School), Amelia Rout (Chislehurst & Sidcup Grammar School), Alexander Song (Westminster School), Roan Talbut (The Perse School), Tommy Walker Mackay (Stretford Grammar School), Naomi Wei (City of London School for Girls), Harvey Yau (Ysgol Dryffyn Taf).

Romanian Master of Mathematics

In 2017, the Romanian Masters of Mathematics was held between February 22nd and 27th in Bucharest. The leader of the UK team was Dominic Yeo, with James Gazet as the deputy and Mary Teresa Fyfe who attended as the Observer with Contestants. The team consisted of : Joe Benton (St Paul's School), Rosie Cates (Hills Road Sixth Form College), Neel Nanda (Latymer School), Thomas Read (The Perse School), Alexander Song (Westminster School) and Harvey Yau (Ysgol Dryffyn Taf).

This year the team came 2nd out of 19 competing teams. They collected two gold, one silver, and one bronze medal, and an Honourable Mention. The leaders report can be found at

https://imo-register.org.uk/2017-rmm-report.pdf

Balkan Mathematical Olympiad

The UK continues to be invited as a guest nation to the Balkan Mathematical Olympiad, a competition for secondary school students which is organised annually by eleven countries in Eastern Europe on a rotation basis. In 2017 the event was held in Ohrid, Macedonia from 2nd to 7th May.

This year the group was led by Dominic Rowland, with Gerry Leversha as deputy and Jill Parker accompanying the students. UKMT rules state that UK students can only attend this competition on a single occasion, thus giving an opportunity for as many students as possible to experience an overseas event. This year the team was: Hugo Aaronson (St. Paul's School), Sam Bealing (Bridgewater High School), Emily Beatty (King Edward VII School, Sheffield), Thomas Pycroft (Whitchurch High School), Yuta Tsuchiya (Queen Elizabeth's School) and Naomi Wei (City of London School for Girls).

This year the team succeeded in gaining four bronze medals. The team leaders report for this year can be found at

https://www.imo-register.org.uk/2017-balkan-report.pdf

European Girls' Mathematical Olympiad

The 6th European Girls' Mathematical Olympiad was held in Zurich, Switzerland, between 6th and 12th April 2017

The UK team attending were: Rosie Cates (Hills Road Sixth Form College), Melissa Quail (Longsands Academy), Alevtina Studenikina (Cheltenham Ladies' College), Naomi Wei (City of London School for Girls).

The Team leader was Jo Harbour and the deputy leaders were Jenny Owladi and Kasia Warburton. The team came home with one gold and three bronze medals, and were 6th out of 33 participating European teams.

Trinity Training Camp

The annual Trinity Training Camp was held at Trinity College, Cambridge, from 30th March to 3rd April 2017. UKMT are very grateful to Trinity College for its continuing support of this event.

Twenty-two students attended the camp this year, including all the candidates for the 2017 International Mathematical Olympiad (IMO) team, and younger students who have the potential to reach future international camps.

Students attending this year were: Hugo Aaronson (St Paul's School), Sam Bealing (Bridgewater High School), Emily Beatty (King Edward VII School, Sheffield), Joe Benton (St Paul's School), Rosie Cates (Hills Road VI Form College), Alex Chen (Westminster School), Jacob Coxon (Magdalen College School), Nathan Creighton (Mossbourne Community Academy, London), Dmitry Filippov (John Lyon School), Shavinda Jayasekera (Wilson's School, Wallington), Neel Nanda (Latymer School), Navonil Neogi (Tiffin School), Michael Ng (Aylesbury Grammar School), Thomas Pycroft (Whitchurch High School), Melissa Quail (Longsands Academy), Thomas Read (The Perse School), Ben Randall

Shaw (Westminster School), Alexander Song (Westminster School), Alevtina Studenikina (Cheltenham Ladies' College), Yuta Tsuchiya (Queen Elizabeth's School), Naomi Wei ((City of London Girls' School), Harvey Yau (Ysgol Dryffyn Taf),

The training camp was led by Dominic Yeo with assistance from the local organiser Oliver Feng and a group of UKMT volunteers.

IMO Selection Camp, Tonbridge

The final camp before the selection of the team of six students who were selected for the International Mathematical Olympiad was again held at Tonbridge School from 27th to 31st May. The camp was led by Geoff Smith and Dominic Yeo, with assistance from other volunteers and visiting speakers.

Students attending the camp this year were: Sam Bealing (Bridgewater High School), Joe Benton (St Paul's School), Rosie Cates (Hills Road VI Form College), Jacob Coxon (Magdalen College School), Neel Nanda (Latimer School), Michael Ng (Aylesbury Grammar School), Thomas Read (The Perse School), Alexander Song (Westminster School), Harvey Yau (Ysgol Dryffyn Taf), Naomi Wei (City of London Girls' School).

The International Mathematical Olympiad

In many ways, a lot of the events and activities described earlier in this book relate to stages that UK IMO team members will go through before they attend an IMO. At this stage, it is worth explaining a little about the structure of the Olympiad, both for its own sake as well as to fit the following report into a wider context.

An IMO is a huge event and takes several years to plan and to execute. In 2017, teams from more than 110 countries went to Rio de Janeiro to participate. A team consists of six youngsters (although in some cases, a country may send fewer) who must be under 20 years of age and not have entered university. The focus of an IMO is really the two days on which teams sit the contest papers. The papers are on consecutive days and each lasts $4\frac{1}{2}$ hours. Each paper consists of three problems, and each problem is worth 7 marks. Thus a perfect score for a student is 42/42. The students are ranked according to their personal scores, and the top half receive medals. These are distributed in the ratios gold:silver:bronze = 1:2:3. The host city of the IMO varies from year to year. Detailed contemporary and historical data can be found at

http://www.imo-official.org/

However, whilst these may be the focus, there are other essential stages, in particular the selection of the problems and, in due course, the co-ordination (marking) of scripts and awarding of medals.

As stated, an IMO team is built around the students but they are accompanied by two other very important people: the Team Leader and the Deputy Leader (many teams also take Observers who assist at the various stages and some of these may turn out to be future Leaders). Some three or four days before the actual IMO examinations, the Team Leaders arrive in the host country to deal with the task of constructing the papers. Countries will have submitted questions for consideration over the preceding months and a short list of questions (and, eventually, solutions) are given to Team Leaders on arrival. The Team Leaders gather as a committee (in IMO parlance, the Jury) to select six of the short-listed questions. This can involve some very vigorous debate and pretty tough talking, but it has to be done! Once agreed, the questions are put into the papers and translations produced into as many languages as necessary, sometimes over 50.

At some stage, the students, accompanied by the Deputy Leader, arrive in the host country. As is obvious, there can be no contact with the Team Leader who, by then, has a good idea of the IMO papers! The Leaders and the students are housed in different locations to prevent any contact, casual or otherwise.

On the day before the first examination, there is an Opening Ceremony. This is attended by all those involved (with due regard to security). Immediately after the second day's paper, the marking can begin. It may seem strange that students' scripts are 'marked' by their own Leader and Deputy. In fact, no actual marks or comments of any kind are put on the scripts themselves. Instead, having looked at scripts and decided what marks they think should be awarded, the Leader and Deputy have to justify their claim to others, called co-ordinators, who are supplied by the host country. Once all the marks have been agreed, sometimes after extremely protracted negotiation, the Jury decides where the medal boundaries should go. Naturally, this is a crucial part of the procedure and results in many tears as well as cheers.

Whilst the co-ordination of marks is going on, the students have time to relax and recover. There are often organised activities and excursions and there is much interaction and getting to know like-minded individuals from all corners of the world.

The grand finale is always the closing ceremony which includes the awarding of medals as well as speeches and numerous items of entertainment – some planned but others accidental.

58th International Mathematical Olympiad, Rio de Janeiro, July 2017, Report by Geoff Smith (UK Team Leader)

The UK Deputy Leader was Dominic Yeo of the Technion, and our Observer C was Jill Parker, formerly of the University of Bath. Here is the UK IMO team of 2017:

Joe Benton	St Paul's School, London
Rosie Cates	Hill's Road Sixth Form College, Cambridge
Jacob Coxon	Magdalen College School, Oxford
Neel Nanda	Latymer School, London
Alexander Song	Westminster School, London
Harvey Yau	Ysgol Dyffryn Taf, Carmarthenshire

The reserves were Sam Bealing, Bridgewater High School; Michael Ng, Aylesbury Grammar School; Thomas Read, The Perse School; Naomi Wei, City of London School for Girls.

The Papers
Contestants have 4 hours 30 minutes to sit each paper. The three problems

on each paper are each marked out of 7. It is intended that the three problems should be in increasing order of difficulty on each day.

Day 1

Problem 1 For each integer $a_0 > 1$, define the sequence $a_0, a_1, a_2, \ldots$ by:

$$a_{n+1} = \begin{cases} \sqrt{a_n} & \text{if } \sqrt{a_n} \text{ is an integer,} \\ a_n + 3 & \text{otherwise,} \end{cases} \quad \text{for each } n \geqslant 0.$$

Determine all values of a_0 for which there is a number A such that $a_n = A$ for infinitely many values of n.

Problem 2 Let $\mathbb{R}$ be the set of real numbers. Determine all functions $f : \mathbb{R} \to \mathbb{R}$ such that, for all real numbers x and y,

$$f\big(f(x)f(y)\big) + f(x + y) = f(xy).$$

Problem 3 A hunter and an invisible rabbit play a game in the Euclidean plane. The rabbit's starting point, A_0, and the hunter's starting point, B_0, are the same. After $n - 1$ rounds of the game, the rabbit is at point A_{n-1} and the hunter is at point B_{n-1}. In the nth round of the game, three things occur in order.

(i)   The rabbit moves invisibly to a point A_n such that the distance between A_{n-1} and A_n is exactly 1.

(ii) A tracking device reports a point P_n to the hunter. The only guarantee provided by the tracking device to the hunter is that the distance between P_n and A_n is at most 1.

(iii) The hunter moves visibly to a point B_n such that the distance between B_{n-1} and B_n is exactly 1.

Is it always possible, no matter how the rabbit moves, and no matter what points are reported by the tracking device, for the hunter to choose her moves so that after 10^9 rounds she can ensure that the distance between her and the rabbit is at most 100?

Day 2

Problem 4 Let R and S be different points on a circle Ω such that RS is not a diameter. Let ℓ be the tangent line to Ω at R. Point T is such that S is the midpoint of the line segment RT. Point J is chosen on the shorter arc RS of Ω so that the circumcircle Γ of triangle JST intersects ℓ at two distinct points. Let A be the common point of Γ and ℓ that is closer to R. Line AJ meets Ω again at K. Prove that the line KT is tangent to Γ.

Problem 5 An integer $N \geqslant 2$ is given. A collection of $N(N + 1)$ soccer players, no two of whom are of the same height, stand in a row. Sir Alex wants to remove $N(N - 1)$ players from this row leaving a new row of $2N$ players in which the following N conditions hold:

    (1)   no one stands between the two tallest players,

    (2)   no one stands between the third and fourth tallest players,

    $\vdots$

    (N) no one stands between the two shortest players.

Show that this is always possible.

Problem 6 An ordered pair (x, y) of integers is a *primitive point* if the greatest common divisor of x and y is 1. Given a finite set S of primitive points, prove that there exist a positive integer n and integers $a_0, a_1, \ldots, a_n$ such that, for each (x, y) in S, we have:

$$a_0 x^n + a_1 x^{n-1} y + a_2 x^{n-2} y^2 + \ldots + a_{n-1} xy^{n-1} + a_n y^n = 1.$$

Problem Authors

Problem 1 was proposed by South Africa (Stephan Wagner),

Problem 2 was proposed by Albania (Dorlir Ahmeti),

Problem 3 was proposed by Austria (Gerhard Woeginger),

Problem 4 was proposed by Luxembourg (Charles Leytem),

Problem 5 was proposed by Russia (Grigory Chelnokov),

Problem 6 was proposed by the United States of America (John Berman).

Here are the results obtained by the UK students in 2017.

Name	P1	P2	P3	P4	P5	P6		award
Joe Benton	7	7	5	7	1	2	29	Gold
Rosie Cates	7	1	0	7	0	3	18	Bronze
Jacob Coxon	7	3	0	7	0	0	17	Bronze
Neel Nanda	7	4	0	7	0	7	25	Gold
Alexander Song	7	1	0	7	0	0	15	Honourable Mention
Harvey Yau	7	1	0	7	7	4	26	Gold

The cut-offs were 16 for bronze, 19 for silver and 25 for gold. The current IMO marks format became stable in 1982. This is the lowest gold cut, and the equal lowest silver cut, since then. This is evidence of the exceptional difficulty of this IMO.

This is the first time that a UK team has secured three gold medals at an IMO since 1981, the last year in which IMO teams comprised 8 people. Joe, Harvey and Neel all obtained well deserved gold medals.

It was very pleasing that EGMO star (41/42) Rosie Cates made the team, and secured a strong bronze medal. Jacob Coxon also earned a good bronze. Alexander Song was unlucky to miss out on a medal by 1 mark, but he has chances to win medals at IMOs 2018 and 2019. His marks were essential in securing a high team ranking for the UK. Harvey is also available for selection for IMO 2018.

Comments on Problems

It was pleasing that the UK team obtained perfect scores on the first problem of each day. Certainly Problem 1 was a completely appropriate choice, and gave lots of students the opportunity to obtain an Honourable Mention. The geometry Problem 4 was amenable to attack by sensible methods, but naturally Harvey Yau found another approach. He began by discussing some barely relevant spiral similarities, and then created an extraordinary collection of circles with curious intersection properties, and concluded by means of a collinearity which follows from the converse of Miquel and Steiner's quadrilateral theorem. Under no circumstances should you try this at home.

The two medium problems, 2 and 5, proved hard this year. Problem 2 was a functional equation which demanded considerable ingenuity. Problem 5 was an *hommage* to the Erdős-Szekeres theorem which, in downmarket form, concerns soccer players of different heights standing in a row. Problem 5 was one of those conceptual combinatorial problems which students find hard to solve under pressure of time.

The two hard problems were indeed hard, especially Problem 3. Again this was a conceptual problem, where the technical mathematics was not demanding but the idea of how to solve the problem was very hard to find. Only two students in the IMO scored perfectly on Problem 3 (Linus Cooper of Australia and Mikhail Ivanov of Russia) and only 26 marks were awarded for that problem in total. Problem 6 was an intriguing and beautiful problem about homogeneous polynomials.

Performances

The joint winner of IMO 2017 was Yuta Takaya of Japan who scored 35/42, securing perfect scores on all problems which did not involve rabbits. Immediately after IMO 2017, he participated in the International Olympiad in Informatics in Iran, and he won that too. Breathing closely down Yuta's neck was the UK's Joe Benton who came 7th in the IMO and 6th at the IOI. Joe was able to say very worthwhile things about invisible leporidae, producing a solution (with correct asymptotic analysis) but with details of the calculation missing because of shortage of time.

There were 111 teams participating at IMO 2017. Hearty congratulations to Korea for finishing ranked 1st, repeating their first win of 2012. All six Korean students (including a girl) won gold medals, and no other team repeated this feat in 2017. We give a list of the teams ranked in the top 40, and by chance this list consists of exactly those teams which scored at least 100 marks.

1 Korea (170), 2 China (159), 3 Vietnam (155), 4 USA (148), 5 Iran (142), 6 Japan (134), 7 Singapore, Thailand (131), 9 Taiwan, United Kingdom (130), 11 Russian Federation (128), 12 Georgia, Greece (127), 14 Belarus, Czech Republic, Ukraine (122), 17 Philippines (120), 18 Bulgaria, Italy, Netherlands, Serbia (116), 22 Hungary, Poland, Romania (115), 25 Kazakhstan (113), 26 Argentina, Bangladesh, Hong Kong (111), 29 Canada (110), 30 Peru (109), 31 Indonesia (108), 32 Israel (107), 33 Germany (106), 34 Australia (103), 35 Croatia, Turkey (102), 37 Brazil, Malaysia (101), 39 France, Saudi Arabia (100).

Anglophone and Commonwealth interest in other scores might include 46 New Zealand (94), 47 Cyprus (93), 52 India (90), 60 South Africa (81), 62 Ireland, Sri Lanka (80), 81 Pakistan (58), 95 Uganda (22), 98 Botswana (19), 99 Myanmar, Trinidad and Tobago [1 person] (15), 107 Kenya (8), 108 Ghana [1 person] (6), 109 Tanzania [2 people] (5), 110 Nepal (3).

China finished 2nd, continuing their extraordinary run of consistently excellent performances. China has not finished outside the top 3 since 1996. As in 2016, the top 10 countries comprise 7 countries from the far east, and three others. In 2016 the three exceptions were Russia, UK and USA, and in 2017 Iran replaced Russia in that trio.

Top monarchy was Japan, and Commonwealth Champion was Singapore. The UK was first among the nations of Europe, and therefore also those of the EU. Note the remarkable performances of Greece and Georgia in finishing equal 12th, so equal third in Europe just behind Russia. Greece was first among nations which use the euro.

From our national perspective, the breadth of the UK performance was very pleasing. Every team has a virtual player Max. This player is deemed to score the maximum of the marks obtained by a team member on each problem. In the Max contest, the clear winner was UK Max who scored 40/42, dropping just two marks on Problem 3. Second equal were Korean Max and Russian Maxim who scored 36/42.

Full scores are available at the IMO official site:

www.imo-official.org/year\underlinecountry\underliner.aspx?year=2017

Forthcoming International Events

This is a summary of the events which are relevant for the UK. Of course there are many other competitions going on in other parts of the world.

The next IMO will be held in Cluj, Romania 2018. More formally, this Transylvanian city is known as Cluj-Napoca. After that the IMOs are: Bath, UK 2019; St Petersburg, Russia 2020; the USA 2021, Norway 2022 and (unconfirmed) Japan 2023.

Forthcoming editions of the European Girls' Mathematical Olympiad will be in Florence, Italy in 2018; Kiev, Ukraine in 2019; Netherlands 2020 and (unconfirmed) Georgia 2021.

The Balkan Mathematical Olympiad of 2018 will be in Serbia.

The Romanian Master of Mathematics competition will continue as an annual event in Bucharest.

The Mathematical Ashes

The United Kingdom retained the Ashes 83-63 in the 2017 match at the pre-IMO camp in Itaipava, Brazil. The UK has held the Ashes since 2009, but the contest of 2018 may see a change of fortunes, with the UK losing four IMO 2017 medallists to higher education.

Acknowledgements

Thanks to everyone in Brazil for making this such an enjoyable IMO, especially the taxi drivers who always sought to minimize journey times. In the land of Ayrton Senna, Nelson Piquet and Emerson Fittipaldi, passengers may wish to use a blindfold.

The UK Mathematics Trust is an astonishing organization, bringing together so many volunteers and a small professional core to focus their energies on maths competitions and more generally, mathematics enrichment. Our collective effort is, I am sure, a significant part of the success story which is secondary school mathematics for able students in the UK. This is not to be complacent, because there are always opportunities to do more things and to do things better, but I thank everyone for what we already accomplish every year.

Hundreds of thousands of lives are touched by our wonderful maths challenges and team competitions, and I thank everyone involved for their marvellous work.

On a personal note, I thank Dominic Yeo for his exceptional work, inspiring so many young people with his passion for good mathematics. Jill Parker kept the team happy and safe while it was in Brazil. The teams which UKMT sends abroad to represent the country (and the associated reserves) continue to conduct themselves in an exemplary fashion in person, in the *Guardian* and on *Radio 4*.

Joseph Myers did splendid work as a co-ordinator of Problem 3 and minute taker for both the IMO Advisory Board and the IMO jury. We were also joined for a few days by Steve Mulligan of the Team Maths Challenge subtrust who came to Rio to promote *Diamond Maths Challenge*, the global outreach project of IMO 2019 in the United Kingdom. Steve made a lot of friends very quickly.

I thank *Oxford Asset Management* for their continuing generous sponsorship of the UK IMO team, and the other donors, both individual and corporate, who give so generously to UKMT. Why not join in?

www.ukmt.org.uk/about-us/

UKMT Mentoring Schemes 2016–2017

The schemes continue to grow at all levels. We are extremely proud that the materials are used by over 1100 schools around the world. The mentoring sheets continue to be offered to all schools who register with us – at no cost, and many schools subscribe to receive all three levels.

Our team of volunteer question setters continue to work on their individual schemes, with each small group of volunteers writing a monthly set of questions and solutions for eight months of the year. This can be time consuming work as each sheet passes through a series of checks and corrections until the group considers it suitable for publication, and then it is sent out to all the participating schools, mentees and mentors. Each of the schemes develops to become more challenging as the year progresses.

Junior Scheme

During this academic year, there were almost 900 schools receiving the Junior materials. This scheme is aimed at years 7-9, some of whom have completed the Junior Maths Challenge and maybe even the Junior Olympiad papers. On these monthly sheets, the authors also offer discussion points and hints to stimulate problem solving at an accessible level.

When a teacher enrols on the scheme, they are sent a new sheet of materials each month, for them to use within their school. At the Junior level all the pupils are mentored internally by their own teachers, who are free to use the resources in the most appropriate way for them, in some schools they are used with whole classes, in others it may be in a maths club, or even with individual students.

Intermediate Scheme

The Intermediate scheme has over 800 schools registered to receive the resources, which again they are free to use within their schools as they wish, with them being used most with pupils in Years 9, 10 and 11. Additionally there were 9 volunteer UKMT mentors working with over 30 individual students on the scheme.

Senior Scheme

The senior materials this year have been sent out to around 450 schools. Aimed at students in Years 11, 12 and 13, these are suitable for students who have experience of Maclaurin Olympiad papers, and BMO1 materials.

There are also a large number of volunteer mentors on the senior scheme, who in this year have been working with over 200 individual mentees. An important role for mentors at this level is to give encouragement to their mentees as the questions become more challenging than material they may have seen before.

All three of these schemes run between October and May and they are open to all schools and individuals, although for individuals access is sometimes limited by the number of volunteer mentors we have available at any one time. Examples of the materials can be found on the UKMT website.

Advanced Scheme

Participation on the Advanced scheme is by invitation only. This level is aimed at potential members of the UK IMO squad, and others for whom the Senior scheme has ceased to be a challenge, and where their mentor has recommended them. The questions are very challenging and are mainly of interest to those who strive for a place on the UK team at a future International Mathematical Olympiad. During this year there were 12 mentors working with 30 mentees.

The mentoring schemes are supported by Oxford Asset Management and we would like to thank them for their continuing support.

Thanks must also go to all the volunteer mentors and question setters and checkers, who have freely given so much time to make the schemes work and encourage the next generation of young mathematicians. Without their help, the mentoring schemes would not exist.

UKMT Team Maths Challenge 2017

Overview

The Team Maths Challenge (TMC) is a national mathematics competition which gives pupils the opportunity to participate in a wide range of mathematical activities and compete against other pupils from schools in their region. The TMC promotes team working and, unlike the Junior, Intermediate and Senior Challenges, students work in groups and are given practical tasks as well as theoretical problems to add another dimension to mathematics.

The TMC is designed for teams of four pupils in:

- Y8 & Y9 (England and Wales)
- S1 & S2 (Scotland)
- Y9 & Y10 (Northern Ireland)

with no more than two pupils from the older year group.

Sample TMC material is available to download from the TMC section of the UKMT website (www.tmc.ukmt.org.uk) for use in school and to help teachers to select a team to represent their school at the Regional Finals.

Report on the 2017 TMC

This was the fifteenth year of the competition. Entries were received from 1757 teams, of which 1642 turned up to take part at one of 69 Regional Finals.

As usual, competition details and entry forms were sent to schools in early October and made available on the UKMT website, which also provided up-to-date information on Regional Final venues and availability of places, as well as past materials for the use of schools in selecting and preparing their team of four. Schools also received a copy of the winning poster from the 2017 National Final, originally created by Sutton Grammar School and professionally reproduced by Arbelos.

Each team signed up to participate in one of the 69 Regional Finals, held between late February and the end of April at a widely-spread set of venues. Each Regional Final comprised four rounds which encouraged the teams to think mathematically in a variety of ways. The Group Round is the only round in which the whole team work together, tackling a set of ten challenging questions. In the Crossnumber the team splits into two pairs; one pair gets the across clues and the other pair gets the down clues. The two pairs then work independently to complete the Crossnumber using logic and deduction. For the Shuttle, teams compete against the clock to answer a series of questions, with each pair working on different questions and the solution of each question dependent on the previous answer. The final round of the day, the Relay, is a fast and lively race involving much movement to answer a series of questions in pairs. Each Regional Final was run by a regional lead coordinator with support from an assistant coordinator and, at some venues, other local helpers. The teachers who accompanied the teams were fully occupied too – they were involved in the delivery and marking of all of the rounds.

TMC National Final

Eighty-eight teams (the winners from each Regional Final plus a few runners-up) were invited to the National Final in London on 19th June. As usual the event was held at the Lindley Hall, part of the prestigious Royal Horticultural Halls, in Westminster, and led with typical energy and expertise by Steve Mulligan. The four rounds from the Regional Finals also featured at the National Final except that the Group Round became the Group Circus: a similar round but with the inclusion of practical materials for use in solving the questions. In addition, the day began with the Poster Competition, which is judged and scored separately from the main event. The Poster theme for 2017 was 'Polyominoes', inspiring some eye-catching designs among the entries, which were all exhibited down the side of the hall throughout the day for the perusal of the participants as well as the judges.

The following schools (a 49:39 split between state and independent), coming from as far north as Nairn and as far south as Plymouth, participated at the National Final:

Adams' Grammar School, Shropshire
All Saint's RC School, York
Aylesbury Grammar School, Buckinghamshire
Bancroft's School, Essex
Birkenhead School
Bishop Wordsworth's School, Salisbury
Bradford Grammar School
Brighton College
Bury St Edmunds All-Through Trust
Caistor Grammar School, Lincolnshire
Cargilfield Preparatory, Edinburgh
Chepstow School, Monmouthshire
City of London School
Clitheroe Royal Grammar School, Lancs
Clounagh Junior High School, Co. Armagh
Colchester Royal Grammar School
Colyton Grammar School, Devon
Devonport High School for Boys, Plymouth
Dorcan Academy, Swindon

Dragon School, Oxford
Durham Johnston School
Edgbarrow School, Berkshire
Ermysted's Grammar School, N. Yorks
Glasgow Academy
Hampton School, Middlesex
Heckmondwike Grammar School, West Yorkshire
Horsforth School, Leeds
Hull Trinity House Academy
Ipswich School
Judd School, Tonbridge, Kent
King Edward VI Camp Hill S. for Boys, Birmingham
King Edward's School, Birmingham
King's School Bruton, Somerset
King's School Ely, Cambridgeshire
Lancaster Royal Grammar School
Lawrence Sheriff School, Rugby
Lenzie Academy, East Dunbartonshire
Loretto School, Musselburgh, Lothian

Loughborough Grammar School
Manchester Grammar School
Matthew Arnold School, Oxford
Merchant Taylors' Boys School, Liverpool
Merchant Taylors' School, Middlesex
Mill Chase Academy, Hampshire
Millfield School, Somerset
Monkseaton Middle School, Tyne and Wear
Monkton Prep School, Bath
Monmouth School
Nairn Academy
Newcastle School for Boys
Newquay Tretherras, Cornwall
Norlington School, London
North London Collegiate School
Norwich School
Nottingham High School
Ounsdale High School, West Midlands
Pate's Grammar School, Cheltenham
Queen Elizabeth's Hospital, Bristol
Queen Elizabeth's School, Barnet
Reading School
Reigate Grammar School, Surrey
Royal Grammar School, Newcastle
Rydal Penrhos School, Colwyn Bay, Conwy

Sale Grammar School, Cheshire
Sheffield High School
Sherborne School for Girls, Dorset
Simon Langton Boys' Grammar Sch., Canterbury
St Catherine's College, Eastbourne
St Olave's Grammar School, Kent
St Paul's Girls' School, Hammersmith
St Paul's School, Barnes, London
St Peter's CE School, Exeter
Stratford Girls' Grammar School, Warwickshire
Stretford Grammar School, Manchester
Sutton Grammar School for Boys, Surrey
The Grange School, Cheshire
The Perse School, Cambridge
The Portsmouth Grammar School
The Royal Latin School, Buckingham
The Trinity Catholic School , Nottingham
Thomas Telford School, Shropshire
Tiffin School, Kingston-upon-Thames
Trinity School, Berkshire
Ulverston Victoria High School, Cumbria
Walton High School, nr Stafford
Westminster Under School, London
Whitgift School, Surrey
Yarm School, nr Stockton-on-Tees

After a very close-run competition, the Team Maths Challenge 2017 trophy went to St Olave's Grammar School (Kent), while the Poster Competition was won by Durham Johnston Comprehensive School.

The team responsible for producing another set of excellent and engaging materials were Madeleine Copin, Jenny Ramsden, Martyn Lawley and Francis Chalmers (the checkers of the questions), Keith Cadman and Dean Bunnell (Group Round), Peter Ransom (Crossnumber), Karl Hayward-Bradley and David Crawford (Shuttle), Sue Essex, Ann Ault and Phil Colville (Relay), Andrew Jobbings, Peter Neumann, Fraser Heywood and Colin Campbell (Poster Competition).

As usual, thanks are due to a great number of people for ensuring another successful year of the TMC: the team of volunteers (listed at the back of this book) who generously give up their time to write, check, trial and refine materials, run Regional Finals and readily carry out countless other jobs behind the scenes; the staff in the UKMT office in Leeds for the way in which the competition is administered (particularly Nicky Bray who has responsibility for the central coordination of the competition, assisted by Shona Raffle-Edwards and Jo Williams, with additional support from Jessica Davis) and the team of packers for their efficient and precise preparation and packing of materials; the teachers who continue to support the competition and take part so willingly, some of whom also undertake the significant task of organising and hosting a Regional Final at their own school and, of course, the pupils who participate so enthusiastically in the competition at all levels. Our thanks also go to additional contacts at schools and other host venues responsible for organising and helping with Regional Finals (listed at the back of this book).

TMC Regional Finals Material

Each of the 69 Regional Finals held across the UK involved four rounds:

1. Group Round
2. Crossnumber
3. Shuttle
4. Relay Race

Group Round

Teams are given a set of 10 questions, which they should divide up among themselves so that they can answer, individually or in pairs, as many as possible in the allotted time.

Question 1

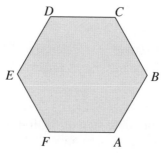

ABCDEF is a regular hexagon.

What is the area of triangle *CDF* as a fraction of the area of the hexagon? Give your answer as a fraction in its lowest terms.

[6]

Question 2

(a) A circle touches the mid-points of the edges of a square. The ratio of the area of the circle to the area of the square is $\pi : x$.

What is the value of x?

[3]

(b) A circle touches the vertices of a square. The ratio of the area of the circle to the area of the square is $\pi : y$.

What is the value of y?

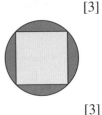

[3]

The area of a circle is equal to π times the square of its radius.

Question 3

(a) What is the *smallest* possible sum of the four non-zero digits that may be placed in the Crossnumber below?

Across	Down
1. A square	1. A square
3. A square	2. A square

[3]

(b) What is the *largest* possible sum of the four non-zero digits that may be placed in the Crossnumber below?

Across	Down
1. A square	1. A square
3. A square	2. A square

[3]

Question 4

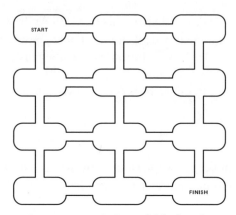

The diagram shows a burrow consisting of 12 chambers.

A mole moves from one chamber to another by passing through a tunnel.

Starting in the top left chamber of the burrow, the mole goes through exactly five tunnels to reach the bottom right chamber.

In how many different ways can this be done?

[6]

Question 5

In a 4 × 4 grid, four cells are shaded, and the numbers 1, 2 and 3 each lie in a cell, as shown below.

The numbers 5, 6, 7, 8, 9, 10, 11, 12 and 14 are to be placed, once each, in an unshaded cell so that the sum of the numbers in each row and in each column is the same.

What number should be placed in the cell labelled x?

[6]

Question 6

Some of the integers between two and fifty are not prime. Some of these are *special integers*. This means that neither the integer nor double the integer is divisible by a square greater than one.

How many of these *special integers* are there?

[6]

Question 7

Dean took 16 minutes to cycle from his home to Andrew's house.

He later took 48 minutes to walk home. Each journey was at a constant speed. On that day Dean cycled 5 miles per hour faster, on average, than he walked.

What is the distance, in miles, between the two houses?

[6]

Question 8

A palindromic number reads the same forwards as backwards.

A two-digit palindromic number is multiplied by 99. The tens digit of the answer is a five.

What is the answer?

[6]

Question 9

(a) Each son in the Jones family has the same number of brothers as sisters. Each daughter has twice as many brothers as sisters.

How many children are there in the Jones family?

[3]

(b) Mrs Jones is currently four times as old as her daughter Hannah.

Twenty years from now, Mrs Jones will be twice as old as Hannah.

How old is Hannah now?

[3]

Question 10

Five children standing in a line each tossed a coin.

At least four of the coins landed the same way up.

Using "H" for Head and "T" for Tail, in how many different ways could the outcome be written down?

[6]

Crossnumber

Teams are divided into pairs, with one pair given the across clues and one pair given the down clues. Each pair answers as many questions as possible on the grid, showing their answers to the supervising teacher who either confirms or corrects them. The correct version is then shown to both pairs. The sole communication permitted between the two pairs is to request, via the supervising teacher, for a particular clue to be solved by the other pair.

Across:

1.	29 Across plus 4 Down	(3)
3.	The sum of the first twelve prime numbers	(3)
6.	$77 \times \dfrac{7 \text{ Down}}{2}$	(3)
8.	This number is a multiple of the sum of its digits	(3)
9.	The sum of the digits of this number is a factor of 10 Down	(2)
12.	A non-square factor of 16 Down	(2)
13.	A palindromic number	(4)
15.	3 Down plus five	(2)

17. Twice a square (2)
18. $9 \times 8 \times 7 \times (6 - 5 + 4 - 3) \times 2 + 1$ (4)
19. x, where $\dfrac{5 \text{ Down} - 2}{x} = 70 - 22 \text{ Across}$ (2)
22. A factor of 23 Down (2)
24. The mean of 16 Down and 24 Across (3)
26. The largest three-digit number that is the sum of a Fibonacci number and a square (3)
28. The sum of its digits is 8 (3)
29. y where $1 : 20 = 2 \text{ Down} : y$ (3)

Down:

1. The product of the first five odd numbers (3)
2. x where $10 \text{ Down} : x = 72 : 1$ (2)
3. A factor of 12 Across (2)
4. An angle, in degrees, of an isosceles triangle that contains a $53°$ angle (2)
5. The factor of 26 Across whose digits add to 8 (3)
7. Twice 6 Across $\div 77$ (2)
10. A multiple of the sum of the digits of 9 Across (4)
11. $\dfrac{14 \text{ Down} + 18 \text{ Across}}{6}$ (3)
14. $(3 + 1 \times 2)^5$ (4)
16. A power of 2 (3)
20. A prime number of the form $n^n + 1$ (3)
21. The mean of 2 Down and 12 Across (2)
23. A multiple of 22 Across (3)
25. x, where $x + 79 = 5 \text{ Down} - 10x$ (2)
26. A multiple of 5 that is the sum of two different squares (2)
27. The remainder when 26 Across is divided by 103 (2)

Shuttle

Teams are divided into pairs, with one pair given Questions 1 and 3 (along with the record sheet on which to record their answers) and the other pair given Questions 2 and 4. The first pair works on Question 1 and then passes the answer to the students in the other pair who use it to help them answer Question 2, for which they can first carry out some preparatory work. This continues with the second pair passing the answer to Question 2 back to the first pair and so on until a full set of answers is presented for marking. Bonus points are awarded to all teams which present a correct set of answers before the 6-minute whistle, then the other teams have a further 2 minutes in which to finish. Four of these shuttles are attempted in the time given.

A1   From 80% of 70, Jocelyn correctly subtracts $\frac{3}{4}$ of 60.
Pass on her answer.

A2   *T is the number you will receive*
A quadrilateral has interior angles $7T°$, $8T°$, $9T°$ and $12K°$.
Pass on the value of K.

A3   *T is the number you will receive*
From a 2.74 m length of rope, $(T - 1)$ pieces of mean length 22 cm are cut.
The remaining piece has length K cm.
Pass on the value of K.

A4   *T is the number you will receive*

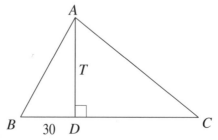

In the diagram, triangle ABC has area 6000. Length $BC = 30$ and $AD = T$.
Write down the area of triangle ADC.

B1
$$(201 + 7x) - (20 + 17x) = 1.$$

Pass on the value of $\dfrac{x}{3}$.

B2   *T is the number you will receive*

In recurring decimal notation, $2.\dot{3}4\dot{5}$ means $2.345\ 345\ 345\ldots$

The fraction $\dfrac{20}{17}$ can be written as the recurring decimal

$1.\dot{1}76\ 470\ 588\ 235\ 294\ \dot{1}$.

Pass on the value of the digit in the $(2017 + T)$th decimal place.

Pass on the value of K.

B3   *T is the number you will receive*

Pass on the lowest common multiple of $20T$ and $32T$.

B4   *T is the number you will receive*

Tilly has drawn a rhombus. The long diagonal of her rhombus is four times the length of the shorter diagonal. The area of the rhombus is T.

Write down the length of the shorter diagonal.

C1
$$K = \dfrac{1}{1} \div \left(\dfrac{1}{2} \times \dfrac{1}{3} \times \dfrac{1}{4} \times \dfrac{1}{5}\right).$$

Pass on the value of K.

C2   *T is the number you will receive*

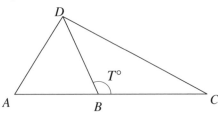

In the diagram, $\angle DBC = T°$, $\angle CDB = 2 \times \angle BCD$ and $\angle BDA = 3 \times \angle BCD$.

$\angle DAB = x°$.

Pass on the value of x.

C3 *T is the number you will receive*

In the diagram, each of the rectangles *ABCD* and *EFGH* is twice as wide as it is long.

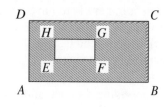

Rectangle *ABCD* is three times as wide as rectangle *EFGH*. The total perimeter of the shaded region is $(T - 12)$ cm.

The area of the shaded region is K cm². Pass on the value of K.

C4 *T is the number you will receive*

$$\frac{1}{8}\left(x + \frac{T}{4}\right) - \frac{1}{2}\left(\frac{1}{16}x + \frac{T}{64}\right) = \frac{1}{4}\left(\frac{1}{2}x + \frac{T}{16}\right).$$

Write down the value of x.

D1 $$A = 123 \div (-4 - 5 + 6) - 7 \times (-8 - 9 + 10).$$

Pass on the value of A.

D2 *T is the number you will receive*

A hexagon has interior angles of $17T°$, $20T°$, $17T°$, $18T°$, $16T°$ and $kT°$.

Pass on the value of k.

D3 *T is the number you will receive*

The Grand Old Duke of Walk, he had T thousand men. He marched them 2 km to the top of a hill and he marched them 2 km down again.

However, 20% of his men stopped after 1 km.

Of those who carried on, 20% stopped after 2 km.

Of those who carried on further, another 20% stopped after 3 km.

Pass on the number of men still walking after 3 km.

D4 *T is the number you will receive*

The mean of five positive integers is $\frac{T}{2}$, the mode is $\frac{3T}{4}$ and the range is $\frac{T}{2}$.

Write down the largest possible value of the median of the set of integers.

Relay

The aim here is to have a speed competition with students working in pairs to answer alternate questions. Each team is divided into two pairs, with each pair seated at a different desk away from the other pair and their supervising teacher.

One member of Pair A from a team collects question A1 from the supervising teacher and returns to his/her partner to answer the question together. When the pair is certain that they have answered the question, the runner returns to the front and submits their answer. If it is correct, the runner is given question B1 to give to the other pair (Pair B) from their team. If it is incorrect, Pair A then has a second (and final) attempt at answering the question, then the runner returns to the front to receive question B1 to deliver to pair B. The runner then returns, empty handed, to his/her partner. Pair B answers question B1 and a runner from this pair brings the answer to the front, as above, then takes question A2 to Pair A. Pair A answers question A2, their runner returns it to the front and collects question B2 for the other pair, and so on until all questions are answered or time runs out. Thus the A pairs answer only A questions and the B pairs answer only B questions. Only one pair from a team should be working on a question at any time and each pair must work independently of the other.

A1   An isosceles triangle has a line of symmetry $y = 3$ and two of its vertices are (3, 3) and (5, 2).

What are the coordinates of the third vertex?

A2   A bat will snooze for 21 hours a day.

For what percentage of the year is the bat not snoozing?

A3   How many of these four statements are true?

1.   There are five single-digit prime numbers.

2.   The area of a square with sides 3 cm long is 0.09 m².

3.   Two of the letters in the word CHIME have rotational symmetry of order 2.

4. $\frac{7}{8}$ is smaller than $\frac{8}{9}$.

A4 A sequence consists of positive and negative integers in this pattern:

1, −2, −2, 3, 3, 3, −4, −4, −4, −4, and so on, ending with

−8, −8, −8, −8, −8, −8, −8, −8.

What is the range of the numbers in the sequence?

A5 "For a laugh", somebody swapped the + and × buttons on Matt's scientific calculator. Matt then punched in 2 × 4 ÷12 + 6 × 3.
What answer did the calculator give?

A6 What is the product of the mean and range of the numbers 2, 0, 1 and 7?

A7 A walker travels 2 km on a bearing of 090° then 2 km on a bearing of 210°.
On what bearing must she walk to return to her starting point?

A8 A path of width 2 m runs along two adjacent sides of a square flower bed, as shown.
The area of the path is 72 m².
What is the area of the flower bed?

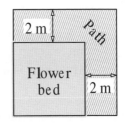

A9 From the integers 1 to 100, all the multiples of 2, 3 and 4 are removed.
How many of the original one hundred integers remain?

A10 The BBC Concert Orchestra has 125 members for a concert.
The woodwind section is made up of three each of flutes, oboes, clarinets and bassoons, two piccolos and two cors anglais.
What percentage of the orchestra is the woodwind section?

A11 Young Jack decides to become serious with saving his pennies.
On 26 May he puts 1p into his piggy bank. The next day he puts 2p into the piggy bank and the day after he puts 4p into the piggy bank, and so on, doubling the amount he puts in each day.
On what date does his piggy bank first hold more than £5?

A12   An integer sequence uses this rule to obtain the next number:
"If odd, then multiply by 5 and subtract 3; if even, divide by 2".
When I start with 14, what is the sum of the four smallest different integers in the entire sequence?

A13   A class of 28 pupils were asked about what they watched at the Rio Olympics. When asked "Did you watch some athletics?", three more said "yes" than when they were asked "Did you watch some gymnastics?", which was three more than the nine pupils who said that they watched neither athletics nor gymnastics.
How many pupils watched ONLY gymnastics?

A14   Four positive integers have a median of 2 and a range of 3.
Let m be the mean of these four numbers.
What is the sum of all the different values that m could take?

A15   Pietro is trying out a road bike with wheels of different sizes; the circumferences of the rear and front wheels are 1.2 m and 1.8 m respectively. During a test race, the rear wheel does 150 more complete turns than the front wheel.
How long is the race?

B1   Excited at the prospect of a bargain, Jane bought 24 books from a market stall advertising 3 books for £5 or £1.99 each.
What is the difference between what Jane paid and the full price?

B2   What is the product of the median and range of the numbers 2, 0, 1 and 7?

B3   My horse, Ned, spends 95% of his time standing.
For how many hours is he not standing this year?

B4   Harry and Martha set off on a 21 km cycle ride.
Harry travels at a steady speed of 14 km per hour, and Martha at 12 km per hour.
For how many minutes does Harry have to wait for Martha to arrive at the end?

B5 A survey taken by the deputy head on how many students ride to school every day received 504 replies. The deputy head draws a pie chart to show the 504 responses and shades 315° as the sector representing "does not ride to school".

How many pupils rode to school?

B6 Three of the coordinates of a square *ABCD* are

$$A\,(20,\,10);\ B\,(30,\,20);\ C\,(20,\,30)\,.$$

The square is reflected in the *x*-axis.

What are the coordinates of the centre of the reflected square?

B7 Cubes-R-Us, a firm that makes boxes, has increased the volume of its most popular box, the deluxe silk-lined jewellery box, by 80%.

The old size was 5 cm × 6 cm × 2 cm.

What is the new volume?

B8 $C = \sqrt{5}$. What is $\dfrac{5}{8}$ of C^4 plus $87\frac{1}{2}\%$ of C^4?

B9 Josh walks 35 metres on a bearing of 260° then walks another 35 metres on a bearing of 140°. He then walks on a bearing of $y°$ for x metres, returning to his starting point.

Calculate the value of $x + y$.

B10 Julie has bought a small canister of helium for filling helium balloons at her party. On the side of the canister it says:

"Will fill 24 large balloons OR 60 medium balloons OR 240 small balloons."

Julie fills 9 large and 25 medium balloons.

How many small balloons can she fill with the remaining helium?

B11 What is the difference between the product of the factors of 26 and the sum of the factors of 26?

B12 A sequence consists of positive and negative integers in this pattern:
1, −2, −2, 3, 3, 3, −4, −4, −4, −4, and so on, ending with
−8, −8, −8, −8, −8, −8, −8, −8.
What is the median?

B13 Julie walks for 1 hour at 1 mph, then for 2 hours at 2 mph, then for 3 hours at x mph.
Her average speed over the entire journey is 2 mph.
What is the value of x?

B14 A sequence follows this rule to obtain the next number:
"If odd, then multiply by 3 and add 1; if even, then divide by 2".
When I start from 14, what is the sum of the four smallest different numbers in the entire sequence?

B15 A right-angled triangle travels along the line AB as shown. It passes through a square of side 8 cm.

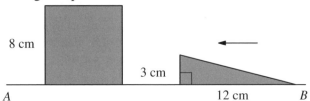

What is the maximum area of the overlap?

TMC National Final Material

At the National Final, the Group Round is replaced by the Group Circus.

Group Circus

Teams move around eight different stations to tackle a variety of activities, some of which involve practical materials.

Station 1

(a) $15(a + b + c)$ = '*abc*', where a, b and c are digits, so that '*abc*' is a 3-digit number.

What is the value of '*abc*'? [2 marks]

(b) $24(d + e + f)$ = '*def*', where d, e and f are digits, so that '*def*' is a 3-digit number.

What is the value of '*def*'? [2 marks]

(c) $11(g + h + i)$ = '*ghi*', where g, h and i are digits, so that '*ghi*' is a 3-digit number.

What is the value of '*ghi*'? [2 marks]

Station 2

(a) The grid below contains a total of 14 squares. The grid has been formed using eight sticks.

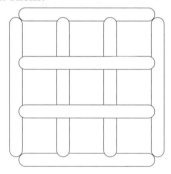

Remove two sticks to leave exactly three squares of different sizes.

[3 marks]

(b) Arrange nine sticks to form a figure which contains exactly six squares.

You are allowed to place one stick over another, but the edges of each square in your answer must be either a full stick or part of a stick.

[3 marks]

204

Station 3

Garron and Zoey take turns shading some of the unshaded cells in the 2 × 4 grid below.

At each turn the unshaded cell, or cells, that they shade are in the shape of a square or a rectangle.

The person who has no cells left to shade loses the game.

Garron starts first and shades just cell A2, as shown.

	1	2	3	4
A		▓		
B				

On Zoey's first turn, she also chooses to shade just one cell.

Mark a cross on the possible cells that Zoey could shade on her first turn in order to force a win.

Station 4

You have three red, three yellow and three green cards to place on a grid. Place one card in each square on the grid below so that:

     Each red card touches a yellow card edge to edge.

     Each yellow card touches a green card edge to edge.

     Each green card touches a red card edge to edge.

     All nine cards are used.

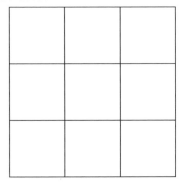

Station 5

The number of positive factors of 30 is eight, namely 1, 2, 3, 5, 6, 10, 15 and 30.

(a) How many positive factors does 210 have?   [2 marks]

(b) How many positive factors does 630 have?   [2 marks]

(c) How many positive factors does 510 510 have?   [2 marks]

Station 6

Divide the L-shape below into eight congruent quadrilaterals.

You are expected to use a pencil and a ruler.

Station 7

You are given two sets of the prime cards 2, 3, 5, 7, 11 and 13. One set is blue (a) and the other is yellow (b).

Using only one colour in each grid, place the cards in the grids below, once each in a blank cell, so that:

(i) the total of the numbers in each of the three rows is equal to a prime less than 25; and

(ii) the total of the numbers in each of the three columns is equal to a prime less than 25;

where

(a) the number of different totals is *more* than four.   [3 marks]

and

(b) the number of different totals is *fewer* than four.   [3 marks]

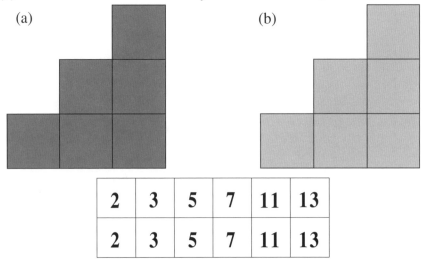

(a)   (b)

Station 8

The 5 × 4 grid below consists of congruent cells. You have been given 14 counters.

Place one counter in each of 14 of the cells of the grid, so that each row and each column contains an even number of counters.

Crossnumber

Across:

1.	A triangular number	(3)
3.	The mean of this number and 22 Across is 15 Down	(5)
6.	A multiple of 11	(3)
7.	The difference between 5 Down and twice 21 Down	(3)
8.	$8^4 + 6^3 + 4^2 + 2^1$	(4)
10.	The digits of this number sum to 14	(4)
12.	The 13th prime number	(2)
14.	x, where $\dfrac{22}{2x + 2} = \dfrac{1}{3}$	(2)
16.	18 Down × 21 Down	(4)
18.	x, where $72 : x = 1 : 48$	(4)
20.	A square	(3)
21.	A factor of 1155	(3)
22.	3 Down × 6 Across + 13 Down	(5)
23.	The sum of the digits of this row is a square	(3)

Down:

1. The mean of this number and 18 Across is 3 Across (5)

2. x, where $x : 13 = 96 : 1$ (4)

3. The 12th prime number (2)

4. A triangular number (3)

5. A square plus 20 Across (3)

8. A multiple of 4 Down (4)

9. A cube (3)

11. The sum of the digits is the same as that of 10 Across (4)

13. A multiple of 13 (3)

15. 13 Down × 21 Across (5)

17. $1^1 + 2^2 + 3^3 + 4^4 + 5^5$ (4)

18. The sum of the digits of this column is a square (3)

19. A square plus 21 Across (3)

21. x, where $\dfrac{180}{3x + 3} = \dfrac{5}{2}$ (2)

A1   Each letter represents the number corresponding to its position in the alphabet.

For example, $A = 1, B = 2, C = 3$ and $Z = 26$.

Pass on the value of $(U - K) \times M - T$.

A2   *T is the number that you will receive.*

$$K = \frac{5}{6}T - \frac{4}{5}T + \frac{2}{3}T - \frac{1}{2}T.$$

Pass on the value of $\frac{1}{2}K$.

A3   *T is the number that you will receive.*

A number sequence is created by subtracting the n th even number from the n th square.

The sequence starts $-1, 0, 3, \ldots$.

Pass on the value of the T th term in this sequence.

A4   *T is the number that you will receive.*

One of the angles in a pentagon is $(T + 1)°$. The other four angles are in the ratio of the first four triangular numbers.

The largest angle is $K°$.

Write down the value of K.

B1 $A = 8 \times \left(-6 - 4 \times (-2)\right) - 7 \times \left(-5 - 3 \times (-1)\right)$.

Pass on the value of A.

B2   *T is the number that you will receive.*

The sizes of the interior angles, in degrees, of a certain quadrilateral form a sequence where each angle is $T°$ more than the previous angle.

The smallest angle is $K°$.

Pass on the value of K.

B3   *T is the number that you will receive.*

In the diagram, the lines *FE* and
AB are parallel.

∠*DEF* = *T*°, ∠*CDE* = 90°
and ∠*ABC* = (3*T* − 10)°.

The size of the obtuse angle
BCD is *x*°.

Pass on the value of $\frac{1}{10}x$.

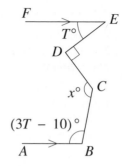

B4   *T is the number that you will receive.*

The diagram shows a shaded triangle bounded by the line $y = \frac{1}{2}x$,
the line $x + y = T$ and the *x*-axis.

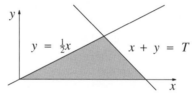

The shaded area has size $(k + \frac{2}{3})$ square units, where *k* is an
integer.

Write down the value of *k*.

C1   *X* is the sum of the *even* numbers from 1 to 100 inclusive.
Y is the sum of the *odd* numbers from 1 to 100 inclusive.
Pass on the value of *X* − *Y*.

C2   *T is the number that you will receive.*

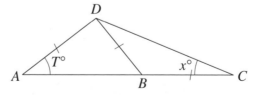

ABC is a straight line. *AD* = *DB* = *BC*.
Pass on the value of $\frac{1}{5}x$.

212

C3   *T is the number that you will receive.*

A cuboid measuring
8 cm × *T* cm ×12 cm is cut into two
equal prisms, as shown.

Each prism has two faces which are
trapeziums, and has total surface
area *P* cm².

Pass on the sum of the digits of *P*.

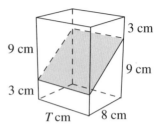

C4   *T is the number that you will receive.*

Tilly has a *T* cm × *T* cm paint-covered
square lying on a piece of paper. She
rotates it 90° clockwise around corner
A, so that *B* moves to *B′*. As the square
rotates it transfers paint to the paper.

The total painted area on the paper
after this quarter turn is
$(a + b\pi)$ cm².

Write down the value of $a + b$.

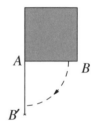

D1
$$\frac{20}{17} + \frac{17}{20} = \frac{A}{B}.$$

where $\dfrac{A}{B}$ is a fraction in its lowest terms.

Pass on the value of $\sqrt{A - 2B}$.

D2   *T is the number that you will receive.*

In the diagram, *X* divides the line *AB* in the ratio 3 : 2 and
Y divides *AB* in the ratio 3 : 1.

$AB = K$ cm and $XY = T$ cm.
Pass on the value of *K*.

D3   *T is the number that you will receive.*

In Miss Sunshine's class there are T pupils.

Half of those who are happy wear glasses. Half of those who are not happy wear glasses.

80% of those who wear glasses are happy.

There are P pupils who are not happy and do not wear glasses.

Pass on the value of P.

D4   *T is the number that you will receive.*

She and he raced each other, and each walked half the distance and ran half the distance.

She walked at R km per hour. He walked at $2T$ km per hour.

She ran twice as fast as she walked. He ran three times as fast as he walked.

She and he started, and finished, at exactly the same time.

Write down the value of R.

214

Relay

A1   Every two minutes my dad's old pocket watch gains 5 seconds.
How many minutes will the watch gain in twenty-four hours?

A2   What is the smallest number that is divisible by every integer from
1 to 10 inclusive?

A3

16	17	18	19
26	27	28	29
36	37	38	39
46	47	48	49

Multiply the only cube in the grid by the sum of the triangular
numbers in the grid.

Write down your answer in the form n^3, where n is an integer.

A4   An official document needs the date to be written in the form
dd/mm/yyyy.

So 1 December this year is 01/12/2017.

When today's date, 19 June, is written like this, what is the mean
of the digits?

A5   How many of these statements are true?

(i)   There is only one Fibonacci number between 20 and 30.

(ii)   A litre is a cubic decimetre.

(iii)   Twelve is a multiple of thirty-six.

(iv)   A set of numbers cannot have the same mean as its median.

A6   The Television Licence costs £12 per month. Of this, £2.33 is
spent on radio, £8.00 on television, £0.60 on on-line services and
£1.07 on miscellaneous charges.

When this information is represented by a pie chart, what is the
angle of the sector for radio to the nearest degree?

A7   Ann, Phil and Sue are given a box of twenty-five chocolates to
share.

Ann eats one every day, Phil eats one every alternate day and Sue
eats one every third day.

They all have their first chocolate on 1 June.

On what date in June is the box emptied?

A8 The digits 1, 3, 5 may be placed in any three consecutive boxes as indicated in the diagram.

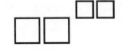

For example 15^3 or 5^{13}.

What is the largest number that can be formed in this way?

Leave your answer in index form.

A9 The sequence 1, 3, . . . , is formed by applying the following to each term, to create the next term:

> Change the sign, multiply by two, add five.

What is the range of the first seven terms of the sequence?

A10 Four cuboids have dimensions in cm, as follows:

> $2 \times 3 \times 3$, $3 \times 5 \times 2$, $5 \times 3 \times 6$, $6 \times 2 \times 5$.

Two of these cuboids are selected and glued together on identical faces to make a new cuboid.

What is the longest edge length of all possible cuboids so formed?

A11 Two gear wheels mesh. Initially the marks on the wheels are perfectly aligned. The large wheel completes one revolution in 20 seconds.

After how many minutes are the two marks again perfectly aligned?

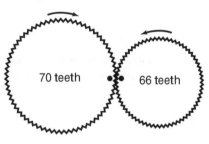

A12 A rectangular sheet of paper *ABCD*, measuring 18 cm by 12 cm, is folded so that the edge *BC* exactly coincides with the edge *BA*.

The fold line, shown in the diagram as a dotted line, crosses the diagonal at *E*.

What is the area of the triangle *FEC*?

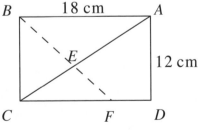

A13 A journey proceeds $A \rightarrow B \rightarrow C \rightarrow D$ in straight lines, where:

- A has coordinates $(-3, 2)$;
- B has coordinates $(1, 5)$;
- C has coordinates $(7, -3)$;
- D has coordinates $(2, 9)$.

What is the total distance covered?

A14 A cuboid has edges whose lengths are in the ratio $1 : 3 : 5$.
The volume of the cuboid is 405 cm^3.
What is the total surface area of the cuboid?

A15 An erratic spider has made a large web made up of 1 cm squares.

The spider can only travel along the threads of the web. For example, in going from the point N to the point A, the shortest distance the spider can travel is 3 cm.

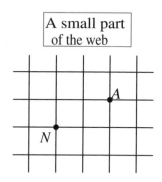

How many points, excluding N itself, are there that the spider could reach from N by travelling not more than 7 cm?

B1

35	36	37	38
45	46	47	48
55	56	57	58
65	66	67	68

What is the sum of all the triangular numbers in this grid?

B2 In 1997 Ronnie O'Sullivan completed the fastest maximum clearance ever in snooker in just 5 minutes 20 seconds.

In 2015 the longest ever frame of snooker in a professional match was played (between McManus and Pinches). The frame lasted 1 hour 40 minutes 24 seconds.

To the nearest whole number, how many times longer was the longest frame than the fastest maximum clearance?

B3   A rhombus has diagonals measuring 3.8 cm and 8.2 cm.
What is the area of the rhombus?

B4   The sequence 1, 3, . . . , is formed by applying the following to
each term, to create the next term:

> Change the sign, add two, multiply by three.

What is the range of the first seven terms of the sequence?

B5   Two is the smallest Fibonacci number that can be written as the
sum of a square and a cube.

$$2 = 1^2 + 1^3$$

What is the next smallest Fibonacci number that can be written as
the sum of a square and a cube, without using either of 1^2 or 1^3?

B6   A hummingbird is found to beat its wings 170 times every nine
seconds.
How many beats does it make in three minutes?

B7   Two circles of diameter 2 cm roll
around a rectangle measuring 6 cm
by 8 cm as shown. They start
exactly at the midpoints, and both
roll anticlockwise around the
rectangle at the same speed.
What is the maximum distance
between the centres of the circles?

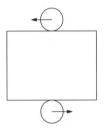

B8   A cuboid has edges whose lengths are in the ratio 2 : 3 : 5.
The volume of the cuboid is 240 cm^3.
What is the total surface area of the cuboid?

B9   The Television Licence costs £15 per month. Of this, £2.50 is
spent on radio, £9.47 on television, £1.40 on on-line services and
£1.63 on miscellaneous charges.
When this information is represented by a pie chart, what is the
angle of the sector for on-line services to the nearest degree?

218

B10 Jack is in charge of the very large maths club noticeboard and has twenty-four A4 notices to pin up, putting a pin in each corner.

By overlapping them slightly, he can use fewer pins, for example, using 8 pins to pin up 3 sheets.

Using Jack's method, what is the smallest number of pins that can be used for the twenty-four sheets?

B11 Four cuboids have dimensions (in cm) as follows:

$3 \times 1 \times 1$,	$3 \times 5 \times 1$.	$5 \times 1 \times 4$,	$4 \times 3 \times 5$.

Two of these cuboids are selected and glued together on identical faces to make a new cuboid.

What is the longest edge length of all possible cuboids so formed?

B12 An ordinary die is to be folded up from the net shown alongside.

The numbers on the faces are 44, 45, 46, 47, 48, 49.

As usual, pairs of opposite faces always have the same total.

$e = 48$

What is the value of $a + c + f$?

B13 A triangle ABC has a right angle at B.

$AC = 12$ cm.

D is a point on AC.

$AD = 4$ cm.

What is the ratio of the area of triangle ABC to the area of triangle CBD?

B14 What is the sum of all the numbers between 500 and 1000 that have exactly 3 factors?

B15 Put the following three numbers in order of decreasing size.

6^9	8^8	9^6

Leave your answer in index form.

Solutions from the Regional Finals

Group Round Answers

1. $\frac{1}{3}$
2. (a) 4; (b) 2
3. (a) 16; (b) 23
4. 10
5. 11
6. 5
7. 2
8. 4356
9. (a) 7; (b) 10
10. 12

Crossnumber

¹9	9	²4		³1	9	⁴7		⁵3
4		⁶6	⁷1	6		⁸4	2	3
⁹5	¹⁰3		6		¹¹8			2
	¹²3	2		¹³3	5	5	¹⁴3	
¹⁵2	1		¹⁶5		7		¹⁷1	8
	¹⁸2	0	1	7		¹⁹2	2	
²⁰2			2		²¹3		²²5	²³5
²⁴5	1	²⁵2		²⁶9	9	²⁷6		5
7		²⁸3	5	0		²⁹9	2	0

220

Shuttle

A1	11
A2	8
A3	120
A4	4200

B1	6
B2	5
B3	800
B4	20

C1	120
C2	60
C3	64
C4	16

D1	8
D2	2
D3	1024
D4	511

Relay

A1	(5, 4)	B1	£7.76
A2	12.5 or $12\frac{1}{2}$	B2	10.5 or $10\frac{1}{2}$
A3	2	B3	438
A4	15	B4	15
A5	7	B5	63
A6	17.5 or $17\frac{1}{2}$	B6	(20, −20)
A7	330	B7	108
A8	289	B8	37.5 or $37\frac{1}{2}$
A9	33	B9	55
A10	12.8 or $12\frac{4}{5}$	B10	50
A11	3 June	B11	634
A12	14	B12	−3
A13	4	B13	$2\frac{1}{3}$ or $2.\dot{3}$ or $\frac{7}{3}$
A14	5	B14	12
A15	540	B15	16

Solutions from the National Final

Group Circus

1. (a) 135; (b) 216; (c) 198

2. For example

   (a) ; (b)

   Others are possible.

3.

	1	2	3	4
A				
B				

4. For example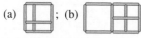

5. (a) 16; (b) 24; (c) 128

6.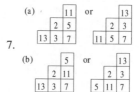

7. (a)

	11		or		13
	2	5		2	3
13	3	7		11	5	7

   (b)

	5		or		13
	2	11		2	3
13	3	7		5	11	7

8. For example,

Crossnumber

¹7	4	²1	■	³3	6	⁴9	5	⁵5
0	■	⁶2	9	7	■	0	■	0
⁷4	5	4	■	⁸4	3	⁹3	0	
5	■	¹⁰8	¹¹1	0	5	■	4	■
¹²4	¹³1	■	0	■	1	■	¹⁴3	¹⁵2
■	0	■	¹⁶7	1	5	¹⁷3	■	4
¹⁸3	4	¹⁹5	6	■	■	²⁰4	0	0
1	■	2	■	²¹2	3	1	■	2
²²1	1	0	9	3	■	²³3	4	4

Shuttle

A1	110
A2	11
A3	99
A4	220

B1	30
B2	45
B3	10
B4	16

C1	50
C2	5
C3	12
C4	216

D1	3
D2	20
D3	2
D4	4.5 etc

Relay

A1	60	B1	202
A2	2520	B2	19
A3	12^3	B3	15.58
A4	3.25 or $3\frac{1}{4}$ or $\frac{13}{4}$	B4	486
A5	2	B5	89
A6	70	B6	3400
A7	13 June	B7	12
A8	3^{51}	B8	248
A9	64	B9	34
A10	9	B10	35
A11	11	B11	7
A12	28.8 or $28\frac{4}{5}$	B12	138
A13	28	B13	3 : 2
A14	414	B14	2331
A15	112	B15	$8^8 > 6^9 > 9^6$

UKMT and Further Maths Support Programme
Senior Team Maths Challenge 2017

Overview

The Senior Team Maths Challenge is now entering into its 11th year and continues to grow in size and popularity. The 2016-17 competition once again had a greater number of Regional Finals and competing schools than ever before, with events taking place at 65 locations across the UK with over 1200 competing schools.

Each team is made up of four students from years 11, 12 and 13 (S5 and S6 in Scotland, and years 12, 13 and 14 in Northern Ireland) and the Regional Competition consists of 3 Rounds; The Group Round, the Crossnumber and the Shuttle. For the Group Round, 10 questions are answered by each team in 40 minutes, while the Crossnumber involves each team solving a mathematical version of a crossword by splitting in two to work on the 'Across' and the 'Down' clues. The competition finishes with the Shuttle, which consists of sets of 4 linked questions, answered in pairs against a timer.

National Final

The culmination of the competition is at the National Final in February, where the top 88 teams were invited to the Royal Horticultural Halls in London to compete for the title of 'National Champions'. Yet again, it was an exciting finale, at which the high level of energy and enthusiasm throughout the day created a wonderful celebration of mathematics. Many thanks to Fraser Heywood for leading the day.

Congratulations to all the schools who took part in the STMC National Final. These schools were:

Alcester Grammar School
Altrincham Grammar School for Girls
Ashcroft Technology Academy
Ashford School
Atlantic College
Aylesbury Grammar School
Backwell School
Bedford School
Belfast Royal Academy
Bilborough VI Form College
Birkenhead School
Bishop Wordsworth's School
Bradford Grammar School

King Edward's School, Edgbaston
King's College London Mathematics School
Lancaster Royal Grammar School
Leicester Grammar School
Lime House School
Loretto School
Magdalen College School
Malvern St James School
Merchant Taylors' Boys School
Moreton Hall School
Myton School
North London Collegiate School
Norwich School

Brentwood School
Bridgewater High School
Brighton College
Bryanston School
Burnham Grammar School
Cardiff Sixth Form College
Carmel College
Caterham School
Cedars Upper School
Chislehurst & Sidcup Grammar School
Churchill Academy
City of London School
Clitheroe Royal Grammar School
Colchester Royal Grammar School
Concord College
Dame Alice Owen's School
Devonport High School for Boys
Durham Johnston School
Eton College
Exeter Mathematics School
Fulford School
Giggleswick School
Headington School
High School of Glasgow
Highgate School
Hills Road VI Form College
Horsforth School
INTO University of East Anglia
King David High School
King Edward VI Camp Hill School for Boys
King Edward's School, Bath

Pate's Grammar School
Peter Symonds College
Pocklington School
Queen Elizabeth's Grammar School
Queen Margaret's School
Queenswood School
Robert Gordon's College
Robert Smyth Academy
Royal Grammar School (Newcastle)
Rugby School
Ruthin School
Ryde School with Upper Chine
Sevenoaks School
Shrewsbury School
Southbank International School
St Paul's School
Stanborough School
Stockport Grammar School
Strathallan School
Sutton Grammar School for Boys
Tapton School
The Glasgow Academy
The Perse School
The Royal School, Haslemere
Tiffin School
Truro College
Wallington County Grammar School
Warwick School
Welbeck, the Defense Sixth Form College
Westminster School
William Brookes School

The Overall Winners were Ruthin School, while the Poster Competition was won by Royal Grammar School, Newcastle.

The National Final consisted of the Group Round, the Crossnumber and the Shuttle with the addition of a new Relay Round, which added another exciting dimension to the day. Teams also took part in a Poster Competition at the start of the day, answering questions on '*Cellular automata*' and setting these in the form of an attractive poster. Thanks to Peter Neumann, Colin Campbell, Fraser Haywood, Alexandra Hewitt and Andrew Jobbings for their hard work in preparing the materials and judging the posters.

As with all UKMT competitions, grateful thanks are due to all of the volunteers who wrote questions, acted as checkers for the materials produced, ran Regional Finals alongside FMSP coordinators and who helped on the day at the National Final.

The checkers of the questions were: Heather Reeve (Lead Checker), Alan Slomson and Jenny Ramsden.

The Round Rulers, who oversaw the materials for each round, were: Charles Oakley (Group round), Peter Hall (Crossnumber), Katie Ray (Shuttle) and James Cranch (Starter questions). Our thanks also to all the STMC volunteers who submitted questions to the Round Rulers.

As ever, many thanks to everyone involved for making 2016-17 another successful year.

Regional Group Round

1   Find the value of:

$$1! \times 1 + 2! \times 2 + 3! \times 3 + 4! \times 4 + 5! \times 5.$$

Note: $n! = n \times (n - 1) \times (n - 2) \times \ldots \times 2 \times 1.$

[6 marks]

2   Andrew and Alan are twins. They are both directors of a small company. They both have to attend a meeting with their new staff.

When Andrew enters the room, the mean age of those in the room increases by four. He is immediately followed by Alan and the mean age increases by a further three. No more people enter the room for the meeting.

How many people are at the meeting including the twins?

[6 marks]

3   In 1929, Farmer Giles took his animals to market. He had some cows, sheep and chickens to sell.

- Cows sold for ten pounds each,
- Sheep sold for one pound each,
- Chickens were sold for one pound for a brood of eight (they were only sold in whole broods).

Farmer Giles had a good day and sold 100 animals for exactly £100.

The day did have its down side; he had to sell Daisy, his favourite cow.

How many sheep did Farmer Giles sell?

[6 marks]

4   The area of the rhombus *PQRS* is twice the area of the square *TUVW*. The side length of *PQRS* is twice the side length of *TUVW*.

What is the ratio of $\angle QRS$ to $\angle PQR$?

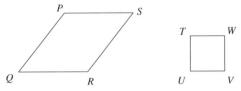

[6 marks]

5   Find the number of distinct triples (x, y, z) of non-negative integers that satisfy the equation

$$2x + y + z = 16.$$

[6 marks]

6   Six circular counters of radius 1 cm are placed on the vertices of a regular hexagon of side length 2 cm as shown. What is the area of the shaded region in cm²?

Give your answer in the form $a\sqrt{p} - b\pi$ where p is a prime number.

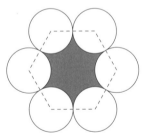

[6 marks]

7   A languages survey is a carried out at a college. Every student at the college has to study at least one language of the four offered; French, German, Spanish and Russian.

F denotes the number of students studying French only. *FS* denotes the number of students studying French and Spanish only. *FGR* denotes the number of students who study only the three languages French, German and Russian, etc.

It was found that:

S, *FS* and *FG* are equal;

F is three times *S*;

R is double *S*;

FRS and *FGS* are both two less than *FG*;

RS and *GS* are equal and four more than *GRS*;

G is one less than *R*;

FGR and *GRS* are both one less than *FS*;

GR + *FGRS* = *R*;

GR is four more than *S*;

FR is seven more than *GRS*.

There were 138 students who were surveyed. How many of them study exactly two languages?

[6 marks]

8   12 boys and n girls made some cupcakes. Every child made the same number of cupcakes. The total number of cupcakes made was $n^2 + 10n - 2$. How many children made cupcakes?

[6 marks]

9   The digit-sum of a positive integer is the sum of its digits. The digit-product of a positive integer is the product of its digits. For example 1234 has a digit-sum of $1 + 2 + 3 + 4 = 10$ and a digit-product of $1 \times 2 \times 3 \times 4 = 24$.

Find the lowest nine-digit positive integer with a digit-sum equal to its digit product.

[6 marks]

10   A large room is in the form of a cuboid that has height 12 m, width 12 m and length 30 m. The room does not contain any furniture.

A spider is on one of the square walls, equidistant from the two side walls and one metre above the floor. A dormant fly is on the opposite square wall, equidistant from the two side walls and one metre below the ceiling. The spider realised that its shortest route to the fly was less than 42 m long.

Find the shortest distance the spider can walk to devour the fly (assuming the fly does not move from its current position).

[6 marks]

Regional Final Crossnumber

Across

1. The value of x^2y^2 where $2y - 3x = 12$ and $3y - 4x = 20$ (4)

3. The value of $\dfrac{10 \text{ Down} \times 73}{15}$ (4)

5. Twice the interior angle, in degrees, of a regular polygon with 16 Down sides   (3)

6. One less than a square   (2)

7. Four less than a triangular number   (2)

9. Twice a cube   (3)

12. A Fibonacci number   (3)

14. The solution of $\dfrac{3 \text{ Down} + 2}{x - 200} = 7$ (3)

15. A prime number between $\dfrac{15 \text{ Down} + 600}{12}$ and 703   (3)

17. The value of $100a + 11b$ when $\dfrac{2\sqrt{3} + 3}{\sqrt{3}}$ is written in the form $a + \sqrt{b}$ for integers a and b (3)

19. A fourth power (2)

21. The difference between $\sqrt{18 \text{ Down}}$ and $\sqrt{19 \text{ Across}}$ (2)

22. The value of d^2 where d is the larger solution of $x^2 - 36x + 155 = 0$ (3)

23. The product of 11 Down and 6 Down added to twice 17 Across (4)

24. The value of $n^{11} + 1$ where n is an integer. (4)

Down

1. Five less than the smallest square greater than 24 Across (4)

2. The square root of $a^2 + 2ab + b^2$ where $a =$ 17 Across and $b = 200$ (3)

3. The solution of $\dfrac{x + 1}{8} + \dfrac{x - 3}{10} + \dfrac{x + 5}{12} = 32$ (3)

4. One more than a common multiple of 6 Across and 7 Across (4)

6. Twice a Fibonacci number (2)

8. Two less than the square root of 22 Across (2)

10. The value of $5xy$, where $x = \dfrac{6 \text{ Across}}{3}$ and $y = \dfrac{9 \text{ Across}}{64}$ (3)

11. The triangle with side lengths (14 Across − 200), (9 Across − 16) and 11 Down is right-angled (3)

13. The value of $(n + 1)^5 - n^5 + (n - 1)^5$ where n is an integer (3)

15. The value of $100xy - 4x$ where $2x - 3y = 19$ and $3x - 4y = 23$ (4)

16. The value of ab when $\dfrac{6\sqrt{3} + 3}{\sqrt{3}}$ is written in the form $a + \sqrt{b}$ (2)

17. Twice the number of factors of (22 Across − 15 Across) (2)

18. The value of a^2 where $a = \dfrac{2016}{32}$ (4)

20. A triangular number (3)

21. A cube (3)

230

A1 The equation

$$8\,(9x + 7) - 7\,(6x - 5) = 1$$

has the solution $x = -k$, where k is a positive integer.
Pass on the value of k.

A2 *T is the number that you will receive.*

The expression

$$64^{-\frac{1}{7}} + 36^{-\frac{1}{2}} + 8^{-\frac{2}{3}}$$

can be simplified to $\dfrac{p}{q}$, where p and q are positive integers with no
common factor greater than 1.
Pass on the value of $p + q$.

A3 *T is the number that you will receive.*

Y is proportional to the reciprocal of the square of X.
$Y = 20$ when $X = 6$.
Pass on the value of Y when $X = T - 1$.

A4 *T is the number that you will receive.*

In the diagram VXY and WXZ are straight lines.
The lines VW and ZY are parallel.
$WX = 36$ cm, $XY = 30$ cm, $ZX = d$ cm and $XV = T$ cm.

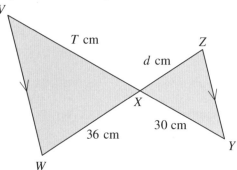

Write down the value of d.

B1
$$(10!) \div (6!) = n!$$
Pass on the value of *n*.

> [*The notation n! means the* factorial *of n, which is n* × (*n* − 1) ×... × 2 × 1.
> *For example*, 6! *means* 6 × 5 × 4 × 3 × 2 × 1.]

B2 *T is the number that you will receive.*

Evaluate $\dfrac{T}{3} - \dfrac{3}{T}$ and write your answer in the form $\dfrac{a}{b}$, where *a* and *b* are positive integers with no common factor greater than 1.
Pass on the value of $a + b - 1$.

B3 *T is the number that you will receive.*

An equilateral triangle has its vertices on a circle of area $\frac{1}{3}\pi T$ cm² , as shown.

The perimeter of the triangle has length *x* cm .

Pass on the value of *x*.

$$[\sin 30° = \cos 60° = \tfrac{1}{2} \text{ and}$$
$$\sin 60° = \cos 30° = \tfrac{\sqrt{3}}{2}.]$$

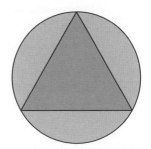

B4 *T is the number that you will receive.*

The graph of $y = x^2 - 6x - T$ meets the *y*-axis at *P*, and the *x*-axis at *Q* and *R*, as shown.

Write down the area of the triangle *PQR* as a simplified surd $a\sqrt{b}$, where *a* and *b* are integers and *b* is not divisible by any square greater than 1.

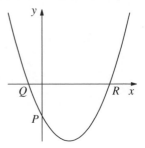

C1 *U, K, M* and *T* are positive integers with

$$1 < U < K < M < T < 10$$

such that

$$U^M = K \times T.$$

Pass on the value of $U + K + M + T$.

232

C2 *T is the number that you will receive.*

The diagram shows parts of two regular polygons with a common edge.

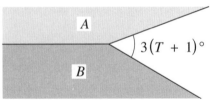

$3(T + 1)°$

Polygon A has five more sides than polygon B and the sum of their exterior angles is $3(T + 1)°$.

Pass on the sum of the numbers of sides of the two polygons.

C3 *T is the number that you will receive.*

The line $y = 4x + T$ intersects the curve $y = x^2 - (T - 14)x - 9T$ at the points (x_1, y_1) and (x_2, y_2).

Pass on the value of $x_1 + x_2$.

C4 *T is the number that you will receive.*

x satisfies the equation

$$256^{\frac{1}{3}x} \times 2^{(T + 1)x} = 16^{3x + T}$$

Write down the value of x.

D1

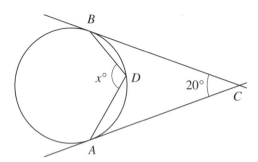

The lines CA and CB are tangents to the circle.

D is a point on the circle on the minor arc between A and B,

The angle $BCA = 20°$.

Pass on the value of x.

D2   *T is the number that you will receive.*

A rectangle is drawn with its vertices on
a circle as shown.
The width of the rectangle is 4 cm.
The height of the rectangle is $\sqrt{T}$ cm.
The area of the circle can be written in
the form $A\pi$ cm^2.
Pass on the value of $2A - 4$.

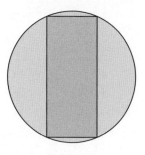

D3   *T is the number that you will receive.*

The integer k is such that the expression

$$k\left(\sqrt{2} + 2\right)\left(\sqrt{3} + 3\right) - \sqrt{T} - \sqrt{2T} - \sqrt{3T}$$

is an integer.
Pass on the value of $6k$.

D4   *T is the number that you will receive.*

A bag contains $(T - 3)$ balls, each of which is red, blue or green.
There is at least one red ball. There are more blue balls than red
balls, and more green balls than blue balls.
If three balls are chosen at random from the bag, without
replacement, the probability that there is one of each colour is $\frac{16}{91}$.
Write down the number of green balls in the bag.

Group Round answers

1.	719	**6.**	$6\sqrt{3} - 2\pi$
2.	8	**7.**	58
3.	21	**8.**	22
4.	5 : 1	**9.**	111 111 129
5.	81	**10.**	40

Crossnumber: Completed grid

¹2	3	0	²4		³1	0	2	⁴2
1	■	■	⁵3	2	0	■		0
1	■	⁶6	3	■	⁷3	⁸2		1
⁹1	¹⁰2	8	■	¹¹1	■	¹²9	¹³8	7
■	1	■	¹⁴2	1	5	■	1	■
¹⁵7	0	¹⁶1	■	3	■	¹⁷2	3	¹⁸3
7	■	¹⁹8	²⁰1	■	²¹5	4	■	9
2	■		²²9	6	1	■	■	6
²³8	1	5	0	■	²⁴2	0	4	9

Shuttle answers

A1	**3**
A2	**5**
A3	**45**
A4	**24**

B1	**7**
B2	**60**
B3	**18**
B4	**54√3**

C1	**19**
C2	**25**
C3	**15**
C4	**9**

D1	**100**
D2	**54**
D3	**18**
D4	**8**

National Final Group Round

1   Find the value of

$$\frac{2017^2 - 2016^2 - 2015^2 + 2014^2}{2017 + 2016 - 2015 - 2014}.$$

[6 marks]

2

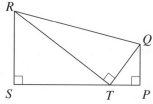

PQRS is a trapezium with *PQ* parallel to *SR*. Each of the angles *TPQ*, *RTQ* and *RST* is a right angle.

     The length of *PT* is 15

     The length of *QP* is 20

     The length of *QR* is 65

A square *ABCD* is equal in area to the trapezium *PQRS*.
What is the length of *AB*?

[6 marks]

3   A positive number x satisfies the equation

$$x^2 + \frac{1}{x^2} = 7.$$

What is the value of

$$x^3 + \frac{1}{x^3}\ ?$$

[6 marks]

4   The crossnumber contains one occurrence of each of the digits 1 to 9.

Across	Down
1. A square	1. 3 times a prime
4. A square	2. A multiple of 11
5. A square	3. Not a multiple of 13

What is the correct answer to 4 Across?

[6 marks]

5   The positive numbers x and y satisfy the equation

$$20x^2 = 17xy - 3y^2.$$

What is the maximum value of

$$\frac{y + 2x}{y - x}?$$

[6 marks]

6

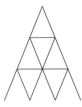

A house of cards, 3 storeys high, requires 15 cards to build. To break the world record you would need to build an 80 storey high house of cards, in the style shown.

How many cards would be needed to build this?

[6 marks]

7   (a) A group of children share marbles from a bag.

The first child takes one marble and a tenth of the remainder.

The second child takes two marbles and a tenth of the remainder.

The third child takes three marbles and a tenth of the remainder and so on until the last child takes whatever is left.

All the children end up with the same number of marbles.

How many children are there?

[3 marks]

(b) Thirteen pirates are trying to share out some gold coins.

There are fewer than 1000 coins and, when they try to share them out equally, there are three coins left over.

They cannot decide on what to do with the remaining coins so one pirate is eliminated and the remaining twelve share the coins out, only to find there are now five left over.

Another pirate is eliminated and then the remaining eleven are able to distribute the coins between them with each pirate receiving the same number of coins.

How many coins were there in total originally?

[3 marks]

8

(a)

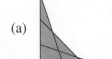

Two adjacent sides of a unit square are trisected and lines drawn between the points as shown.

What fraction of the square is shaded?

[3 marks]

(b)

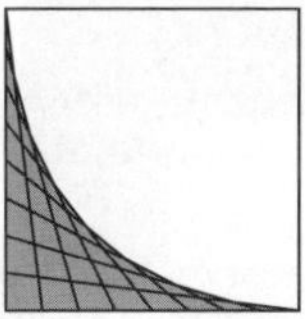

Two adjacent sides of a unit square are divided into n equal parts and a similar pattern is formed. (The resulting areas for $n = 5$ and $n = 8$ are shown above.)

For which value of n is the shaded area equal to one-fifth of the area of the square?

[3 marks]

9   In this question the letters A, C, F, H, I, L, M, N, S and T represent different digits.

The digits A, C, H, M, S and T satisfy

$$
\begin{array}{rcccc}
 & S & T & M & C \\
 & & & \times & 4 \\
\hline
M & A & T & H & S \\
\end{array}
$$

What is the value of $F + I + N + A + L$?

[6 marks]

10   A pair of integers has a sum of 294 and a lowest common multiple of 420.

What is the smaller number of the pair?

[6 marks]

Across

1. 9 Down plus a solution of $x^2 - 57x - 25$ Across $= 0$ (3)

3. $3^3 + 4^4 + 3^3 + 5^5$ (4)

6. A prime factor of 4 Down   (3)

8. $a + b$ where $ab = 100\,000$ but neither a nor b is a multiple of 10   (4)

10. x where 11 Across : 12 Down $= 252 : x$ (3)

11. The number of different arrangements of the letters in the word CIRCLE   (3)

13. $100b + a$ when $\dfrac{c - 800 - (d - 1900)\sqrt{3}}{2 - \sqrt{3}}$, where $c = 19$ Across and $d = 22$ Across, is expressed in the form $a + b\sqrt{3}$ (4)

16. The sum of its digits is five   (4)

19. Sum of the first seven factorials starting with 0! [Note: 0! = 1]   (3)

21. The mean of 7 Down and 11 Across   (3)

22. Five less than a square   (4)

23. 1 Across + 21 Across   (3)

24. A cube   (4)

25. A multiple of 7 Down   (3)

Down

2. Six greater than the largest prime factor of $(4 \text{ Down})^2 - (8 \text{ Across})^2$ (3)

3. 15 Down − 8 Across   (5)

4. A multiple of 19   (4)

5. $100a + b$ when $\dfrac{c - 820 - (d - 1900)\sqrt{5}}{2 - \sqrt{5}}$, where $c = 19$ Down
   and $d = 22$ Across, is expressed in the form $a + b\sqrt{5}$ (4)

7. The smallest sum of five consecutive positive integers none of
   which are prime   (3)

9. A palindromic triangular number   (3)

12. A Fibonacci number   (3)

14. The remainder when 8 Across is divided by 11 Across   (3)

15. $4! + 0! + 5! + 8! + 5!$ [Note: 0! = 1]   (5)

17. A prime factor of 3 Across   (3)

18. $1 + (2 \times 3 + 4 + 5 + 6 + 7) \times 8 \times 9$ (4)

19. 25 Across plus a solution of $x^2 + 44x - 21 \text{ Across} = 0$ (3)

20. A multiple of 11   (4)

22. The number of degrees in each angle of a regular polygon with n
    sides, where $n = 11$ Across   (3)

National Final Shuttle

A1   Solve for x the equation

$$\sqrt{x + 1} = 2 - \sqrt{x}.$$

Write x as a fraction in the form $\dfrac{a}{b}$, where a and b are positive integers with no common factor other than 1.

Pass on the value of $b - a$.

A2   *T is the number that you will receive.*

Solve for x the equation

$$256^{x + 1} = 32^{T + 1}.$$

Pass on the value of x.

A3   *T is the number that you will receive.*

$ABCD$ is a square that lies within another square $AEFG$. The point C lies on the circumference of the circle with centre F that also passes through points E and G.

$FG = T - 2$.

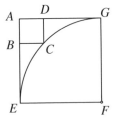

The area of $ABCD$ can be written in the form $a - b\sqrt{2}$, where a and b are positive integers.

Pass on the value of $a + b$.

A4   *T is the number that you will receive.*

The number $\dfrac{\sqrt{T!}}{5!}$ can be written in the form $\sqrt{a}$, where a is an integer.

Write down the value of a.

[*The notation n! means the* factorial *of n, which is* $n \times (n - 1) \times \ldots \times 2 \times 1$. *For example,* 6! *means* $6 \times 5 \times 4 \times 3 \times 2 \times 1$.]

B1 *ABCDEFGH* is a regular octagon.
Pass on the size, in degrees, of
∠*GBE*.

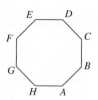

B2 *T is the number that you will receive.*

A bag contains $\frac{1}{5}T$ counters, of which some are red and the rest are blue. The probability of removing two red counters, one after the other, without replacement, is $\frac{1}{6}$.

Pass on the number of red counters in the bag,

B3 *T is the number that you will receive.*

The mode of five integers is two less than the median. The mean is *T* more than the mode.

Pass on the largest possible value of the range of the data.

B4 *T is the number that you will receive.*

The expression $\dfrac{\sqrt{3T} + \sqrt{5T}}{\sqrt{5} - \sqrt{3}}$ can be simplified to $b + \sqrt{a}$, where *a* and *b* are positive integers.

Write down the value of *a* + *b*.

C1
$$P = 2^4 \times 3^4 \times 5^7,$$
$$Q = 2^7 \times 3^5 \times 5^3 \qquad \text{and}$$
$$R = 2^8 \times 3^3 \times 5^6.$$

The highest common factor of *P*, *Q* and *R* is $2^a \times 3^b \times 5^c$ where *a*, *b* and *c* are positive integers.

The lowest common multiple of *P*, *Q* and *R* is $2^d \times 3^e \times 5^f$ where *d*, *e* and *f* are positive integers.

Pass on the value of *a* + *b* + *c* + *d* + *e* + *f*.

C2 *T is the number that you will receive.*

$$\left(\frac{8}{125}\right)^{-\frac{1}{3}} - \frac{1}{2}\left(\frac{16}{81}\right)^{-\frac{3}{4}} - \left(\frac{4}{T+6}\right)^{\frac{1}{2}} - \left(\frac{9}{2T+12}\right)^{\frac{2}{3}} = \frac{a}{b},$$

where *a* and *b* are positive integers with no common factor other than 1.

Pass on the value of *a* + *b* + 1.

C3   *T is the number that you will receive.*

The line $2x + y = 3$ is rotated $90°$ clockwise about the origin. The rotated line can be given by the equation $ax + by = T - 48.$ for a suitable choice of a and b.

Pass on the value of $a - 4b$.

C4   *T is the number that you will receive.*

The line CE is the tangent to the circle at C. The line FE is the tangent to the circle at A. $AD = CD$ and $\angle AEC = (3T + 2)°$.

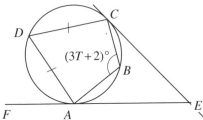

Write down the sum, in degrees, of $\angle AEC$ and $\angle FAD$.

D1   The frustum shown shaded in the diagram is obtained by removing the top circular cone, whose base has a diameter of 6 cm, from the circular cone whose base has a diameter of 10 cm.

The volume of the circular cone that is removed is V cm^3.

The volume of the frustum is 392 cm^2.

Pass on the value of V.

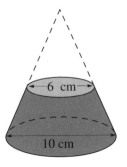

D2   *T is the number that you will receive.*

Solve for x the equation

$$\frac{12x}{T - 12x} + \frac{36x}{T + 36x} = 1.$$

Pass on the positive solution.

D3   *T is the number that you will receive.*

The diagram shows the straight line $y = 2x + T$, the part of the curve $y = \dfrac{9T}{x}$ in the positive quadrant, and a line segment joining the point of intersection of the curve and the line to the point $(5,\ 0)$.

Pass on the value of the shaded area.

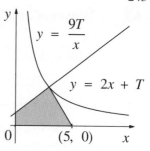

D4   *T is the number that you will receive.*

The diagram shows the quadratic curve $y = ax^2 + bx + c$. The curve meets the x-axis at $\left(\frac{1}{3}T,\ 0\right)$ and has a maximum point at $\left(\frac{1}{9}T,\ 36\right)$.

Write down the value of c.

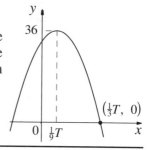

National Final Relay

A1   What is the value of

$$\sqrt{1^2 + 2^3 + 3^4 + 4^5 - 5^2}\ ?$$

A2 $$11^2 \times 22^2 \times 33^2 = 66^2 k.$$

What is the value of k?

A3   The four-digit integers 5634 and 6435 share the following two properties:

   (i)   they consist of four consecutive digits in some order;

   (ii) they are divisible by 3.

How many such four-digit integers are there?

A4   Shona, Jo and Bev run round a 400 m athletic track in the same direction. Shona runs at a constant speed of 3 m/s, Jo runs at a constant speed of 4 m/s whilst Bev runs at a constant speed of 5 m/s.

They start together.

How many metres in total do the three of them run before they are together again?

A5 The operation $A \otimes B$ is defined by

$$A \otimes B = 20A - B - 7AB.$$

What is the value of

$$2 \otimes \big(0 \otimes (1 \otimes 7)\big)?$$

A6 For how many integers n, is it true that

$$\frac{3}{47} < \frac{1}{n} < \frac{4}{37}?$$

A7 In the triangle ABC, AB has length 7, BC has length 8 and CA has length 9.

D is the midpoint of BC.

What is the length of AD?

A8 For $a > 0$, the triangle with vertices at the points $(0, a)$, $(2a, 10)$ and $(10, 0)$ has area $4a^2$.

What is the value of a?

A9 A circle with centre A and radius 12 has diameter BC. A second circle with diameter AC is drawn. The tangent shown from B to this circle meets circle centre A at the point D.

What is the length of BD?

Give your answer in fully simplified form.

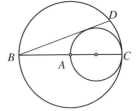

A10 The positive integers x and y are such that

$$20x + 17y = 2017.$$

What is the maximum value of $x + y$?

A11 'abc' is a three-digit prime. Its individual digits a, b and c are different primes.

Write down all such three-digit primes 'abc'.

A12 For each value of x, $F(x)$ is defined to be the minimum value of $x + 5$, $-2x - 4$ and $-5x - 7$.

What is the maximum value of $F(x)$?

B1 What is the value of

$$\sqrt{1^1 + 2^2 + 3^3 + 4^4 + 5^5 - 7^2}\,?$$

B2
$$\frac{88^4}{22^2 \times 44^2} = 2^k.$$

What is the value of k?

B3 For how many integer values of x is $\dfrac{24}{x - 6}$ an integer?

B4 A match takes place between two teams, each of 11 players. There are three referees.

Before the match, each player exchanges handshakes with each of their opponents and each of the referees.

What was the total number of handshakes?

B5 What is the sum of all digits that cannot be the units digit of the square of an integer?

B6 For which integer values of x is $x^4 - 40x^2 + 144$ negative?

B7 In the triangle ABC, AB has length 20, BC has length 11 and CA has length 13.

The line through A perpendicular to BC meets the line through B and C at D.

What is the length of AD?

B8 The diagram shows three congruent rectangles of height 5 and breadth 13.

As shown, two pairs of rectangles share a vertex. Two rectangles are placed so that a vertex of each lies on the long side of the third rectangle.

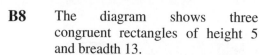

What is the area of the region where all three rectangles overlap?

B9 A circle centre A has diameter BC.

A second circle with diameter AC is drawn. The tangent shown from B to this circle meets circle centre A at the point D.
BD has length 16.

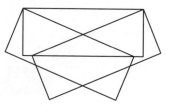

What is the length of the radius of the circle centre A?

Give your answer in fully simplified form.

B10 The sum of all two-digit primes, in which all the individual digits are prime, is A.

The sum of all single-digit primes is B.

The integer $A + B$ is the product of two primes p and q.

What are p and q?

B11 a, b, c, d and e are nonzero digits.

The five-digit integers '$abcde$' and '$edcba$' satisfy the multiplication sum shown alongside.

What is the digit c?

$$\begin{array}{r} a\ b\ c\ d\ e \\ \times\ 4 \\ \hline e\ d\ c\ b\ a \end{array}$$

B12 For every value of x, $f(x)$ satisfies the equation

$$f(x) + 3f(1-x) = 2x.$$

What is the value of $f(25)$?

Group Round answers

1.	1	6.	9640
2.	42	7.	(a) 9 (b) 341
3.	18	8.	(a) $\frac{5}{18}$ (b) 10
4.	784	9.	24
5.	5.5 or $\frac{11}{2}$ or $5\frac{1}{2}$	10.	84

Crossnumber: Completed grid

	¹5	8	²2		³3	4	⁴3	5	
⁵7			⁶1	6	7		1		⁷1
⁸3	1	⁹5	7		¹⁰4	2	7		3
2		9			2		¹¹3	¹²6	0
¹³1	¹⁴2	5	5		8			1	
	7			¹⁵4		¹⁶1	¹⁷2	0	¹⁸2
¹⁹8	7	²⁰4		0			2		0
6		²¹2	4	5		²²1	9	3	1
1		1		²³8	2	7			7
	²⁴3	3	7	5		²⁵9	1	0	

Shuttle answers

A1	7
A2	4
A3	10
A4	252

B1	45
B2	4
B3	15
B4	255

C1	30
C2	60
C3	36
C4	95

D1	108
D2	3
D3	27
D4	27

Relay answers

A1	33	A7	7	B1	58	B7	12
A2	14641	A8	$\frac{10}{3}$ or $3\frac{1}{3}$	B2	6	B8	$\frac{605}{48}$ or $12\frac{29}{48}$
A3	66	A9	$16\sqrt{2}$	B3	16	B9	$6\sqrt{2}$
A4	4800	A10	116	B4	187	B10	7, 29
A5	−500	A11	257, 523	B5	20	B11	9
A6	6	A12	2	B6	±5, ±4, ±3	B12	$\frac{-97}{4}$ or $-24\frac{1}{4}$

In A11, B6 and B10, the order does not matter.

Other aspects of the UKMT

As well as the Maths Challenges, the UKMT is involved in other events and activities.

Mathematical Circles

The Mathematical Circles developed from two trial events in spring 2012. Following on from the success of these we have since significantly expanded the programme.

Local schools are invited to select two students from Year 10 (or S3 in Scotland) to send to the two-day events, which are comprised of mathematically demanding work through topics such as geometry, proof and modular arithmetic. Students have the opportunity to discuss mathematics and make new friends from other schools around their region.

Our thanks go to the following people who ran the 2016-17 events, and to the schools who supported these:

Aberdeen, University of Aberdeen

Birmingham, Aston University Academy

Cardiff, Cardiff University

Leeds, University of Leeds

Leicester, Leicester Grammar School

Rickmansworth, Royal Masonic School

Wells, Wells Cathedral School

Weymouth, All Saints School

Winchester, St Swithun's School

Many thanks are also given to those people who ran sessions (a list of which is given in the Volunteers section of the Yearbook).

Mathematical Circles are being held throughout the next academic year. If you would like to find out more about how you can become involved in the Mathematical Circles, either through your school hosting an event or by supporting us in running a session, please do contact us at enquiry@ukmt.org.uk.

Primary Team Maths Resources

In recognition and support of the growing number of secondary schools organising and hosting local team maths events for their feeder schools, UKMT developed a set of Primary Team Maths Resources (PTMR) intended for use at such events. The first ever PTMR were made available free of charge in spring 2012. At the start of each calendar year, a new set of material has since been made available.

Schools may choose to use the materials in other ways, e.g. a primary school may use the materials to run a competition for their own Year 5 and 6 pupils (and equivalent), or a secondary school may use the materials as an end of term activity for their Year 7 pupils.

The PTMR include more materials than would be needed for any one competition, allowing schools to pick and choose those most appropriate for their purposes. Some of the rounds are familiar from the UKMT Team Challenges (the Group Round, Crossnumber, Relay and Mini Relay) and the material included some new rounds (the Logic Round, Make a Number, Open Ended Questions, Primary Kangaroo, and Speed Test).

The 2017 PTMR and full instructions for suggested use is available to download from our website at:

http://www.ukmt.org.uk/team-challenges/primary-team-maths-resources/

Best in School Events

Since 2007, the UKMT has partnered with the Royal Institution to invite top scoring IMC candidates to attend RI masterclass celebration events, held in the summer term. These events give students from Year 9 and S3, and sometimes Year 12, the opportunity to attend inspiring lectures, meet mathematicians from their local area, and have a go at 'hands-on' mathematics.

In 2017, these events took place in Bath, Edinburgh, Liverpool, London (Year 9 / S3 events) Newcastle, and Plymouth.

Website – www.ukmt.org.uk

Visit the UKMT's website for information about all the UKMT's activities, including the Maths Challenges, team events, latest UKMT news and newsletters, contact details, and to purchase publications and past papers.

There are online resources featuring past questions from the Challenges, mentoring questions, and sample Primary Team Maths Challenge materials. Also links to sponsors, supporters and other mathematical bodies providing further resources for young mathematicians.

Other similar bodies overseas

The UKMT has links of varying degrees of formality with several similar organisations in other countries. It is also a member of the World Federation of National Mathematics Competitions (WFNMC). What follows is a brief description of some of these other organisations. Some of the information is taken from the organisations' web sites but a UK slant has been applied.

"Association Kangourou sans Frontières"

http://www.aksf.org/

The obvious question is: why Kangaroo? The name was given in tribute to the pioneering efforts of the Australian Mathematics Trust. The Kangaroo contest is run by local organisers in each country under the auspices of the 'Association Kangourou sans Frontières', which was founded by a small group of countries in 1991. There are now over 50 countries involved and more than six million participants throughout Europe and beyond, from the UK to Mongolia and from Norway to Cyprus.

In the UK in 2016, over 7000 children in the years equivalent to English Years 9, 10 and 11 took part in the 'Cadet' and 'Junior' levels of the Kangaroo competition, as a follow-up to the Intermediate Maths Challenge. Four representatives of the UK Mathematics Trust, Andrew Jobbings, Paul Murray, Rachel Greenhalgh and David Crawford, attended the meeting in Sweden, at which these Kangaroo papers were constructed.

The main objective of the Kangaroo, like all the competitions described in this section, is to stimulate and motivate large numbers of pupils, as well as to contribute to the development of a mathematical culture which will be accessible to, and enjoyed by, many children and young people. The Association also encourages cross-cultural activities; in some countries, for example, prize-winners are invited to attend a mathematics 'camp' with similar participants from other nations.

The Australian Mathematics Trust

www.wfnmc.org

For over twenty-five years, the Australian Mathematics Competition has been one of the major events on the Australian Education Calendar, with about one in three Australian secondary students entering each year to test their skills. That's over half a million participants a year.

The Competition commenced in 1978 under the leadership of the late Professor Peter O'Halloran, of the University of Canberra, after a successful pilot scheme had run in Canberra for two years.

The questions are multiple-choice and students have 75 minutes in which to answer 30 questions. There are follow-up rounds for high scorers.

In common with the other organisations described here, the AMC also extends its mathematical enrichment activities by publishing high quality material which can be used in the classroom.

Whilst the AMC provides students all over Australia with an opportunity to solve the same problems on the same day, it is also an international event, with most of the countries of the Pacific and South-East Asia participating, as well as a few schools from further afield. New Zealand and Singapore each enter a further 30,000 students to help give the Competition an international flavour.

World Federation of National Mathematics Competitions – WFNMC

www.amt.canberra.edu.au/wfnmc.html

The Federation was created in 1984 during the Fifth International Congress for Mathematical Education.

The Federation aims to provide a focal point for those interested in, and concerned with, conducting national mathematics competitions for the purpose of stimulating the learning of mathematics. Its objectives include:

- Serving as a resource for the exchange of information and ideas on mathematics competitions through publications and conferences.
- Assisting with the development and improvement of mathematics competitions.

- Increasing public awareness of the role of mathematics competitions in the education of all students and ensuring that the importance of that role is properly recognised in academic circles.
- Creating and enhancing professional links between mathematicians involved in competitions around the world.

The World Federation of National Mathematics Competitions is an organisation of national mathematics competitions affiliated as a Special Interest Group of the International Commission for Mathematical Instruction (ICMI).

It administers a number of activities, including

- The Journal *Mathematics Competitions*
- An international conference every four years.
- David Hilbert and Paul Erdős Awards for mathematicians prominent on an international or national scale in mathematical enrichment activities.

The UKMT sent two delegates, Tony Gardiner and Bill Richardson, to the WFNMC conference in Zhong Shan in 1998 and provided support for several delegates who attended ICME 9 in Tokyo in August 2000, at which the WFNMC provided a strand.

In August 2002, the WFNMC held another conference, similar to the one in 1998. The venue for this was Melbourne, Victoria. On this occasion, the UKMT provided support for two delegates: Howard Groves and Bill Richardson.

In July 2006, WFNMC 5 was held in the UK at Robinson College, Cambridge. This event was a tremendous success with around 100 delegates from many parts of the world.

In July 2008, WFNMC had a strand at ICME 11 in Mexico. UKMT was represented by Bill Richardson.

In July 2010, WFNMC 6 was held in Riga. The UKMT was represented by Howard Groves, Dean Bunnell, David Crawford and James Welham.

In July 2014, WFNMC 7 was held in Colombia. The UKMT was represented by David Crawford.

Lists of volunteers involved in the UKMT's activities

BMO2 markers

James Aaronson (University of Oxford)
Lex Betts (University of Oxford)
Alison Fisher (Willis Towers Watson)
John Haslegrave (University of Warwick)
Maria Holdcroft (Queen's College, Oxford)
Gerry Leversha (ex St Paul's School)
Martin Orr (Imperial College, London)
Dominic Rowland (Winchester College)
Geoff Smith (University of Bath)
Karthik Tadinada (Featurespace)

Ben Barrett (Trinity College, Cambridge)
James Cranch (University of Sheffield)
Richard Freeland (Trinity College, Cambridge)
Tim Hennock (Jane Street Capital)
Andras H. Harris (Westminster 6th Form)
Joseph Myers (CodeSourcery)
Jenny Owladi (Bank of England)
Paul Russell (Churchill Coll., Cambridge)
Zhivko Stoyanov (University of Reading)
Kasia Warburton (Trinity, Cambridge)

MOG Markers

Olivia Aaronson	Philiip Beckett	Natalie Behague
Andrea Chlebikova	Philip Coggins	James Cranch
Chris Eagle	Paul Fannon	Nicole Few-Durnall
Richard Freeland	Mary Teresa Fyfe	Gabriel Gendler
Adam Goucher	Tim Hennock	Jack Hodkinson
Maria Holdcroft	Daniel Hu	Andrew Jobbings
Vesna Kadelburg	Eszter Kiss	Daniel Low
Georgina Majury	Sam Maltby	Matei Mandache
David Mestel	Joseph Myers	Vicky Neale
Peter Neumann	Sylvia Neumann	Roger Patterson
David Phillips	Eve Pound	Linden Ralph
Paul Russell	Jon Stone	Kasia Warburton
Jerome Watson		

Markers for IMOK and JMO

Anne Baker	IMOK	Philip Beckett	IMOK
Maya Brock	IMOK	Valerie Chapman	IMOK/JMO
Andrea Chlebikova	IMOK/JMO	Philip Coggins	IMOK/JMO
James Cranch	IMOK	David Crawford	IMOK/JMO
Tim Cross	IMOK	Sue Cubbon	IMOK
Wendy Dersley	IMOK/JMO	David Forster	IMOK
Mary Teresa Fyfe	IMOK	Carol Gainlall	IMOK/JMO
Gwyn Gardiner	IMOK/JMO	James Gazet	IMOK
Michael Griffiths	IMOK	Howard Groves	IMOK
James Hall	IMOK	Stuart Haring	IMOK
Hugh Hill	IMOK	Jack Hodkinson	IMOK
Carl James	IMOK	Andrew Jobbings	IMOK/JMO

Zoe Kelly	IMOK	Mark Knapton	IMOK/JMO
David Knipe	IMOK	Gerry Leversha	IMOK
Aleksandar Lishkov	IMOK	Daniel Low	IMOK/JMO
Georgina Majury	IMOK	Sam Maltby	IMOKJOM
Matthew Miller	IMOK	Joseph Myers	IMOK
Peter Neumann	IMOK/JMO	Sylvia Neumann	IMOK/JMO
Roger Patterson	IMOK	Jenny Perkins	IMOK
David Phillips	JMO	Eve Pound	IMOK
Stephen Power	IMOK/JMO	Catherine Ramsay	IMOK/JMO
Jenny Ramsden	IMOK/JMO	Christine Randall	IMOK
Peter Ransom	IMOK/JMO	Jenni Sambrook	IMOK
Fiona Shen	IMOK/JMO	Anne Strong	IMOK
Stephen Tate	IMOK	Alex Voice	JMO
Christopher Walker	IMOK	Mairi Walker	IMOK
Paul Walter	IMOK	Lynn Walton	IMOK
Jerome Watson	IMOK	David Webber	IMOK/JMO
Michaela Weiserova	IMOK/JMO	Rosie Wiltshire	IMOK/JMO
Dorothy Winn	JMO	Heather Yorston	IMOK

Problems Groups
The chairs of the Problems groups are:

BMO Dr Jeremy King	IMOK (Olympiad) Dr Andrew Jobbings
IMC Mr Howard Groves	JMC Mr Howard Groves
JMO Dr Alex Randolph	SMC Mrs Karen Fogden
Senior Kangaroo Mr Carl James	Grey Kangaroo Dr David Crawford
Pink Kangaroo Mr Paul Murray	Junior Kangaroo Dr David Crawford
MOG Dr Vesna Kadelburg	PTMR Mr Dennis Pinshon

Group Members

Mr Steve Barge	SMC
Mr Lex Betts	BMO
Mr Dean Bunnell	SMC, IMOK, JMO
Dr James Cranch	IMOK
Dr David Crawford	GK, SK, JK, JI GK JK
Mrs Karen Fogden	SMC, JI, JMO SMC
Mrs Mary Teresa Fyfe	SMC, IMOK, JMO
Ms Carol Gainlall	JI
Dr Tony Gardiner	JI, IMOK, JMO
Dr Julian Gilbey	BMO
Mr Michael Griffiths	SMC, IMOK

258

Mr Daniel Griller	BMO
Mr Howard Groves	SMC, JI, IMOK, JMO IMC JMC
Mr Carl James	SK SK
Mr Paul Jefferys	BMO
Dr Andrew Jobbings	SMC, JI, IMOK, JMO IMOK
Dr Vesna Kadelburg	MOG
Dr Calum Kilgour	JMO
Dr Jeremy King	BMO
Dr Gerry Leversha	IMOK, BMO
Mr Paul Murray	JI, JMO, PK PK
Mr Andy Parkinson	IMOK
Mr Dennis Pinshon	PTMR
Mr Stephen Power	JI
Dr Alexandra Randolph	JMO
Mr Peter Ransom	JI
Mrs Mary Read	IMOK
Mr Lionel Richard	SMC
Mr Dominic Rowland	BMO
Ms Fiona Shen	SMC
Mr Jack Shotton	BMO
Dr Alan Slomson	SMC, JI
Dr Geoff Smith	BMO
Mr Alex Voice	JI, JMO

Checkers of Challenges Subtrust are: Dr David Crawford; Prof Adam McBride; Miss Jenny Ramsden; Prof Chris Robson; Mrs Lyn Robson; Dr Alan Slomson and those papers are typeset by Bill Richardson.

Primary Team Maths Resources Group

Dennis Pinshon (Chair)	Lyndon Baker	Dorothy Ball
Andy Bell	Elizabeth Bull	Dean Bunnell
Sue Essex	Rachel Greenhalgh	Fraser Heyward
Trish Lunel	Lorna Piper	Alan Slomson

Summer School Staff

Robin Bhattacharyya	Michael Bradley	Katie Chicot
Sue Cubbon	Oliver Feng	Richard Freeland
Tony Gardiner	James Gazet	Howard Groves
Adrian Hemery	Jack Hodkinson	Maria Holdcroft
Andrew Jobbings	Elizabeth Kimber	Gerry Leversha
Georgina Majury	Vicky Neale	Martin Orr

David Phillips   Lorna Piper   Peter Price
Catherine Ramsay   George Robinson   Dominic Rowland
Paul Russell   John Slater   Alan Slomson
Geoff Smith   Charlotte Squires-Parkin   Dorothy Winn

TMC event coordinators, writers (W) and checkers (C)

Hugh Ainsley   Patricia Andrews   Ann Ault (W)
Joe Bailey   Martin Bailey   Anne Baker
Bridget Ballantyne   Andrew Bell   James Beltrami
Zillah Booth   Elizabeth Bull   Dean Bunnell (W)
Kerry Burnham   Keith Cadman (W)   Colin Campbell (W)
Francis Chalmers (C)   Robert Chapman   Phil Colville (W)
Madeleine Copin (C)   Elaine Corr (C)   James Cranch
David Crawford (W)   Rosie Cretney   Mark Dennis
Wendy Dersley   Geoffrey Dolamore   Sue Essex (W)
Sheldon Fernandes   Jackie Fox   Roy Fraser
Mary Teresa Fyfe   Helen Gauld   Peter Hall
Karl Hayward-Bradley (W) Terry Heard   Fraser Heywood (W)
Sue Hughes   Sally Anne Huk   Pam Hunt
Andrina Inglis (C)   Andrew Jobbings (W)   Martyn Lawley (C)
Tricia Lunel   Pat Lyden   Patricia Matheson
Lin McIntosh   Matthew Miller   Steve Mulligan
Helen Mumby   Peter Neumann (W)   Pauline Noble
Andy Parkinson   Dennis Pinshon   Valerie Pinto
Vivian Pinto   Peter Price   Jenny Ramsden (C)
Peter Ransom (W)   Wendy Rathbone   Heather Reeve
Valerie Ridgman   Syra Saddique (C)   John Slater
Alan Slomson   Anne Strong   Penny Thompson
James Welham   Tim Whalley   Ian Wiltshire
Rosie Wiltshire

Additional local helpers and organisers at TMC host venues

Anthony Alonzi   Morag Anderson   Sharon Austin   David Bedford
Helena Benzinski   Steven Birtle   Peter Boyle   Richard Bradshaw
Frank Bray   Maya Brock   Nigel Brookes   Helen Burton
Joseph Carthew   Sue Childs   Maxine Clapham   Anastasia Cobbs
Nicki Cologne-Brookes   Rebecca Cotton-Barratt
Tim Cox   Ladi Dariya   Andrew Davies   Laura Davies
Adam Ealden   Ruth Earl   Charlotte Fine   Gary Higham

Stephen Hope	Paul Howl	Nia Innes	Ian Ironmonger
Beth Kellham	Hayley Key	George Kinnear	Neil Maltman
Helen Martin	Iain Mitchell	Jen Moat	Marijke Molenaar
Heather Morgan	Julie Mundy	Damian Murphy	Deborah Parnell
Mark Patterson	Sarah Powell	Alice Ratheram	Norman Revie
Valentina Reynolds	Peter Richmond	John Robinson	Andrew Rogers
Amelia Rood	Amanda Smallwood	Mark Smith	Richard Stakes
Gerald Telfer	Paul Thomas	Annette Thompson	Rachel Tindal
Danny Walker	Jo Walker	Liz Ward	Dan Wenman
Dave Widdowson			

STMC coordinators and regional helpers

Hugh Ainsley	Patricia Andrews	Ann Ault	Joe Bailey
Gillian Baker	Phillip Beckett	Andrew Bell	Zillah Booth
Dean Bunnell (Round Ruler)		Kerry Burnham	Colin Campbell
Robert Chapman	Tony Cheslett	Elaine Corr	James Cranch
David Crawford	Rosie Cretney	George Engelhardt	Sue Essex
Karen Fogden	Mary Teresa Fyfe (Round Ruler)		Helen Gauld
Douglas Hainline	Peter Hall	James Hall	Paul Healey
Terry Heard	Fraser Heywood (National Final leader)		Sally Anne Huk
Pam Hunt	Andrina Inglis	Andrew Jobbings	John Lardner
Peter Neumann	Charles Oakley (Round Ruler)		Andy Parkinson
Dennis Pinshon	Lorna Piper	Stephen Power	
Jenny Ramsden (Checker)		Alexandra Randolph	
Peter Ransom (Round Ruler)		Katie Ray (Round Ruler)	
Heather Reeve (Checker)		Peter Richmond	Valerie Ridgman
Syra Saddique (Checker)		John Slater	
Alan Slomson (Checker)		Anne Strong	Penny Thompson
Neil Turner	Lynn Walton	James Welham	Rosie Wiltshire

Maths Circles Speakers and Event Leaders (L)

Ann Ault	Tom Brunt	Sarah Cassidy
Valerie Chapman	Tony Cheslett	Andrea Chlebikova
Philip Coggins (L)	James Cranch	Sue Cubbon (L)
Howard Fay	Malcolm Findlay	Mary Teresa Fyfe (L)
Gwyn Gardiner	Tony Gardiner (L)	James Hall
Hugh Hill	Jack Hodkinson (L)	Maria Holdcroft
Susie Jameson (L)	Andrew Jobbings	Elizabeth Kimber
Vince Knight	Gerry Leversha	Danielle Lewis
Kevin Lord	Ben Martin	Vicky Neale
Peter Neumann	Sophie Parker	David Phillips

Stephen Power (L) David Pritchard Catherine Ramsey
Peter Ransom Dominic Rowland Alastair Rucklidge
Jason Semeraro Anindya Sharma John Slater
Alan Slomson (L) Geoff Smith Bart Vlaar

BMOS Mentoring Schemes

Mentoring Committee 2016-17

Anne Andrews Richard Freeland Jack Hodkinson
Freddie Illingworth Zoe Kelly Vicky Neale
David Phillips John Slater

Advanced Scheme Co-ordinator: Richard Freeland

Mentors:

James Aaronson Richard Freeland Gabriel Gendler
Tim Hennock Freddie Illingworth Warren Li
Matei Mandache Joseph Myers Kasia Warburton
Dominic Yeo Renzhi Zhou

Senior Scheme co-ordinators: Anne Andrews, Freddie Illingworth

Senior external mentors:

Olivia Aaronson Alice Ahn Anne Andrews
Jamie Beacom Philip Beckett Natalie Behague
Don Berry Ruth Carling Nicholas Chee
Katie Chicot Andrea Chlebikova Gabriel Craciun
Sam Crew John Cullen Jan Dangerfield
Josh Dixon Chris Eagle Chris Ellingham
Oliver Feng Nicole Few-Durnall Liam Franz
Mary Teresa Fyfe James Gazet Julian Gilbey
Esteban Gomezllata Marmolejo James Hall
Danny Hamilton Paul Healey Fraser Heywood
Edward Hinton Jack Hodkinson Lawrence Hollom
Ina Hughes Mihail Hurmuzov Michael Illing
Sam Kittle Mark Knapton Robert Lasenby
Jasmina Lazic Gerry Leversha Michael Lipton
Daniel Low Georgina Majury Gareth McCaughan
Harry Metrebian Vicky Neale Pavlena Nenova
Peter Neumann Robin Oliver-Jones Keith Porteous
Peter Price Jerome Ripp Julia Robson
Peter Scott Ben Spells Stephen Tate

In memoriam

Brian Wilson, February 2017   Member of the Trust
Jenni Sambrook, March 2017   IMOK marker

UKMT Publications

The books published by the UK Mathematics Trust are grouped into series.

The *YEARBOOKS* series documents all the UKMT activities, including details of all the challenge papers and solutions, lists of high scorers, accounts of the IMO and Olympiad training camps, and other information about the Trust's work during each year.

1. 2016-2017 Yearbook

This is our 19th Yearbook, having published one a year since 1998-1999. Edited by Bill Richardson, the Yearbook documents all the UKMT activities from that particular year. They include all the challenge papers and solutions at every level; list of high scorers; tales from the IMO and Olympiad training camps; details of the UKMT's other activities; and a round-up of global mathematical associations.

Previous Yearbooks are available to purchase. Please contact the UKMT for further details.

CHALLENGES

1. *Ten Years of Mathematical Challenges 1997 to 2006*

Edited by Bill Richardson, this book was published to celebrate the tenth anniversary of the founding of UKMT. This 188-page book contains question papers and solutions for nine Senior Challenges, ten Intermediate Challenges, and ten Junior Challenges.

2. *Ten Further Years of Mathematical Challenges*

This book includes all thirty of the Mathematical Challenge papers set between autumn 2006 and summer 2016, and their solutions:

Senior 2006-2015   Intermediate 2007-2016   Junior 2007-2016

3. *Intermediate Problems*

This book includes all 500 problems from the twenty Intermediate Mathematical Challenge papers set by the UKMT between 1997 and 2016. The problems–which are not given as multiple-choice questions–have been grouped together in two ways: by difficulty; and by topic. The answer to every problem in the book is included.

4. *Junior Problems*

Similarly, this book includes all 500 problems and solutions from the twenty Junior Mathematical Challenge papers set by the UKMT between 1997 and 2016.

The *HANDBOOKS* series is aimed particularly at students at secondary school who are interested in acquiring the knowledge and skills which are useful for tackling challenging problems, such as those posed in the competitions administered by the UKMT.

1. *Plane Euclidean Geometry: Theory and Problems*,
   AD Gardiner and CJ Bradley

An excellent book for students aged 15-18 and teachers who want to learn how to solve problems in elementary Euclidean geometry. The book follows the development of Euclid; contents include Pythagoras, trigonometry, circle theorems, and Ceva and Menelaus. The book contains hundreds of problems, many with hints and solutions.

2. *Introduction to Inequalities*, CJ Bradley

Introduction to Inequalities is a thoroughly revised and extended edition of a book which was initially published as part of the composite volume 'Introductions to Number Theory and Inequalities'. This accessible text aims to show students how to select and apply the correct sort of inequality to solve a given problem.

3. *A Mathematical Olympiad Primer*, Geoff C Smith

This UKMT publication provides an excellent guide for young mathematicians preparing for competitions such as the British Mathematical Olympiad. The book has recently been updated and extended and contains theory including algebra, combinatorics and geometry, and BMO1 problems and solutions from 1996 onwards.

4. *Introduction to Number Theory*, CJ Bradley

This book for students aged 15 upwards aims to show how to tackle the sort of problems on number theory which are set in mathematics competitions. Topics include primes and divisibility, congruence arithmetic and the representation of real numbers by decimals.

5. *A Problem Solver's Handbook*, Andrew Jobbings

This recently published book is an informal guide to Intermediate Olympiads, not only for potential candidates, but for anyone wishing to tackle more challenging problems. The discussions of sample questions aim to show how to attack a problem which may be quite unlike anything seen before.

6. *Introduction to Combinatorics*, Gerry Leversha and Dominic Rowland

The subject of combinatorics provides a rich source of material for mathematics competitions. At one level it can be thought of as a sort of extreme counting–how do we enumerate the number of ways of different ways of doing something? However, the subject is broader than that. It addresses situations which involve organising things so as to satisfy certain 'criteria–placing' tiles on a chessboard, seating people in a circle, chopping up a cube; and then asks whether or not a certain outcome is possible. This accessible text aims to give the enthusiastic student plenty of tips on how to tackle questions of this nature. For ages 16+.

7. *First Steps for Problem Solvers*, Mary Teresa Fyfe and Andrew Jobbings

This book is a guide to pupils aged 11-13 who are attempting problems in competitions such as the Junior Mathematical Olympiad, which are administered by the UKMT and similar organisations. Written with the pupil in mind, the book covers all of the section B questions set in the Junior Mathematical Olympiad papers over sixteen years of the competition. For ages 11-13.

8. *Mathematical Olympiad Companion*

This text will enable enthusiastic students to deal with confidence with secondary school mathematics competitions at the highest level. The book is a sequel to *A Mathematical Olympiad Primer* by the same author, but contains harder problems.

The *EXCURSIONS IN MATHEMATICS* series consists of monographs which focus on a particular topic of interest and investigate it in some detail, using a wide range of ideas and techniques. They are aimed at high school students, undergraduates, and others who are prepared to pursue a subject in some depth, but do not require specialised knowledge.

1. *The Backbone of Pascal's Triangle*, Martin Griffiths

Everything covered in this book is connected to the sequence of numbers: 2, 6, 20, 70, 252, 924, 3432, ... Some readers might recognize this list straight away, while others will not have seen it before. Either way, students and teachers alike may well be astounded at both the variety and the depth of mathematical ideas that it can lead to.

2. *A Prime Puzzle*, Martin Griffiths

The prime numbers 2, 3, 5, 7, ... are the building blocks of our number system. Under certain conditions, any arithmetic progression of positive integers contains infinitely many primes, as proved by Gustave Dirichlet. This book seeks to provide a complete proof which is accessible to school students possessing post-16 mathematical knowledge. All the techniques needed are carefully developed and explained.

The *PATHWAYS* series aims to provide classroom teaching material for use in secondary school. Each title develops a subject in more depth and detail than is normally required by public examinations or national curricula.

1. *Crossing the Bridge*, Gerry Leversha

This book provides a course on geometry for use in the classroom, re-emphasising some traditional features of geometrical education. The bulk of the text is devoted to carefully constructed exercises for classroom discussion or individual study. It is suitable for students aged 13 and upwards.

2. *The Geometry of the Triangle*, Gerry Leversha

The basic geometry of the triangle is widely known, but readers of this book will find that there are many more delights to discover. The book is full of stimulating results and careful exposition, and thus forms a trustworthy guide. Recommended for ages 16+.

The *PROBLEMS* series consists of collections of high-quality and original problems of Olympiad standard.

1. *New Problems in Euclidean Geometry*, David Monk

This book should appeal to anyone aged 16+ who enjoys solving the kind of challenging and attractive geometry problems that have virtually vanished from the school curriculum, but which still play a central role in national and international mathematics competitions. It is a treasure trove of wonderful geometrical problems, with hints for their solutions.

We also sell:

1. *The First 25 Years of the Superbrain*, Diarmuid Early & Des MacHale

This is an extraordinary collection of mathematical problems laced with some puzzles. This book will be of interest to those preparing for senior Olympiad examinations, to teachers of mathematics, and to all those who enjoy solving problems in mathematics.

2. *The Algebra of Geometry*, Christopher J Bradley

In the 19th century, the algebra of the plane was part of the armoury of every serious mathematician. In recent times the major fronts of research mathematics have moved elsewhere. However, those skills and methods are alive and well, and can be found in this book. The Algebra of Geometry deserves a place on the shelf of every enthusiast for Euclidean Geometry, amateur or professional, and is certainly valuable reading for students wishing to compete in senior Mathematical Olympiads. For age 16+ mathematicians.

3. The UKMT is the European agent for a large number of books published by the Art of Problem Solving (http://www.artofproblemsolving.com/).

To find out more about these publications and to order copies, please go to the UKMT website at www.publications.ukmt.org.uk.

In addition to the books above, UKMT continues to publish its termly Newsletter, giving the latest news from the Trust, mathematical articles, examples from Challenge papers and occasional posters for the classroom wall. This is sent free to all schools participating in the UKMT Maths Challenges.